Macmillan Building and Surveying Series

Series Editor: Ivor H. Seeley
Emeritus Professor, Nottingham Trent University

(continued overleaf)

Series Standing Order (Macmillan Building and Surveying Series)
If you would like to receive future titles in this series as they are published, you can make use of our standing order facility. To place a standing order please contact your bookseller or, in case of difficulty, write to us at the address below with your name and address and the name of the series. Please state with which title you wish to begin your standing order. (If you live outside the United Kingdom we may not have the rights for your area, in which case we will forward your order to the publisher concerned.)

Customer Services Department, Macmillan Distribution Ltd
Houndmills, Basingstoke, Hampshire, RG21 2XS, England.

APPLIED VALUATION

SECOND EDITION

DIANE BUTLER

MPhil, FRICS

Senior Lecturer in Valuation
Department of Surveying
The Nottingham Trent University
Nottingham

MACMILLAN

First edition 1987
Second edition 1995

Published by
MACMILLAN PRESS LTD
Houndmills, Basingstoke, Hampshire RG21 2XS
and London
Companies and representatives
throughout the world

ISBN 0–333–64133–7

A catalogue record for this book is available from the British Library.

10   9   8   7   6   5   4   3   2   1
04   03   02   01   00   99   98   97   96   95

Printed in Great Britain by Antony Rowe Ltd., Chippenham, Wilts

To John and Pauleen

CONTENTS

PREFACE TO THE FIRST EDITION

The contents of this book evolved as a result of work that I prepared for second year degree students, in the Department of Surveying at Trent Polytechnic, who were experiencing difficulty in their approach to Valuation examinations. The aim is therefore to consider typical examination questions at intermediate level and demonstrate ways of attempting the answers.

It must be stressed that the answers provided are in no way intended as model answers; rather they are suggested answers and, in some cases, alternative approaches are demonstrated. Valuation, art or science, is not exact and this inevitably means that there can never be universal agreement regarding all methods and approaches. This is perhaps particularly true of topic areas where statute and case law leave room for differing interpretations and also in the case of modern valuation techniques, where arguments continue among advocates of change. Differences of opinion regarding the choice of yields in a valuation can additionally cause appreciable differences in the end result. That there is rarely one precise answer to a valuation problem is a fact which students of the subject often find difficult to accept. However, examiners are generally looking for a sound approach to a question and a demonstration that the underlying concepts are understood rather than an answer which exactly matches that of the examiner.

To gain the greatest benefit from this book, it is suggested that the student should attempt each question without first referring to the answer. The book is arranged in topic areas with questions and suggested answers presented separately, and students are advised to consult the latter only when they have exhausted their own initiative. For reasons already mentioned, there should not be undue concern if the student's answer conflicts with the one produced in the book, unless, of course, this is due to an error in the basic method or understanding of the topic area.

There is a deliberate bias in the book towards calculation questions, since these are usually the type of question with which students tend to need the greatest guidance. Difficulties with essay questions usually stem from poor structuring; therefore, where they are included, consideration is concentrated on the general approach and the main points that should be highlighted, rather than detailed discussion of the points which may be obtained from

Preface

All the calculations are annotated and the importance of this cannot be over-stressed. For instance, a brief explanation of the choice of yields in a valuation may go a long way towards convincing the examiner that the student has not merely produced the valuation by a memorised format, but has grasped the underlying concepts. In fact, annotation is often a requirement of a question and marks will certainly be lost if this is omitted.

One final word of advice — read each question carefully. Frequently, students produce quite impressive answers to questions which they think have been asked. Be quite sure what the examiner requires before embarking on your answer.

I would like to express my appreciation to Professor Ivor Seeley, the Series Editor, for his invaluable advice and encouragement. My friends and colleagues in the Department of Surveying at Trent Polytechnic, particularly David Richmond and Neil Crosby, have, as always, provided excellent moral support. Students of valuation must also be given a mention — without them the idea would not have emerged. Finally, my thanks go to Mrs Susan Williams for her efficient typing of the manuscript.

Nottingham Diane Butler
Spring 1987

PREFACE TO THE SECOND EDITION

Since the first edition of this book in 1987, there have been many changes for valuers to come to terms with. Students of Valuation find this more difficult, since changes occur as they are in the process of grasping principles and statutory rules.

This text is arranged in the same topic areas as the first edition and values have been updated throughout.

The bias towards calculation questions remains, but the opportunity has been taken to expand the answers to questions requiring a discursive response, mainly because students have commented that they would find this beneficial.

Since the first edition, there appears to be a more general acceptance of modern valuation techniques and a readiness to challenge accepted valuation practice, and this is reflected in the approach to the consideration of Valuation Theory in Chapter 1.

Just as students are beginning to feel some confidence with valuation principles, they are introduced to statutory interference, producing complications that do not always seem to follow logical valuation reasoning.

Leasehold Enfranchisement is one such topic that readily springs to mind in this respect, but the sections in this text dealing with Capital Gains Tax, Rating, Compulsory Purchase and the relationship of Landlord and Tenant in business premises, are all very much affected by statutory rules.

Rating in particular has passed through a very disturbed period, especially in respect of domestic property, with rating of such property being replaced by the Community Charge (or Poll Tax) and this in turn now replaced by the Council Tax. However, the rating system in respect of business property remains, in principle, very little changed and is considered in Chapter 5.

I would like to take this opportunity to express thanks to all my friends in the Department of Surveying at The Nottingham Trent University, particularly David Richmond, for their continuing friendship and support. I hope that students continue to derive benefit from this text. Thanks to Professor Ivor Seeley, the Series Editor, for his usual help and encouragement and also Stef Lubynskyj, for her careful and efficient typing of the manuscript.

Finally to avoid constant repetition in the text, I would like to stress that when the masculine gender is used, it is intended that this should equally refer to feminine or masculine gender.

Nottingham   Diane Butler
Spring 1995

1   VALUATION THEORY

At intermediate level, the study of valuation theory extends beyond a basic understanding and application of techniques, to a more in-depth consideration of valuation concepts.

This chapter begins with the demonstration of a purely traditional approach to the analysis of comparable transactions and the application of evidence to the valuation of freehold and leasehold interests. An explanation of the underlying logic is provided, together with an illustration of how this logic may be adapted to contemporary market conditions.

Accepted traditional methods have been increasingly challenged over the past few years and consideration is given in this section to alternative approaches that have evolved.

Examples first of all illustrate techniques which seek only to modify rather than replace traditional valuation methods – horizontal slicing and an equivalent yield approach in the case of freehold interests and sinking fund, double sinking fund, annual equivalent and Pannell's method in the case of leasehold interests.

Leasehold interests are particularly problematical and examination questions will often seek to test a student's understanding of the difficulties involved in the valuation of these interests. A critical appraisal of the underlying mathematical problem is often required of the student (see question 1.2), as is an understanding of the various methods that have been formulated in an effort to overcome the inadequacies of the traditional approach (see questions 1.3 and 1.4).

Contemporary critics of valuation methods have, over recent years, suggested alternative approaches to those conventionally accepted. Students will usually be expected to show awareness of the evolution of modern valuation models and demonstrate the ability to apply these to a variety of situations. Questions 1.5 and 1.6 provide illustrations.

Throughout this book, the Valuation Tables referred to and adopted for calculations, are those still generally used in practice – *Parry's Valuation and Investment Tables*. Over the past few years, alternative tables have been introduced and a consideration of the use and relative merits of these and Parry's Tables is provided in question 1.7.

Choice of yields in a valuation is vital to its accuracy and reliability. It is an aspect which the valuer may be called upon to defend, but one which students invariably find perplexing. For this reason, throughout this chapter, and in other chapters where appropriate, a brief explanation is given of why a particular yield, or yield pattern, has been adopted.

Figures taken from the Valuation Tables are generally shown to three decimal places, and this is considered to be sufficient. There is a danger of being over-precise in an unrealistic manner, since resultant capital values are usually rounded off.

VALUATION THEORY – QUESTIONS

1.1. The lessee of a shop, No. 12 High Street, holds the property from the freeholder on a 20 year lease with 5 year rent reviews. The lease has 4 years unexpired, is on full repairing and insuring terms and the present rent passing is £37 000 per annum. The shop consists of ground floor sales accommodation with first floor sales over, each measuring 8 m frontage by 17 m depth.

The lessee wishes to purchase the freehold interest and *you are required to calculate the total marriage value produced by merging the two interests.*

You are aware of the following comparables, similar in all respects except for size and the number of floors:

No. 10 High Street. The freehold interest was recently sold with vacant possession for £435 000. The shop has ground floor accommodation only, measuring 7 m frontage by 16.5 m depth.

No. 8 High Street. This shop also has only ground floor sales accommodation, measuring 8 m frontage by 18 m depth. It has recently been let on a 20 year full repairing and insuring lease with 5 year rent reviews at £36 400 per annum. The freehold interest has just been sold for £520 000.

No. 6 High Street. Let recently on a 20 year full repairing and insuring lease with 5 year rent reviews at £42 000 per annum. The shop has ground and first floor sales areas, each measuring 7 m frontage by 18 m depth.

1.2. Outline mathematical and conceptual criticisms that have been raised regarding the valuation of leasehold investments by the application of dual rate, tax adjusted Years' Purchase to a variable profit rent.

Construct examples to illustrate your answer.

1.3. Explain the underlying assumptions of the following approaches to the valuation of a variable profit rent:

(i) the sinking fund approach
(ii) the double sinking fund approach
(iii) the annual equivalent approach.

Value a profit rent of £14 000 per annum for the next 4 years, increasing to
£19 000 per annum for a further 5 years, using all three of these methods.

1.4. A, the freeholder, let a shop to B, 6 years ago on a 14 year lease at a fixed
rent of £40 000 per annum, on full repairing and insuring terms.

B sublet the property 2 years ago, for the remainder of the term, on full
repairing and insuring terms, at a rent of £75 000 per annum, on the basis
of 5 year reviews. The current full rental value of the shop on these terms
is £85 000 per annum. Similar rack rented freehold shops are selling for
yields of 7.5 per cent.

(a) Value A's interest using both vertical and horizontal slicing.

(b) Value B's interest using Pannell's Method.

(c) Briefly explain how A's interest might be valued using an equivalent yield.

1.5. Value the freehold and leasehold interests in office premises, using either a
discounted cash flow at equated yield or a real value approach. The
property is let on a full repairing and insuring lease with 10 years unexpired
at a fixed rent of £50 000 per annum. The current net rack rental value of the
property, based on a 5 year review pattern is £85 000 per annum.

Assume that similar rack rented freehold office properties are achieving
yields of 7 per cent when sold and that gilt edged stock currently yields 10
per cent.

Comment on your choice of yield at each stage of your valuations.

1.6. A shop is held from the freeholder on a full repairing and insuring lease
with 15 years unexpired at a fixed rent of £20 000 per annum and the
leaseholder wishes to sublet. The property measures 7 m frontage by
16 m depth and is on the ground floor only.

A similar shop nearby, measuring 9 m frontage by 17 m depth, has
recently been let on full repairing and insuring terms at £47 500 per
annum on a 21 year lease with 7 year reviews.

Calculate the rent which might be expected on subletting the subject
property and value the head leasehold interest, using a real value
approach, to show an equated yield of 20 per cent, assuming that rental
values will grow at 5 per cent per annum.

1.7. Consider the various valuation tables now available to valuers and
compare their bases, application and relevance to market activities.

VALUATION THEORY – SUGGESTED ANSWERS

Question 1.1

The first step is to analyse the comparable information. It is not necessary to
analyse these transactions in the order presented in the question. In this case,

the information regarding No. 8 High Street should be considered first. It will reveal the rental value per square metre achieved from the recent letting and the all risks yield from the subsequent sale of the freehold interest. Both of these can then be utilised in analysing the information obtained in respect of No. 6 and No. 10 High Street.

No. 8 High Street
The recent letting at £36 400 per annum can be analysed to find the Zone A rental value per square metre. Two 5 m zones and a remainder will be used, halving back – that is, assuming that Zone B is half the value of Zone A per square metre and the remainder is half the value of Zone B. It is not essential to use 5 m zones, but whatever zone depths are adopted, they must be used consistently throughout the analysis and subsequent valuations. This ensures that all the shops are treated on a comparable basis.

Let Zone A rental value per m^2 = £X

$$Zone\ A = 8\ m \times 5\ m \times X\ \ = 40X$$
$$Zone\ B = 8m \times 5m \times \tfrac{1}{2}X\ = 20X$$
$$Remainder = 8\ m \times 8\ m \times \tfrac{1}{4}X = 16X$$
$$rental\ value\ \ \ \ \ = 76X$$
$$76X = £\ 36\,400$$
$$and\ X = £478.95\ per\ m^2$$
$$say\ \ \ £479\ per\ m^2$$

The all risks yield (ARY) can also be discovered from this comparable, since the freehold interest has just been sold.

$$ARY = \frac{£36\,400}{£520\,000} \times 100 = 7\ per\ cent$$

This yield can be verified by applying the Zone A rental value per m^2 to No. 10 High Street, to determine its current rental value. Using this information, together with the sale price of the freehold interest in No. 10, will once again reveal an all risks yield of 7 per cent.

No. 10 High Street
Current rental value:

$$Zone\ A = 7\ m \times 5\ m\ \ \times £479\ \ \ = £16\,765$$
$$Zone\ B = 7\ m \times 5\ m\ \ \times £239.5\ = £\ 8\,383$$
$$Remainder = 7\ m \times 6.5\ m \times £119.75 = £\ 5\,449$$
$$current\ rental\ value\ \ \ \ £30\,597$$
$$say\ \ \ £30\,600\ per\ annum$$

Alternatively, the area of the shop may be expressed as a total in terms of Zone A. This is then multiplied by the Zone A rental value per m^2.

$$\text{Zone A} = 7 \text{ m} \times 5 \text{ m} \qquad = 35 \text{ m}^2$$

$$\text{Zone B} = 7 \text{ m} \times 5 \text{ m} \times \tfrac{1}{2} \qquad = 17.5 \text{ m}^2$$

$$\text{Remainder} = 7 \text{ m} \times 6.5 \text{ m} \times \tfrac{1}{4} \qquad = 11.375 \text{ m}^2$$

$$\text{area in terms of Zone A} \qquad 63.875 \text{ m}^2$$

$$\text{current rental value} = 63.875 \text{ m}^2 \times £479 = £30\,596$$

say £30 600 per annum

$$\text{ARY} = \frac{£30\,600}{£435\,000} \times 100 = 7.03 \text{ say 7 per cent}$$

This confirms the all risks yield obtained from No. 8 High Street.

No. 6 High Street
Using the Zone A rental value per m^2 determined from No. 10 High Street, together with the recent letting of No. 6, will enable the rental value per m^2 of first floor sales accommodation to be derived.

Current rental value   £42 000 pa
(assuming the recent letting is at current full rental value)

less rental value of ground floor sales area:

$$\text{Zone A} = 7 \text{ m} \times 5 \text{ m} \times £479 \qquad = £16\,765$$

$$\text{Zone B} = 7 \text{ m} \times 5 \text{ m} \times £239.5 \quad = £\,8\,383$$

$$\text{Remainder} = 7 \text{ m} \times 8 \text{ m} \times £119.75 = £\,6\,706 \qquad £31\,854 \text{ pa}$$

rental value of first floor sales area   £10 146 pa

area of first floor sales $= 7 \text{ m} \times 18 \text{ m} = 126 \text{ m}^2$

$$\text{rental value per m}^2 = \frac{£10\,146}{126 \text{ m}^2} = £80.52$$

say £80.50

This information may now be applied in the valuation of the subject property.

No. 12 High Street
Current rental value on full repairing and insuring terms with a 5 year review pattern:

ground floor sales

$$\text{Zone A} = 8 \text{ m} \times 5 \text{ m} \times £479 = £19\,160$$

$$\text{Zone B} = 8 \text{ m} \times 5 \text{ m} \times £239.5 = £\,9\,580$$

$$\text{Remainder} = 8 \text{ m} \times 7 \text{ m} \times £119.75 = £\,6\,706$$

$$£35\,446$$

first floor sales 8 m × 17 m × £80.50   = £10 948

current rental value   £46 394

say   £46 400 per annum

Value of freehold interest

Net rent received	£ 37 000 pa	
YP 4 years at 6 per cent [see note 1]	3.465	£128 205
reversion to full net rental value	£ 46 400 pa	
YP in perpetuity deferred 4 years		
at 7 per cent [see note 1]	10.899	£505 714
Capital value		£633 919

say   £635 000

Note

1: Traditional yield pattern. All risks yield, from comparables, used to capitalise the current rental value, deferred for the duration of the term at the same yield. The term income is capitalised at one per cent less than the all risks yield, to reflect the assumed security of the income – the income is currently being received and it is below full rental value, therefore the tenant is enjoying a profit rent and is less likely to default.

In the traditional yield pattern shown above, the yields adopted were logical in an economy where inflation and growth were neither recognised, nor expected. It is now generally accepted that adopting a low yield implies the expectation of rental growth. Thus, the 7 per cent yield used to capitalise the current rental value, correctly reflects market expectations of rental growth, realised every 5 years at rent review.

However, adopting a 6 per cent yield to value the income received during the first 4 years, implies rental growth in a situation where no growth is possible – the income is fixed for those 4 years. Indeed, because the yield is lower than the all risks yield, this implies greater growth in the term income than the reversionary income, which is totally incorrect. Consequently, the term income is over-valued.

On the other hand, the reversion tends to be under-valued, not because the current rental value is capitalised at the all risks yield, but because receipt of that income is *deferred* at the all risks yield. This reflects some degree of growth in the current rental value during the 4 years of the unexpired term, but it may not allow sufficiently for that growth.

A modified yield pattern is now often adopted in the traditional approach, in an attempt to address these problems.

Alternative valuation of freehold interest

Net rent received		£37 000 pa	
YP 4 years at 13 per cent [see note 1]		2.975	£110 075
reversion to full net rental value		£46 400 pa	
YP in perpetuity at 7 per cent			
[see note 2]	14.286		
×PV of £1 in 4 years at 6 per cent			
[see note 3]	0.792	11.315	£525 016
Capital value			£635 091
		say	£635 000 [see note 4]

Notes

1: Income is fixed and inflation prone. The yield achieved by a fixed income from property is expected to at least match that of other fixed income investments, such as long-dated gilt edged stock, plus a margin to reflect the additional problems associated with property investments. This margin is usually accepted as being in the region of 2 per cent, so the 13 per cent yield assumes that gilts are yielding 11 per cent.

2: All risks yield from comparable transactions reflects the partially inflation proof nature of the current rental value, with rent reviews every 5 years.

3: Deferred at one per cent below the all risks yield, to reflect growth in the current rental value during the 4 years of the unexpired term.

4: The capital value, although a little higher, is almost the same as that produced when using a traditional yield pattern. The reason is that, in this case, the over-valuation of the term income in the traditional approach, almost matches its under-valuation of the reversion. It might be argued that, since the traditional approach produces an acceptable capital value, there is no need to consider alternatives. However, if a valuation is to have credibility, the reasoning behind it must be defensible.

For a consideration of contemporary approaches, see question 1.5.

Value of leasehold interest

Full net rental value	£46 400 pa
less rent paid [see note 1]	£37 000 pa
profit rent	£ 9 400 pa
YP 4 years at 8 per cent and 3 per cent	
(tax 40 per cent) [see note 2]	2.090
Capital value	£19 646
say	£19 650

Notes

1: Rent paid is on the same terms as full rental value – both are on full repairing and insuring terms – therefore there is no need to make any adjustments.

2: Traditional yield pattern. Remunerative yield is one per cent above freehold all risks yield, because of the added risks perceived in investing in leasehold interests compared with freehold interests. An annual sinking fund is assumed available at 3 per cent and income tax payable at 40p in the £.

Calculation of marriage value

Value of freehold in possession:		
Full net rental value		£ 46 400 pa
YP in perpetuity at 7 per cent		14.286
Capital value		£662 870 [see note 1]
less		
value of freehold interest	£635 000	
value of leasehold interest	£ 19 650	£654 650 [see note 2]
marriage value		£ 8 220

Notes

1: This is the value of the unencumbered freehold that the lessee will obtain if the freehold interest is purchased.

2: The leaseholder must purchase the present freehold interest and, effectively, his own leasehold interest, in order to become the owner of the unencumbered freehold. The value of these two interests must therefore be deducted from the value of the freehold in possession to reveal the marriage value.

It appears that £635 000 is the price that the leaseholder must pay for the freehold interest. However, merging the freehold and leasehold interests will release marriage value of £8 220. To persuade him to sell, the freeholder will probably require some proportion of this marriage value. It could be shared equally, in which case the freehold interest would be purchased for, say, £639 000. Alternatively, the freeholder might argue that he should receive a larger share of the marriage value, since the freehold interest contributes the majority of this value. The marriage value might then be apportioned according to the relative values of the present interests and, although the question does not require it, the calculation is shown below, to demonstrate the method.

Proportion of marriage value contributed by freehold interest:

$$8\,220 \times \frac{£635\,000}{£654\,650} = £7\,973$$

Price required for freehold interest:

$$£635\,000 + £7\,973 = £642\,973 \quad \text{say} \quad £643\,000$$

Question 1.2

The answer should first of all explain that when dual rate, tax adjusted Years' Purchase is used in the valuation of variable profit rents, a mathematical error occurs. It is also important to note that an error will be present whether or not tax adjustment is incorporated in the Years' Purchase.

There are various ways in which the error may be illustrated, and these are demonstrated below. In an examination it is usually sufficient to produce only one method of showing the error and the individual student should adopt whichever method they personally find most convincing. In all of the examples that follow, it will be assumed that a remunerative yield of 8 per cent is required, an annual sinking fund is available at 2½ per cent and tax is payable at 35p in the £.

Method (i)
A constant profit rent is valued for a period of years, say 10 years, firstly capitalising it over the full 10 year period. The valuation is then repeated, *at the same remunerative and accumulative yields and tax rate*, this time splitting the 10 years into two (or more) periods of years.

Since the profit rent remains constant, the yields adopted are identical and the profit rent is valued for the same total number of years, it would be expected that the two calculations should produce the same answer. The example below shows that this is not so.

Example

Compare the value of a constant profit rent of £10 000 per annum
(a) for 10 years, and
(b) for 4 years and 6 years.

(a) *Valuation over 10 years*

Profit rent	£10 000 pa
YP 10 years at 8 per cent and 2½ per cent	
(tax 35 per cent)	4.602
Capital value	£46 020

(b) *Valuation over 4 years and 6 years*

Profit rent	£10 000 pa	
YP 4 years at 8 per cent and 2½ per cent		
(tax 35 per cent)	2.220	£22 200
Profit rent	£10 000 pa	
YP 6 years at 8 per cent and		
2½ per cent (tax 35 per cent) 3.117		
× PV of £1 in 4 years at 8 per cent 0.735	2.291	£22 910
Capital value		£45 110

an error of −£910

If the 10 year period is split into a different pattern of years for term and reversion, the magnitude of the error will change. For example, if the term is 7 years and the reversion 3 years:

Profit rent	£10 000 pa	
YP 7 years at 8 per cent and		
2½ per cent (tax 35 per cent)	3.523	£35 230
Profit rent	£10 000 pa	
YP 3 years at 8 per cent and		
2½ per cent (tax 35 per cent) 1.724		
× PV of £1 in 7 years at 8 per cent 0.583	1.005	£10 050
Capital value		£45 280

an error of −£740

Method (ii)

A constant profit rent is valued for a period of years, as in Method (i). Adopting the same yields, the valuation is then repeated, this time with an increased profit rent for part of the period. The difference between the two valuations should be the value of the extra profit rent in the second valuation. Once again, an example will show that this is not the case.

Example
Compare
(a) the value of a constant profit rent of £10 000 per annum for 10 years, with
(b) the value of a profit rent of £10 000 per annum for 5 years, rising to a profit rent of £15 000 per annum for a further 5 years.

(a) The value of a constant profit rent of £10 000 per annum for 10 years is £46 020, from Method (i)(a).

(b)	Profit rent		£10 000 pa	
	YP 5 years at 8 per cent and			
	2½ per cent (tax 35 per cent)		2.683	£26 830
	Profit rent		£15 000 pa	
	YP 5 years at 8 per cent and			
	2½ per cent (tax 35 per cent)	2.683		
	× PV of £1 in 5 years at 8 per cent	0.681	1.827	£27 405
	Capital value			£54 235

At first sight, there does not seem to be anything wrong with these two valuations – one would expect valuation (b) to be higher than valuation (a).

The difference between the two is that in (b) an extra £5 000 per annum profit rent is enjoyed for the last 5 years.

The value of this is:

extra profit rent		£5 000 pa
YP 5 years at 8 per cent and		
2½ per cent (tax 35 per cent)	2.683	
× PV of £1 in 5 years at 8 per cent	0.681	1.827
Capital value of extra profit rent		£9 135

£9 135 should be the difference in capital value between valuation (a) and valuation (b). In fact, the actual difference is:

$$£54 235 - £46 020 = £8 215$$

$$\text{There is an error of } -£920$$

Method (iii)
This is, in fact, an alternative form of Method (ii). In some cases, the use of dual rate Years' Purchase results in a leasehold interest with a lower profit rent than a similar leasehold interest, apparently having the higher capital value of the two.

This may be illustrated using an example similar to that used for Method (ii). It is perhaps, not such a satisfactory approach to demonstrating the error, since the valuation may not always appear incorrect, as the example in Method (ii) indicates. Should this occur in an example constructed to illustrate the answer to an examination question, there is no need to abandon it, wasting valuable time. All the student need do is revert to Method (ii), comparing the difference in values with the value of the extra profit rent.

Example

Compare

(a) the value of a constant profit rent of £10 000 per annum for 20 years, with

(b) the value of a profit rent of £10 000 per annum for 15 years, rising to a profit rent of £11 000 per annum for a further 5 years.

The profit rent in (b) is obviously more valuable than that in (a), since an extra £1 000 per annum is enjoyed for the last 5 years. However, the capital values of the two profit rents do not correctly reflect their relative merits.

(a)	Profit rent		£10 000 pa	
	YP 20 years at 8 per cent and			
	2 ½ per cent (tax 35 per cent)		7.131	
	Capital value		£71 310	
(b)	Profit rent		£10 000 pa	
	YP 15 years at 8 per cent and			
	2 ½ per cent (tax 35 per cent)		6.032	£60 320
	Profit rent		£11 000 pa	
	YP 5 years at 8 per cent and			
	2 ½ per cent (tax 35 per cent)	2.683		
	× PV of £1 in 15 years at 8 per cent	0.315	0.845	£ 9 295
	Capital value			£69 615

The *inferior* investment has the *higher* capital value, even though the remunerative and accumulative yields and the rate of tax are the same throughout both valuations.

It was noted at the beginning of this answer that the mathematical error still manifests itself even though tax adjustment does not feature in the Years' Purchase. This may be illustrated by repeating one of the examples used earlier, but omitting the adjustment for tax from the Years' Purchase.

In this case, the example used in Method (i) will be adopted.

(a) *Valuation over 10 years*

Profit rent	£10 000 pa	
YP 10 years at 8 per cent and 2½ per cent	5.908	
Capital value	£59 080	

(b) *Valuation over 4 years and 6 years*

Profit rent		£10 000 pa	
YP 4 years at 8 per cent and 2½ per cent		3.117	£31 170
Profit rent		£10 000 pa	
YP 6 years at 8 per cent and			
2½ per cent	4.227		
×PV of £1 in 4 years at 8 per cent	0.735	3.107	£31 070
Capital value			£62 240

an error of +£3 160

The error has still occurred without the adjustment for tax, but it is interesting to note that both the magnitude and direction of the error have changed. Not only is the error now greater, but it is positive rather than negative.

When a tax adjusted Years' Purchase is adopted, the error will also vary according to the rate of tax.

A brief summary would be useful at this stage, noting the various factors that can affect the magnitude of the error:

(i) the length of time over which the profit rent is valued
(ii) how that length of time is divided up into years, that is, the relative lengths of term and reversion
(iii) the remunerative yield, or yields
(iv) the accumulative yield, and
(v) whether or not adjustment is made for income tax and, if so, the rate of tax.

Methods of correcting the mathematical error in the valuation of variable profit rents are considered in questions 1.3 and 1.4.

As far as conceptual criticisms are concerned, the answer should note that exponents of contemporary valuation techniques argue against using profit rent in the valuation of leasehold interests. There may be a difference in growth potential between the rent received and rent paid by the leaseholder, which cannot be correctly reflected in the profit rent. For instance, the rent paid may be fixed, whereas the rent received may be subject to regular rent reviews.

Example

A holds land on ground lease with 45 years unexpired at a fixed rent of £50 000 per annum net. A has built a factory unit on the land and this has recently been let on a full repairing and insuring lease with 5 year reviews at its full rental value of £100 000 per annum.

B holds land on ground lease with 45 years unexpired at a fixed rent of £75 000 per annum, net. B has also built a factory unit on this land, and it has similarly been recently let on a full repairing and insuring lease with 5 year reviews, at its full rental value of £125 000 per annum.

Thus both A and B each have an initial profit rent of £50 000 per annum, and a traditional valuation approach may well ascribe the same capital value to both head leasehold interests.

Profit rent	£ 50 000 pa
YP 45 years at 10 per cent and 2½ per cent	
(tax 35 per cent)	8.412
Capital value	£420 600

However, depending upon the rate of rental growth, the situation at first review in the subleases, in 5 years' time, will be quite different.

Assuming rental growth is 4 per cent per annum:

Head leaseholder A

Current rental value	£100 000 pa
× Amount of £1 in 5 years at 4 per cent	1.217
rental value in 5 years' time	£121 700 pa
less rent paid	£ 50 000 pa
profit rent in 5 years' time	£ 71 700 pa

This is an increase in profit rent of 43.4 per cent.

Head leaseholder B

Current rental value	£125 000 pa
× Amount of £1 in 5 years at 4 per cent	1.217
rental value in 5 years' time	£152 125 pa
less rent paid	£ 75 000 pa
profit rent in 5 years' time	£ 77 125 pa

This is an increase in profit rent of 54.25 per cent.

At the second review in the subleases, similar calculations reveal that A's profit rent is expected to have increased by 96 per cent over 10 years, and B's by 120 per cent. In 15 years, the anticipated increases are 160 per cent and 200 per cent respectively, and so on.

It is evident that the growth potential of B's profit rent is superior to that of A's, but this was not apparent from the traditional valuation of the two interests.

The concept of allowing for an annual sinking fund should also be considered. The validity of this is questionable when investors rarely trouble to invest in a sinking fund. This is a further aspect under attack from those who favour contemporary valuation techniques. If allowance *is* made for a sinking fund, the rate of interest adopted is also debateable. It is accepted practice to assume a net yield in the region of 3 per cent – a low, safe rate, to ensure that capital is recouped – but it could be argued that investors are unlikely to accept such a low yield if better returns are available elsewhere.

Adjustment for income tax in a dual rate Years' Purchase is also considered by many to be unwarranted, since the majority of investors in leasehold interests are likely to be non-taxpayers. Choice of remunerative yield is a further area of difficulty. It is often impossible to ascertain from comparable transactions, since one leasehold interest is rarely directly comparable with another. All leases are unique in some way – length of unexpired term, terms of the lease and so on. Because of this, it is customary to derive the remunerative yield from that of similar freehold interests, usually increasing it by one or two per cent to allow for the extra problems and risks associated with leasehold interests. This 'rule of thumb' approach cannot be entirely satisfactory and, if a leasehold interest cannot be said to be comparable with any other leasehold interest, it is difficult to argue that it is comparable with a freehold interest.

Question 1.5 considers examples of contemporary approaches to the valuation of leasehold interests, which overcome the difficulties discussed above.

Question 1.3

The answer should begin with a brief explanation that the approaches mentioned have all been suggested as alternatives to the application of dual rate Years' Purchase in the valuation of varying profit rents. This latter method can be shown to produce a mathematical error (see question 1.2) and the 'sinking fund', 'double sinking fund' and 'annual equivalent' are methods that eliminate or greatly reduce this error.

(i) The underlying assumption of the 'sinking fund' approach is that the accumulated annual sinking funds to replace the capital value of the varying profit rents will exactly replace the total capital value of the leasehold investment. Thus, if the total accumulation of the annual sinking funds is calculated, this should be equal to the required capital value.

(ii) The underlying assumption of the 'double sinking fund' approach is that although the varying profit rents are normally valued separately, which implies separate annual sinking funds, an investor would not provide these separately. He would provide only one, constant annual sinking fund, over the total life of the investment, recouping the total capital value.

(iii) The underlying assumption of the 'annual equivalent' approach is that if, instead of valuing the varying profit rents separately, a constant profit rent equivalent to the varying profit rents, is valued over the total life of the investment, there should be no error since the point at which the error occurs in the valuation is eliminated.

The three valuations which follow are all carried out on the assumption of an 8 per cent remunerative yield for the next 4 years and 9 per cent for the following 5 years. It is assumed that an annual sinking fund is available at 3 per cent and that tax is paid at 40p in the £.

Valuation using the 'sinking fund' approach

Let capital value $= £X$
Next 4 years
Profit rent $= £14\,000$ pa
gross sinking fund $=$ total income $-$ spendable income
                     $= £14\,000 - 0.08X$ [see note 1]
net sinking fund $= (£14\,000 - 0.08X)\,0.6$ [see note 2]
                     $= £8\,400 - 0.048X$

Following 5 years
Profit rent $= £19\,000$ pa
gross sinking fund $= £19\,000 - 0.09X$ [see note 3]
net sinking fund $= (£19\,000 - 0.09X)\,0.6$ [see note 2]
                     $= £11\,400 - 0.054X$

The accumulation of the net sinking funds is now calculated.
Next 4 years
net sinking fund $=$ £ $8\,400 - 0.048X$
  × Amount of £1 pa in 4 years
    at 3 per cent   4.184 [see note 4]
  × Amount of £1 in 5 years
    at 3 per cent [see note 5] 1.159   4.849   £ $40\,731.6 - 0.233X$

Following 5 years
net sinking fund $=$ £11\,400 $- 0.054X$

× Amount of £1 pa in 5 years at 3 per cent [see note 6]	5.309	£ 60 522.6 − 0.287X
Total accumulation of annual sinking funds		£101 254.2 − 0.52X

The total annual sinking fund accumulation should equal the capital value, that is, X. Therefore

$$X = £101\,254.2 - 0.52X$$
$$1.52X = £101\,254.2$$
$$X = £\,66\,615$$

Capital value, say £ 66 000

Notes

1: Return required by the investor as spendable income is 8 per cent of capital value, that is, 8 per cent of X, the capital value being unknown at this point in the calculation. After deducting the investor's return on capital, any remaining income is available for investment in the annual sinking fund.

2: Forty per cent of income is payable in tax, therefore of the total amount available for investment in the annual sinking fund, only 60 per cent remains after tax.

3: Return required by the investor as spendable income is 9 per cent of capital value, that is, 9 per cent of X.

4: This shows how much the net sinking fund instalments will accumulate to if invested at the end of each of the next 4 years at an interest rate of 3 per cent per annum.

5: After 4 years, the amount accumulated in the sinking fund continues to gain compound interest at 3 per cent per annum over the last 5 years.

6: This shows how much the net sinking fund instalments will accumulate to if invested at the end of each of the last 5 years at an interest rate of 3 per cent per annum.

Valuation using 'double sinking fund' approach

Let capital value = £X		
Next 4 years		
Profit rent		£14 000 pa
less annual sinking fund to replace X in 9 years at 3 per cent	0.098X	[see note 1]
Adjusted for tax at 40 per cent [see note 2]	1.667	0.163X
Spendable income		£14 000 − 0.163X

YP 4 years at 8 per cent [see note 3]	3.312	£46 368 − 0.540X

Following 5 years
Profit rent   £19 000 pa
less annual sinking fund to
  replace X in 9 years at
  3 per cent (tax 40 per cent)
  [see notes 1 & 2]   0.163X

Spendable income		£19 000 − 0.163X	
YP 5 years at 9 per cent	3.890		
× PV of £1 in 4 years			
at 9 per cent	0.708	2.754	£52 326 − 0.449X

                                                            £98 694 − 0.989X
                                                            [see note 4]

plus present value of capital value replaced by single rate annual sinking fund		
X × PV of £1 in 4 years at 8 per cent	0.735	
× PV of £1 in 5 years at 9 per cent	0.650	+0.478X

Capital value   £98 694 − 0.511X

but the capital value = X
          therefore X = £98 694 − 0.511X
                 1.511X = £98 694
                      X = £65 317
          Capital value, say £66 000

Notes

1: A constant annual sinking fund provision is assumed over the total 9 years unexpired of the investment.

2: The annual sinking fund is grossed up to account for tax at 40 per cent, otherwise it will be insufficient to recoup capital value when the tax is deducted. The figure of 1.667 can be obtained either from the 'Tax Adjustment Factor' table in *Parry's Valuation and Investment Tables*, or by using the formula $100/100 - t$ where t is the rate of tax. The gross sinking fund instalment is then deducted from the profit rent, leaving the spendable income available to the investor.

3: Single rate Years' Purchase can now be used to value the profit rent, since the annual sinking fund has been explicitly provided for.

4: If the valuation were left at this point, the investment would be undervalued, because two annual sinking funds have been provided – the explicit provision of a 3 per cent annual sinking fund (adjusted for tax at 40 per cent) and the annual sinking fund implicit in the Years' Purchase single rate used to value the spendable income. The present value of the capital value provided by the annual sinking fund in the single rate Years' Purchase must therefore be added back.

Valuation using 'annual equivalent' approach

Next 4 years			
Profit rent		£14 000 pa	
YP 4 years at 3 per cent [see note 1]		3.717	£52 038
Following 5 years			
Profit rent		£19 000 pa	
YP 5 years at 3 per cent	4.580		
× PV of £1 in 4 years at 3 per cent	0.888	4.067	£77 273

Annual equivalent incomes:

First 4 years

$$\frac{£52\,038}{\text{YP 9 years at 3 per cent [see note 2]}} = \frac{£52\,038}{7.786} = £6\,684 \text{ pa}$$

Following 5 years

$$\frac{£77\,273}{\text{YP 9 years at 3 per cent [see note 2]}} = \frac{£77\,273}{7.786} = £9\,925 \text{ pa}$$

Valuation:		
First 4 years	£6 684 pa	
YP 9 years at 8 per cent and 3 per cent		
(tax 40 per cent) [see note 3]	4.097	£27 384
Following 5 years	£9 925 pa	
YP 9 years at 9 per cent and 3 per cent		
(tax 40 per cent) [see note 4]	3.936	£39 065
Capital value		£66 449
	say	£66 000

Notes

1: The two profit rents are both capitalised using single rate Years' Purchase at the sinking fund rate, but the capital values of the term and reversion remain separate.

2: The separate capital values of the two profit rents are amortised over the total 9 years, to derive the constant annual profit rents for 9 years equivalent to £14 000 per annum for 4 years and £19 000 per annum for a further 5 years. In other words, a profit rent of £6 684 per annum for 9 years is equivalent to £14 000 per annum for the first 4 years and a profit rent of £9 925 per annum for 9 years is equivalent to £19 000 per annum for the last 5 years.

3: The annual equivalent of the profit rent for the first 4 years is capitalised over 9 years, but at the remunerative yield for the term, of 8 per cent (dual rate, tax adjusted).

4: The annual equivalent of the profit rent for the last 5 years is capitalised over 9 years at the reversionary yield of 9 per cent (dual rate, tax adjusted). By capitalising in this way, the point in the calculation where the mathematical error normally occurs, has been removed.

Harker, Nanthakumaran and Rogers (1988) in *Double Sinking Fund Correction Methods, an Analysis and Appraisal*, considered the effectiveness of the various methods of correcting the mathematical error in leasehold valuations involving a varying profit rent. They concluded that the 'sinking fund' method was the most satisfactory, since it both achieved correct recoupment of capital and ensured the investor obtained the required return. The only circumstance in which the return fell short of that required was when, at any time, the income itself was less than the required return. This they called the 'negative sinking fund problem' – a problem shared by the other correction methods and one which is considered beyond the scope of this book.

The 'double sinking fund' method was found to be not as accurate as the 'sinking fund' method in achieving the investor's required rate of return and ensuring correct recoupment of capital. One basic flaw identified was deferment of the reversionary income at the reversionary yield, rather than the term yield. If deferment is carried out at the term yield in the example under consideration, it produces the following result:

value of term income, as before			£ 46 368 − 0.540X
reversion			
Spendable income		£19 000 − 0.163X	
YP 5 years at 9 per cent	3.890		
×PV of £1 in 4 years at			
8 per cent	0.735	2.859	£ 54 321 − 0.466X
			£100 689 − 1.006X
plus present value of capital value replaced by single rate annual sinking fund, as before			+ 0.478X
Capital value			£100 689 − 0.528X

$$X = £100\,689 - 0.528X$$
$$1.528X = £100\,689$$
$$X = £\ 65\,896$$

Capital value, say   £ 66 000

The accuracy of the 'annual equivalent' method was found to depend upon the yields adopted. Where the term and reversion were valued at the same remunerative yield and the sinking fund yield was used to determine the annual equivalent incomes, then the annual equivalent method proved to be algebraically equal to the sinking fund method. However, if different yields were used to value term and reversion, or the sinking fund yield was not used to calculate the annual equivalent incomes, then the method did not allow for correct recoupment of capital, or the achievement of the investor's required return.

Question 1.4

(a) *Value of A's Interest*

Vertical slicing
This is a traditional valuation in conventional form. The term and reversionary incomes are valued entirely separately.

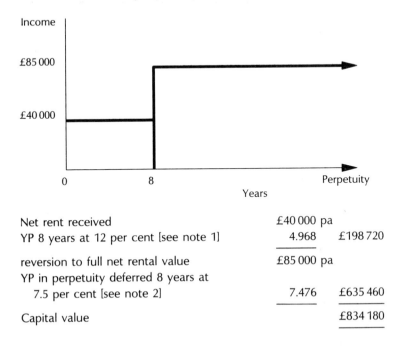

Net rent received	£40 000 pa	
YP 8 years at 12 per cent [see note 1]	4.968	£198 720
reversion to full net rental value	£85 000 pa	
YP in perpetuity deferred 8 years at		
7.5 per cent [see note 2]	7.476	£635 460
Capital value		£834 180

Notes
1: Income is fixed and inflation prone for 8 years, therefore a high yield is adopted. See question 1.1 for a general consideration of the traditional approach.
2: All risks yield obtained from transactions involving similar properties.

Horizontal slicing
Using this method, the rent currently being received is treated as perpetual and valued as such. This is referred to as the bottom slice, or hardcore income. Indeed this approach to a valuation is alternatively called the 'hardcore' method.

   The top slice, or marginal income, is the amount of rent which is required, over and above the hardcore income, to raise the rent to full rental value. This is also valued into perpetuity, but not until full rental value is being received in 8 years' time.

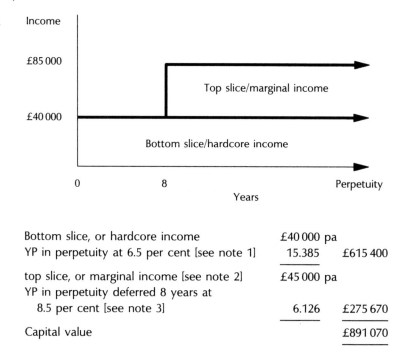

Bottom slice, or hardcore income	£40 000 pa	
YP in perpetuity at 6.5 per cent [see note 1]	15.385	£615 400
top slice, or marginal income [see note 2]	£45 000 pa	
YP in perpetuity deferred 8 years at		
8.5 per cent [see note 3]	6.126	£275 670
Capital value		£891 070

Notes
1: This element of the income is regarded as secure, as reflected in the 6.5 per cent yield. The tenant has covenanted to pay this rent and is actually doing so. The yield adopted is one per cent below the all risks yield as would be used to value the term income in a strictly traditional vertical slicing approach, both sharing the problem of using a low, growth-implicit yield to value a fixed income.

2: £45 000 is the income over and above the bottom slice, which takes the rent to full rental value. It is not yet being paid, therefore there is uncertainty regarding its receipt in the future. A yield higher than the all risks yield is adopted to reflect the risk involved. The risks attached to this element of the income are treated as being entirely separate from those of the hardcore income, even though both are assumed to be received at this stage.

3: The 8.5 per cent yield used to value the marginal income is an estimate, bearing in mind the 7.5 per cent being achieved from similar rack rented freehold properties. It is usual to adopt a rule of thumb adjustment of one per cent above all risks yield in this stage of the valuation. The difference of £56 890 between the vertically and horizontally sliced valuations, tends to suggest that 8.5 per cent is incorrect.

A preliminary calculation must be performed to derive a more accurate yield to apply to the marginal income.

Full rental value	£85 000 pa	
YP in perpetuity at 7.5 per cent [see note 1]	13.333	£1 133 305
less hardcore income	£40 000 pa	
YP in perpetuity at 6.5 per cent	15.385	£ 615 400
Capital value of marginal income [see note 2]		£ 517 905

The yield on the marginal income may now be derived from

$$\frac{\text{marginal income}}{\text{capital value of marginal income}} \times 100$$

$$= \frac{£45\,000}{£517\,905} \times 100 = 8.689 \text{ per cent}$$

say 8.7 per cent

Notes
1: All risks yield from similar rack rented properties.
2: The difference between the capital value of the full rental value in perpetuity and the capital value of the hardcore income in perpetuity, must be the capital value of the difference between the two incomes, that is, the marginal income.

The valuation now becomes:

hardcore income	£40 000 pa	
YP in perpetuity at 6.5 per cent	15.385	£615 400
marginal income	£45 000 pa	

YP in perpetuity at 8.7 per cent	11.494		
× PV of £1 in 8 years at			
8.7 per cent	0.513	5.896	£265 320
Capital value			£880 720

This is £46 540 more than the valuation using vertical slicing. Such a large difference cannot be attributed to rounding and is in fact due to the different yields that have been adopted in the two valuations rather than their different formats. In order to compare horizontal and vertical slicing valuations, the same yields should be used in both.

The preliminary calculations necessary for the horizontal slicing approach will now be repeated, adopting a yield of 12 per cent to value the hardcore income, bringing the yields into line with the vertically sliced valuation

Full rental value		£85 000 pa	
YP in perpetuity at 7.5 per cent		13.333	£1 133 305
less hardcore income		£40 000 pa	
YP in perpetuity at 12 per cent		8.333	£ 333 320
Capital value of marginal income			£ 799 985

$$\text{Yield on marginal income} = \frac{£45\,000}{£799\,985} \times 100 = 5.625 \text{ per cent}$$

say 5.6 per cent

The valuation now becomes:

hardcore income		£40 000 pa	
YP in perpetuity at 12 per cent		8.333	£333 320
marginal income		£45 000 pa	
YP in perpetuity at 5.6 per cent	17.857		
× PV of £1 in 8 years at			
5.6 per cent	0.647	11.553	£519 885
			£853 205

The two valuations are now closer although there is still a difference of £19 025. This is probably due to the relatively long period to reversion. The longer this is the greater the difference between the two valuation approaches tends to be. For example, if the reversion in the situation under consideration were two years rather than eight, both vertical and horizontal slicing produce values close to £1 050 000.

(b) *Value of B's interest using Pannell's method*

The valuation is carried out using a traditional yield pattern, assuming a 7.5 per cent yield for the term income and 8.5 per cent for the reversionary income. It is also assumed that an annual sinking fund is available at 3 per cent and that income tax is payable at 35p in the £.

Pannell's method is one of various approaches used to reduce or eliminate the error which occurs in the valuation of variable profit rents by dual rate, tax adjusted Years' Purchase. For illustration of the error, see the answer to question 1.2 and question 1.3 for other suggested methods of dealing with this situation.

The valuation is first of all carried out using single rate Years' Purchase:

Next 3 years		
Rent received	£75 000 pa	
less rent paid	£40 000 pa	
net income	£35 000 pa	
YP 3 years at 7.5 per cent	2.601	£ 91 035
Following 5 years		
Full net rental value	£85 000 pa	
less rent paid	£40 000 pa	
net income	£45 000 pa	
YP 5 years at 8.5 per cent	3.941	
×PV of £1 in 3 years at		
8.5 per cent	0.783	3.086	£138 870
Capital value on single rate basis		£229 905

The £229 905 is now decapitalised over the total 8 years using the average of the term and reversionary yields, to determine the single, constant net income that, if received for 8 years, would have the same capital value as the two differing net incomes.

The simple arithmetic average of 7.5 per cent and 8.5 per cent is 8 per cent. However, the average should be weighted, to account for the fact that 7.5 per cent is applied in the valuation for only 3 years, whereas 8.5 per cent is applied for 5 years.

A simple method of weighting the yield is as follows:

$$3/8 \times 7.5 = 2.8125 \text{ [see note 1]}$$

$$5/8 \times 8.5 = 5.3125 \text{ [see note 2]}$$

weighted average yield 8.125 per cent

Notes

1: 7.5 per cent is used in the valuation for 3 out of the 8 years remaining of the leasehold interest, so 3/8 of 7.5 per cent is assumed to be contributed to the weighted average yield.

2: 8.5 per cent is used in the valuation for 5 of the 8 years, so 5/8 of 8.5 per cent is assumed to be contributed to the weighted average yield.

In the remainder of this valuation, a yield of 8.125 per cent will be used, but, in an examination, it would be acceptable to round off the yield to 8 per cent, having demonstrated an understanding of the concept of a weighted average yield.

$$\frac{£229\,905}{\text{YP 8 years at 8.125 per cent [see note 1]}}$$

$$= \text{weighted average income, or constant rent,}$$

$$\frac{229\,905}{5.719} = £40\,200 \text{ per annum}$$

Note

1: Years' Purchase calculated using the formula

$$\frac{1 - \dfrac{1}{(1+i)^n}}{i}$$

where i = yield expressed as a decimal (0.08125)

$\qquad n$ = number of years (8).

This constant rent can now be capitalised using a dual rate, tax adjusted Years' Purchase over the full 8 years. This should eliminate, or at least reduce, the mathematical error that occurs when varying profit rents are valued separately, since the point at which the error arises has been eliminated from the calculation.

Constant rent	£ 40 200 pa
YP 8 years at 8.125 per cent and	
3 per cent (tax 35 per cent)	3.933 [see note 1]
Capital value of B's interest	£158 107
say	£158 000

Note

1: YP calculated using the formula

$$\frac{1}{i + \left[\dfrac{i(a)}{(1+i(a))^n - 1} \cdot \dfrac{1}{1-t} \right]}$$

where
i = remunerative yield, expressed as a decimal (0.08125)
$i(a)$ = accumulative yield, expressed as a decimal (0.03)
t = rate of tax, expressed as a decimal (0.35)
n = number of years (8).

(c) How A's interest might be valued using an equivalent yield
In the answer to part (a), using a vertical slicing approach, a yield of 12 per cent was used to value the term income and 7.5 per cent to value the reversionary income.

The equivalent yield is the weighted average of these two yields and is used to value *both* the term and reversion.

For example, from the yields of 12 per cent and 7.5 per cent, it might be estimated that the equivalent yield is in the region of 7.75 per cent. This yield is employed throughout the valuation.

Net rent received	£40 000 pa	
YP 8 years at 7.75 per cent	5.802	£232 080
reversion to full net rental value	£85 000 pa	
YP in perpetuity		
deferred 8 years at 7.75 per cent	7.102	£603 670
Capital value		£835 750

This reconciles with the valuation of £834 180 achieved using yields of 12 per cent and 7.5 per cent, but it would obviously be more satisfactory if the equivalent yield could be derived in a more precise manner. However, the question does *not* ask for the equivalent yield to be *calculated*. All that is required is a *brief* explanation of the equivalent yield approach and the above should satisfy the examiner's requirements.

Although these comments would apply in answering an examination question, a demonstration of the method of calculating the equivalent yield is now given for the benefit of the student.

If information from transactions involving comparable properties is available, this can be analysed to determine the appropriate equivalent yield. For example, assume that the freehold interest in a similar shop nearby has recently been sold for £730 000. It is let with 8 years unexpired on full repairing and insuring terms at a fixed rent of £35 000 per annum. The current full rental value on full repairing and insuring terms and on the basis of 5 year reviews is estimated to be £74 375 per annum.

Equivalent yield may be defined as the *internal rate of return of an investment in terms of the current income flow*, therefore the simplest way of determining the equivalent yield from this transaction is to calculate the internal rate of return. It is important to note the words *current income flow*, which mean that no attempt is made to explicitly incorporate future anticipated growth in the calculation.

Trial rate 8 per cent

Net rent received	£35 000 pa	
YP 8 years at 8 per cent	5.747	£201 145
reversion to full net rental value	£74 375 pa	
YP in perpetuity deferred 8 years		
at 8 per cent	6.753	£502 254
present value of inflows		£703 399 [see note 1]
less present value of outflows		£730 000 [see note 2]
net present value at 8 per cent		− £ 26 601

Notes

1: This is the present value of the right to receive £35 000 per annum for the next 8 years, followed by the full rental value in perpetuity, at a yield of 8 per cent.

2: The price that has been paid for the freehold interest.

A negative net present value indicates that a yield of less than 8 per cent has been achieved. It is necessary to find the yield at which the net present value is nil. A lower trial rate must therefore be tested and 7.5 per cent will be adopted.

Trial rate 7.5 per cent

Net rent received	£35 000 pa	
YP 8 years at 7.5 per cent	5.857	£204 995
reversion to full net rental value	£74 375 pa	
YP in perpetuity deferred 8 years		
at 7.5 per cent	7.476	£556 028
present value of inflows		£761 023
less present value of outflows		£730 000
net present value at 7.5 per cent		+ £ 31 023

The positive net present value means that a 7.5 per cent yield is achieved and the equivalent yield must lie between 7.5 per cent and 8 per cent.

Using similar triangles to discover the equivalent yield:

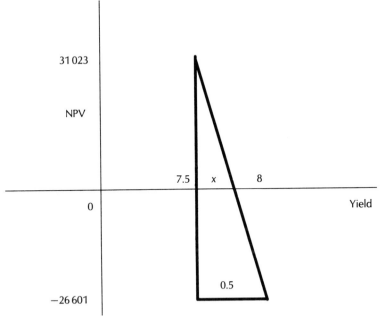

$$\frac{X}{31\,023} = \frac{0.5}{57\,624}$$

$$57\,624X = 15\,511.5$$

$$X = 0.27$$

internal rate of return and equivalent yield

$$= 7.5 \text{ per cent} + 0.27 \text{ per cent} = 7.77 \text{ per cent}$$

(For further consideration of the calculation of internal rates of return, see questions 2.1 and 2.2).

This yield can now be applied in the valuation of A's interest in the subject property.

Net rent received	£40 000 pa	
YP 8 years at 7.77 per cent [see note 1]	5.797	£231 880
reversion to full net rental value	£85 000 pa	
YP in perpetuity at 7.77 per cent [see note 2]	12.870	

× PV of £1 in 8 years at 7.77 per cent [see note 3]	0.550	7.079	£601 715
Capital value			£833 595
		say £834 000	

Notes

1: Years' Purchase calculated using the formula

$$\frac{1 - \dfrac{1}{(1+i)^n}}{i}$$

where $i = 0.0777$
$ n = 8$ years.

2: Years' Purchase calculated by $\dfrac{1}{0.0777}$

3: Present value of £1 calculated using the formula

$$\frac{1}{(1+i)^n}$$

where $i = 0.0777$
$ n = 8$ years.

The capital value of £834 000 reconciles with the valuation using separate yields of 12 per cent and 7.5 per cent.

The transaction involving the similar property in this case is a perfect comparable – the current rent to full rental value ratio and the unexpired term are exactly the same as those of the subject property. A valuer would be extremely pleased, and probably equally surprised, to find such a comparable. Normally the circumstances surrounding similar properties differ in some respects from those of the subject property. A valuer will have to make subjective adjustments in the valuation to allow for these differences.

When an equivalent yield is used in a valuation, either vertical or horizontal slicing may be used. If horizontal slicing is adopted, there is no need for the preliminary calculations to determine the yield at which to value the marginal income, since the same yield is used throughout the valuation.

hardcore income		£40 000 pa	
YP in perpetuity at 7.77 per cent		12.870	£514 800
marginal income		£45 000 pa	
YP in perpetuity at 7.77 per cent	12.870		

× PV of £1 in 8 years at 7.77 per cent	0.550	7.079	£318 555
Capital value			£833 355
		say	£834 000

For a further consideration of equivalent yield valuation, see Chapter 9 of *Advanced Valuation* by Diane Butler and David Richmond (Macmillan, 1990).

Question 1.5

The question requires the valuation of freehold and leasehold interests using *either* a discounted cash flow *or* a real value approach, but both will be shown here to demonstrate the methods.

Freehold interest discounted cash flow approach
Before this valuation may proceed, it is necessary to determine the equated yield and the annual rate of rental growth.

To obtain the equated yield for a freehold interest, it is generally considered acceptable to add 2 or 3 per cent to the yield on gilt edged stock (see question 1.1). The equated yield is the overall yield from an investment; it is the internal rate of return, including any rental and capital growth.

It is stated in the question that gilts currently yield 10 per cent, therefore an equated yield of 12 per cent will be adopted.

The implied rental growth rate may be derived by analysing the 7 per cent yield achieved from similar freehold properties, using the formula:

$$(1+g)^t = \frac{\text{YP in perpetuity at } y - \text{YP } t \text{ years at } e}{\text{YP in perpetuity at } y \times \text{PV of £1 in } t \text{ years at } e}$$

where g = annual rate of rental growth expressed as a decimal
y = all risks yield from transactions involving comparable properties
e = equated yield
t = number of years in rent review pattern of comparables.

$$(1+g)^5 = \frac{\text{YP in perpetuity at 7 per cent} - \text{YP 5 years at 12 per cent}}{\text{YP in perpetuity at 7 per cent} \times \text{PV of £1 in 5 years at 12 per cent}}$$

$$(1+g)^5 = \frac{14.2857 - 3.6048}{14.2857 \times 0.5674} = \frac{10.6809}{8.1057} = 1.3177$$

$$1+g = \sqrt[5]{1.3177} = 1.05673$$

$$g = 0.05673$$

The implied rate of rental growth is therefore 5.673 per cent per annum.

$$\frac{1}{1+.12}$$ $$\left(\frac{1}{1.08}\right)$$ $$\frac{1}{1.1 66^4}$$

This means that the acceptance of a 7 per cent yield implies an expectation that rents will grow at 5.673 per cent per annum, realised every 5 years at review, to produce an overall yield of 12 per cent.

Valuation of freehold interest using a discounted cash flow at equated yield approach

Years	Rent	Amount of £1 at 5.673 per cent[a]	Inflated rent	Years' Purchase at 12 per cent[c]	PV of £1 at 12 per cent	Present value
	£		£[b]			£
1–10	50 000	—	50 000	5.650	1	282 500
11–15	85 000	1.736	147 560	3.605	0.322	171 289
16–20	85 000	2.288	194 480	3.605	0.183	128 301
21–25	85 000	3.015	256 275	3.605	0.104	96 083
26–30	85 000	3.973	337 705	3.605	0.059	71 828
30 +[d]	85 000	5.235	444 975	14.286[e]	0.033[f]	209 778

Capital value £959 779

say £960 000

Notes to tabulation

[a]Rental growth at 5.673 per cent per annum, realised every 5 years, excluding years 1–10 when the rent is fixed.

[b]Future anticipated rental growth is shown explicitly in the calculation.

[c]Capitalisation of income at equated yield.

[d] It is accepted practice to terminate the explicit discounted cash flow after 30 years, valuing the projected income at that point into perpetuity.

[e]The Years' Purchase in perpetuity at 7 per cent. This is the all risks yield (obtained from transactions involving similar properties) and implies the anticipated growth rate of 5.673 per cent per annum, realised at each 5 year review. Up to year 30, this has been made explicit, by inflating the rent at the annual growth rate and discounting at the equated yield.

[f]Rental growth up to this point has been made explicit, therefore the value is deferred at the equated yield.

The explicit nature of a discounted cash flow valuation is an obvious benefit of this approach. It enables the investor to see how the income flow is expected to change in the future. Other items may also be incorporated. For example, if refurbishment of a property is planned at some future date, the anticipated cost may be inserted as a negative cash flow at the appropriate point.

However, the calculation can be lengthy and tedious, particularly if carried out manually and/or extended beyond 30 years. This problem may be overcome by adopting a real value approach.

Valuation of freehold interest using a real value approach
The method shown here is more correctly described as a real value/equated
yield hybrid. It adopts the equated yield model assumptions regarding rental
growth, but incorporates use of the inflation risk free yield from the real value
model of Dr Ernest Wood. The inflation risk free yield may be defined as the
real return from an investment. It reflects all the risks attaching to that
investment, but excludes any additional return for the effects of inflation. The
inflation risk free yield is used to value a completely inflation proof income.

In order to proceed with the valuation, it is first of all necessary to calculate
the inflation risk free yield. This may be determined using the formula:

$$\frac{1+e}{1+g} - 1 = i$$

where e = equated yield
        g = annual growth rate $\Big\}$ all expressed as decimals
        i = inflation risk free yield (IRFY).

$$\frac{1.12}{1.05673} - 1 = i$$

$$= 0.0599$$

and IRFY = 5.99 per cent

It would be acceptable, in an examination, to round off this yield to 6 per cent,
for ease of reference to the valuation tables, but, if this is done, the fact should
be clearly stated.

Net rent received		£50 000 pa	
YP 10 years at 12 per cent [see note 1]		5.650	£282 500
reversion to full net rental value		£85 000 pa	
YP in perpetuity at 7 per cent			
[see note 2]	14.286		
× PV of £1 in 10 years at			
5.99 per cent [see note 3]	0.559	7.986	£678 810
Capital value			£961 310
		say	£960 000

Notes
1: Current income is fixed for 10 years. There is no prospect of realising rental
growth during that time, therefore the valuation is at a yield which reflects a
fixed income – the equated yield.

2: All risks yield from transactions involving similar properties. This yield reflects rental growth at 5.673 per cent per annum with 5 year reviews, to produce an overall (equated) yield of 12 per cent.

Alternatively, the Years' Purchase in perpetuity may be derived using the formula:

$$\text{YP for } n \text{ years} = \text{YP } n \text{ years at } i \times \frac{\text{YP } t \text{ years at } e}{\text{YP } t \text{ years at } i}$$

where n = total number of years (perpetuity in the example)
$\quad i$ = IRFY
$\quad t$ = rent review pattern of income
$\quad e$ = equated yield.

YP in perpetuity

$$= \text{YP in perpetuity at 5.99 per cent} \times \frac{\text{YP 5 years at 12 per cent}}{\text{YP 5 years at 5.99 per cent}}$$

$$= 16.694 \times \frac{3.605}{4.214} = 14.281$$

(slight error, due to rounding)

3: Deferment at the inflation risk free yield reflects 5.673 per cent per annum growth in full rental value during the 10 years before reversion (from the DCF calculation the rental value is expected to be £147 560 per annum in 10 years' time). Thus the full rental value is inflation proofed on reversion. The present value of £1 in 10 years at 5.99 per cent has been calculated by

$$\frac{1}{(1.0599)^{10}}$$

Alternative approach
Using this approach, the term income is valued at the equated yield, as in the previous calculation, but on reversion, anticipated growth in the full rental value during the term is shown explicitly.

Net rent received		£ 50 000 pa	
YP 10 years at 12 per cent		5.650	£282 500
reversion to full net rental value		£ 85 000 pa	
× Amount of £1 in 10 years at			
5.673 per cent [see note 1]		1.736	
estimated full rental value in 10 years' time		£147 560 pa	
YP in perpetuity at 7 per cent			
[see note 2]	14.286		

× PV of £1 in 10 years at 12 per cent [see note 3]	0.322	4.600	£678 776
Capital value			£961 276
		say	£960 000

Notes

1: Growth in full rental value at 5.673 per cent per annum during the 10 years up to reversion.

2: Alternatively, the Years' Purchase in perpetuity may be derived using the '3 YPs' as demonstrated in the previous valuation.

3: Deferment at the equated yield. Rental growth in the 10 years up to reversion has been shown explicitly in the full rental value, therefore there is no need to reflect it in the yield.

Valuation of the leasehold interest using a discounted cash flow at equated yield approach

In the example under consideration, the leaseholder is paying a fixed rent of £50 000 per annum for the next 10 years. However, if the leaseholder were to sublet, he could do so at the full rental value of £85 000 per annum with 5 year reviews. So for the first 5 years the leaseholder's profit rent would be £35 000 per annum, but considerably more for the following 5 years. Using a traditional approach, the initial profit rent would merely be valued for 10 years and any anticipated future growth said to be reflected in the yield adopted by the valuer (usually based upon yields achieved by similar freehold properties). In a discounted cash flow calculation, although profit rent is used as a basis, future growth expectation is shown explicitly in the profit rent, taking into account the partially inflation proof full rental value available to the leaseholder should he sublet, and the fixed, inflation prone income paid by the leaseholder.

An equated yield of 12 per cent was used in the valuation of the freehold interest, but, for the leasehold interest, an equated yield considerably higher than this will be required, to allow for the extra risks perceived as attaching to leasehold interests. A yield of 18 per cent will be adopted in the valuation that follows.

Years	Rent received £	Amount of £1 at 5.673 per cent[a]	Inflated rent £	Rent paid £	Profit rent £	YP at 18 per cent[b]	PV at 18 per cent	Present value £
1–5	85 000[c]	—	85 000	50 000[d]	35 000	3.127	1	109 445
6–10	85 000	1.318	112 030[e]	50 000	62 030	3.127	0.437	84 764

Capital value £194 209
say £195 000

Notes to tabulation
[a]Rent received by the leaseholder is expected to grow at 5.673 per cent per annum, realisable every 5 years on review.
[b]Profit rent is fixed for each period of 5 years, therefore valued at the equated yield.
[c]The leaseholder is able to let the property now at its full rental value.
[d]The rent paid by the leaseholder is fixed for the remaining 10 years of the lease.
[e]In 5 years' time the rent received by the leaseholder is expected to rise to £112 030, increasing the profit rent by £27 030 per annum.

Valuation of leasehold interest using a real value approach
The real value/equated yield hybrid model abandons profit rent as a basis for the valuation. The rent received and rent paid by the leaseholder are first capitalised separately. This is because of their differing growth potentials, the rent received being on the basis of 5 year reviews and the rent paid being fixed for 10 years. The capital value of the rent paid is then deducted from the capital value of the rent received, the resultant figure being the capital value of the leasehold interest.

It is first of all necessary to recalculate the inflation risk free yield for the leasehold interest on the basis of an equated yield of 18 per cent.

$$\frac{1+e}{1+g} - 1 = \frac{1.18}{1.05673} - 1 = 0.1167$$

IRFY = 11.67 per cent
Capital value of rent received:
Full net rental value   £ 85 000 pa

YP 10 years at 11.67 per cent × $\dfrac{\text{YP 5 years at 18 per cent [see note 1]}}{\text{YP 5 years at 11.67 per cent}}$

$$= 5.727 \times \frac{3.127}{3.634}$$

                                                                    4.928
                                                                    ——————
                                                        £418 880 [see note 2]

less
Capital value of rent paid:
    rent paid   £50 000 pa
YP 10 years at 18 per cent
    [see note 3]   4.494   £224 700 [see note 4]
                                        ——————   ——————
Capital value of leasehold interest   £194 180
                                                      ——————

                                              say   £195 000
                                                      ——————

Notes

1: Three YPs reflect the fact that the income is received for 10 years, also that anticipated future rental growth is 5.673 per cent per annum, realised every 5 years, on review, to give an overall yield of 18 per cent.

2: Capital value of rent received if the leaseholder were to sublet the property.

3: The rent paid by the leaseholder is fixed and inflation prone for 10 years and is therefore valued at equated yield.

4: Capital value of rent paid by the leaseholder.

As an alternative, the discounted cash flow valuation of the leasehold interest may also be calculated using a format which separates the capitalisation of rent received and rent paid.

Years	Rent	Amount of £1 at 5.673 per cent	Inflated rent	YP at 18 per cent	PV at 18 per cent	Present value
	£		£			£
Capital value of rent received:						
1–5	85 000	—	85 000	3.127	1	265 795
6–10	85 000	1.318	112 030	3.127	0.437	153 089
						£418 884
less Capital value of rent paid:						
1–10	50 000	—	50 000	4.494	1	£224 700

Capital value of leasehold interest £194 184

say £195 000

For a further consideration of contemporary valuation techniques the reader is recommended to refer to Chapter 9 of *Advanced Valuation* by Diane Butler and David Richmond (Macmillan, 1990).

Question 1.6

In the first instance, the transaction involving the similar shop must be analysed and this information used to find the current rental value of the subject property.

The zoning method is employed and in this example two 5 m zones and a remainder are used (see also question 1.1).

Let Zone A rental value per $m^2 = £X$

Zone A	$= 9 \text{ m} \times 5 \text{ m} \times X$	$= 45X$
Zone B	$= 9 \text{ m} \times 5 \text{ m} \times \frac{1}{2}X = 22.5X$ [see note 1]

Remainder $= 9 \text{ m} \times 7 \text{ m} \times \frac{1}{4}X = 15.75X$

rental value $= 83.25X$

but rental value $= £ \ 47\,500$ pa
therefore $£47\,500 = \quad 83.25X$
$$X = £570.57 \text{ per m}^2$$

The Zone A rental value of the comparable property is £570.57 per m², *on the basis of 7 year rent reviews.*

Note
1: Halving back. Zone A is assumed to be the most valuable part, with value decreasing towards the rear of the shop. Zone B is assumed to be half the value of Zone A and the remainder assumed to be half the value of Zone B.
  This information is now applied to find the current rental value of the subject property. Zone depths used must be the same as those adopted to analyse the comparable transaction.

Zone A $= 7 \text{ m} \times 5 \text{ m} \times £570.57 \quad = £19\,970$
Zone B $= 7 \text{ m} \times 5 \text{ m} \times £285.285 = £ \ 9\,985$
Remainder $= 7 \text{ m} \times 6 \text{ m} \times £142.6425 = £ \ 5\,991$

Current rental value $= £35\,946$

                          say   £35 950 per annum

Alternatively, the area of the shop may be expressed as a total in terms of Zone A. This is then multiplied by the Zone A rental value per m².

Zone A $= 7 \text{ m} \times 5 \text{ m} \qquad = 35 \text{ m}^2$
Zone B $= 7 \text{ m} \times 5 \text{ m} \times \frac{1}{2} = 17.5 \text{ m}^2$
Remainder $= 7 \text{ m} \times 6 \text{ m} \times \frac{1}{4} = 10.5 \text{ m}^2$

Area in terms of Zone A $= 63 \text{ m}^2$

Current rental value $= 63 \text{ m}^2 \times £570.57 = £35\,946$
                          say   £35 950 per annum

The rent which might be expected on letting the subject property is £35 950 per annum, on full repairing and insuring terms, with a *7 year rent review* pattern.
  However, since the head lease has 15 years unexpired, it might be more practical to try and achieve a subletting on the basis of *5 year rent reviews.* If this were done, the head leaseholder would be in a position to accept a lower initial rent, since it would be reviewed two years earlier. For the same reason, the sub-lessee would expect to pay a lower initial rent.

The £35 950 per annum on a 7 year review pattern can easily be converted to the appropriate rental value on the basis of 5 year rent reviews. It would not be essential to show this alternative in answering an examination question, although a brief consideration of the possibility would certainly enhance the overall impression given by the answer. The alternative approach is produced here to demonstrate the methodology.

Conversion of the rental value to a 5 year review pattern will, in fact, make no difference to the capital value of the head leasehold interest. This will be demonstrated by providing real value calculations on the basis of both 7 year reviews and 5 year reviews (although the question requires only one valuation).

Valuation of the head leasehold interest using a real value approach, assuming a 7 year rent review pattern in the sublease.
The inflation risk free yield (IRFY) must first of all be calculated from the equated yield (20 per cent) and the annual growth rate (5 per cent).

$$\frac{1+e}{1+g} - 1 = i \text{ (see question 1.5)}$$

$$\frac{1.2}{1.05} - 1 = 0.1429$$

$$\text{IRFY} = 14.29 \text{ per cent}$$

In an examination, it would be acceptable to round this off to 14 per cent, for ease of reference to the valuation tables, but this should be clearly stated.

The valuation method adopted is a real value/equated yield hybrid and an explanation of the approach to valuing leasehold interests is given in question 1.5.

Capital value of rent received:

rent received £ 35 950 pa

$$\text{YP 15 years at 14.29 per cent} \times \frac{\text{YP 7 years at 20 per cent } \left[\text{see note 1}\right]}{\text{YP 7 years at 14.29 per cent}}$$

$$= 6.054 \times \frac{3.605}{4.251}$$

5.134

£184 567 [see note 2]

less capital value of rent paid:

rent paid	£20 000 pa	
YP 15 years at 20 per cent [see note 3]	4.676	£ 93 520 [see note 4]
Capital value of head leasehold interest		£ 91 047
	say	£ 90 000

Notes

1: Indicates the length of the unexpired term (15 years), also that rental growth is expected to be 5 per cent per annum, which is realised every 7 years on review to give an overall yield of 20 per cent.

2: Capital value of rent received by head leaseholder.

3: The rent paid by the head leaseholder is fixed for 15 years and is therefore valued at a yield reflecting a fixed income, the equated yield.

4: Capital value of rent paid by the head leaseholder. This is deducted from the capital value of the rent received to determine the capital value of the head leasehold interest.

Valuation of the head leasehold interest using a real value approach, assuming a 5 year rent review pattern in the sublease

For this valuation, the current full rental value of the shop on a 5 year review pattern needs to be determined. This may be calculated using the formula:

$$X = Y \times \frac{YP\ t\ years\ at\ e}{YP\ t\ years\ at\ i} \times \frac{YP\ T\ years\ at\ i}{YP\ T\ years\ at\ e}$$

where X = rental value on new review pattern
Y = known rental value on existing review pattern
t = number of years in existing review pattern
e = equated yield
i = IRFY
T = number of years in new review pattern.

$$\frac{Rent\ on\ 5\ year}{review\ pattern} = \frac{Rent\ on\ 7\ year}{review\ pattern}$$

$$\times \frac{YP\ 7\ years\ at\ 20\ per\ cent}{YP\ 7\ years\ at\ 14.29\ per\ cent}$$

$$\times \frac{YP\ 5\ years\ at\ 14.29\ per\ cent}{YP\ 5\ years\ at\ 20\ per\ cent}$$

$$= £35\,950 \times \frac{3.605}{4.251} \times \frac{3.409}{2.991} = £34\,748$$

say   £34 750 per annum

Valuation

Capital value of recent received:

rent received £ 34 750 pa

$$\text{YP 15 years at 14.29 per cent} \times \frac{\text{YP 5 years at 20 per cent [see note 1]}}{\text{YP 5 years at 14.29 per cent}}$$

$$= 6.054 \times \frac{2.991}{3.409}$$

5.312
_____

£184 592 [see note 2]

less Capital value of rent paid:		
rent paid	£20 000 pa	
YP 15 years at 20 per cent	4.676	£ 93 520
Capital value of head leasehold interest		£ 91 072
	say	£ 90 000

Notes

1: Three YPs still indicate, as in the previous calculation, the 15 year unexpired term and rental growth of 5 per cent per annum, but now this growth is realised every 5 years on review, rather than every 7 years.

2: Capital value of rent received by head leaseholder subletting on 5 year reviews is the same as that on 7 year reviews. The 3 YPs have adjusted the Years' Purchase for 15 years to allow for the changed review pattern and consequent change in rental value (compare the Years' Purchase of 5.312 in this calculation with the Years' Purchase of 5.134 in the previous calculation where rental value was on the basis of 7 year reviews and therefore higher).

Question 1.7

The valuation tables most familiar to both students and valuers in practice, are Parry's – *Parry's Valuation and Conversion Tables* by Richard Parry, first published in 1913. The work is now in its eleventh edition, under the title *Parry's Valuation and Investment Tables* by A. W. Davidson.

The answer to this question should consider the basis of construction of these tables and compare it with those of other tables available, the main ones being *Property Valuation Tables* by Philip Bowcock and *Rose's Property Valuation Tables* by J. J. Rose. There are also more specialised tables, such as *Donaldson's Investment Tables* by Philip Marshall, but the question would only require a consideration of general valuation tables.

Parry's tables were, until the eleventh edition of 1989, constructed solely on the basis that both income is received and interest is added annually in arrear. However, the eleventh edition now contains additional tables of Years' Purchase in perpetuity, constructed on the assumption that income is received quarterly in advance.

The derivation of all the tables calculated upon the annual in arrear assumption, stems from the basic compound interest formula:

$$(1 + i)^n$$

where i = annual rate of interest, expressed as a decimal
      n = number of years.

This is the Amount of £1 formula and it can be seen as a common factor in the formulae of all other tables, for example:

Present value of £1 $= \dfrac{1}{(1 + i)^n}$

Amount of £1 per annum $= \dfrac{(1 + i)^n - 1}{i}$

Annual sinking fund $= \dfrac{i}{(1 + i)^n - 1}$

Present value of £1 per annum (Years' Purchase) single rate $= \dfrac{1 - \dfrac{1}{(1 + i)^n}}{i}$

Present value of £1 per annum, dual rate $= \dfrac{1}{i + \dfrac{i}{(1 + i)^n - 1}}$

Students who wish to refresh their memories on the construction of these tables and the mathematics involved should refer to Chapters 2 and 5 of *Introduction to Valuation* (third edition, 1994) by David Richmond (Macmillan).

Bowcock and Rose both produced valuation tables on different assumptions to those of Parry's, in an attempt to follow more closely what actually happens in the market. Both agree that in most modern leases provision is made for payment of rent quarterly in advance, but differ upon when interest is added. Bowcock's tables assume that:

(i) income is received quarterly in advance and
(ii) interest is added half yearly.

Rose's tables assume that:

(i) income is received quarterly in advance and
(ii) interest is added annually.

Although Bowcock's tables are therefore more market realistic, care must be taken when using them that *nominal* and *effective* rates of interest are not confused. The *nominal* rate of interest is that achieved when interest is received as a single payment at the end of the year. The *effective* rate of interest will be greater than the nominal rate of interest if interest is added at intervals of less than one year. It will also be dependent upon the number of times each year that interest is added.

Example
A loan of £5 000 is taken out at the beginning of the year at a nominal rate of interest of 8 per cent. If repayments are made annually, but interest is added half yearly, the following calculation shows that the effective rate of interest is 8.16 per cent:

loan	£5 000
plus interest at 4 per cent for first 6 months	£ 200
loan outstanding after 6 months	£5 200
plus interest at 4 per cent for second 6 months	£ 208
loan outstanding at end of year	£5 408

$$\text{effective rate of interest} = \frac{408}{£5\,000} \times 100 = 8.16\text{per cent}$$

If interest is added quarterly:

loan	£5 000
plus interest at 2 per cent, first quarter	£ 100
loan outstanding at end of first quarter	£5 100
plus interest at 2 per cent, second quarter	£ 102
loan outstanding at end of second quarter	£5 202
plus interest at 2 per cent, third quarter	£ 104.04
loan outstanding at end of third quarter	£5 306.04
plus interest at 2 per cent, last quarter	£ 106.1208
loan outstanding at end of year	£5 412.1608

$$\text{effective rate of interest} = \frac{£412.1608}{5\,000} \times 100 = 8.24 \text{ per cent}$$

The effective rate of interest may be calculated by the formula:

$$e = \left(1 + \frac{i}{m}\right)^m - 1$$

where e = effective rate of interest $\}$ expressed as
 i = nominal rate of interest $\}$ decimals
 m = number of times per annum that interest is added.

Applying this formula in the example above:

$$e = \left(1 + \frac{0.08}{4}\right)^4 - 1$$

$$= (1.02)^4 - 1 = 0.0824$$

and the effective rate of interest is 8.24 per cent.

What has to be borne in mind when referring to Bowcock's tables, is that the columns are headed with nominal rates of interest, but the figures are calculated using the effective rate of interest. The differing assumptions mean that figures from Bowcock's and Parry's tables, which might be expected to be identical, in fact are not.

For example, the Years' Purchase in perpetuity at 9 per cent, with income receivable quarterly in advance:

 from Parry's tables   = 11.7294
 from Bowcock's tables = 11.4847

Examples of the formulae used to calculate the figures in Bowcock's tables, are as follows:

Amount of £1 = $(1 + r)^n$

where r = effective rate of interest
 n = number of years.

Present value of £1 = $(1 + r)^{-n}$

Amount of £1 per annum $= \dfrac{(1 + r)^n - 1}{4[1 - (1 + r)^{-\frac{1}{4}}]}$

assuming that £4 is invested quarterly in advance, accumulating at the effective rate of interest, r.

Annual sinking fund $= \dfrac{4[1 - (1 + s)^{-\frac{1}{4}}]}{(1 + s)^n - 1}$

where s = annual, effective, net of tax, rate of interest

Present value of £1 per annum (Years' Purchase), single rate

$$= \frac{1 - (1 + r)^{-n}}{4[1 - (1 + r)^{-\frac{1}{4}}]}$$

Present value of £1 per annum, dual rate

$$
= \cfrac{1}{4[1-(1+r)^{-\frac{1}{4}}] + \cfrac{4[1-(1+s)^{-\frac{1}{4}}]}{[(1+s)^n - 1](1-t)}}
$$

The formulae used in Rose's tables are similar, except that different notation is used and interest is assumed to be added annually. A further difference is that calculations are based upon *nominal* rates of interest. Similar comments apply to the formula used to calculate the Years' Purchase in perpetuity, quarterly in advance figures, in Parry's tables.

Some consideration should be given in the answer to the application and use of the various tables. A valuer analyses market transactions and then applies the results to value interests in similar properties. For the straightforward situation of a perpetual income, if results of analysis are used directly in a valuation, it will make no difference which tables are used, since the Years' Purchase will be the same.

Example comparing Parry's with Bowcock's tables
You are required to value the freehold interest in a property recently let at its full rental value of £50 000 per annum.

The freehold interest in a similar property has recently been sold for £750 000. Just prior to sale, this property was let at its full rental value of £45 000 per annum.

Analysis reveals that the Years' Purchase is 16.7:

$$
\text{Years' Purchase} = \frac{£750\,000}{£45\,000} = 16.7
$$

Valuation using Parry's tables

Full rental value	£ 50 000 pa
YP in perpetuity at nominal rate of interest 6 per cent	16.7
Capital value	£835 000

Valuation using Bowcock's tables

Full rental value	£ 50 000 pa
YP in perpetuity at nominal rate of interest 6.13 per cent	16.7
Capital value	£835 000

However, if a term and reversion valuation is involved, the two valuations may not be the same.

Example

Value the freehold interest in a property let with 8 years unexpired at a fixed rent of £30 000 per annum. The full rental value of the property is £50 000 per annum.

Assuming nominal rates of interest at full rental value to be the same as the previous example with a one per cent reduction for valuation of the term income, the following results are obtained:

Valuation using Parry's tables

Rent received	£30 000 pa	
YP 8 years at 5 per cent	6.463	£193 890
reversion to full rental value	£50 000 pa	
YP in perpetuity deferred 8 years		
at 6 per cent	10.457	£522 850
Capital value		£716 740

Valuation using Bowcock's tables

Rent received	£30 000 pa	
YP 8 years at 5.13 per cent	6.621	£198 630
reversion to full rental value	£50 000 pa	
YP in perpetuity deferred 8 years		
at 6.13 per cent	10.313	£515 650
Capital value		£714 280

Each valuation is in the region of £715 000, but this does not result from equality throughout the two valuations. Rather, it results from a cancelling-out effect between the values of term and reversion in the respective valuations.

Figures from Bowcock's tables produce a higher valuation of the term income than Parry's, but a lower valuation of the reversion. The effect upon the final valuation will depend upon the nominal yields adopted, the length of the unexpired term and the magnitude of the term income relative to the reversionary income.

The RICS *Report into Property Valuation Methods* (Interim Report, 1980) found reluctance within the profession to move away from the use of Parry's tables, even though, Bowcock's tables in particular, reflect market activity more accurately. Rose's tables always produce higher values than Parry's and were considered 'more at variance with current practice' than Bowcock's. Although valuers generally agreed that Bowcock's tables were more realistic than Parry's, it was concluded in the report that the two main reasons for valuers being reluctant to change were:

(i) the fact that Parry's tables are commonly used by most valuers and have been for many years. This could mean that adopting alternative tables would result in a valuer working on a different basis from the majority of colleagues in the profession
(ii) possible resistance from both practitioners and students to accepting and understanding the more complex mathematical nature of the alternative tables.

The RICS Report recommended that a wider understanding and use of Bowcock's tables should be encouraged within the profession, because they reflect the activities of investors more correctly.

This report was prepared in 1980, but resistance to change still persists and Parry's remain the most widely used of the available valuation tables. It is perhaps a pity that when the eleventh edition of *Parry's Valuation and Investment Tables* was produced, the opportunity was not taken to incorporate more extensive tables on a quarterly in advance basis.

2 VALUATION AND TAXATION

A working knowledge of taxation (on both income and capital) is essential to a valuer, since individual clients may require advice regarding the taxation implications of their investment decisions. Indeed, such advice will often be crucial before these decisions are made.

Consideration is given in this section to various aspects of valuation/taxation. The way in which the return from investments is affected by Income Tax and Capital Gains Tax is demonstrated, showing the influence this can have on the actual choice of investments by individual investors. These matters are dealt with in questions 2.1 and 2.2, illustrating the effects on the return taxpayers achieve with their individual tax rates, compared with the non-taxpaying investor.

Examination questions often require computation of the chargeable gain for Capital Gains Tax purposes on the disposal of interests in property.

The *Finance Act 1988* changed the base date for the taxation of chargeable gains on disposals after 5 April 1988, from 6 April 1965 to 31 March 1982. Unfortunately, the result has been to complicate rather than simplify many chargeable gain computations, and an explanation of this is given in question 2.3(b). This example involves the disposal of a freehold interest and part (a) of the question considers the extent of the exemption available on disposal of a person's principal private residence.

Question 2.4 concerns the part disposal of an interest in property and, in particular, deals with the treatment of allowable expenditure. One specific type of transaction, considered to be a part disposal, is the granting of a lease subject to the payment of a premium. An example of such a situation is provided in question 2.6, which also illustrates the resulting interaction of Capital Gains Tax and Schedule A Income Tax.

The tax situation on granting of a sublease is beyond the scope of this text, but the interested reader is recommended to refer to Chapter 4 of *Advanced Valuation* by Diane Butler and David Richmond (Macmillan, 1990), where this aspect is given full consideration.

Calculation of the chargeable gain, on disposal of a short leasehold interest (a lease with 50 years or less unexpired), is complicated by the assumption that such interests are wasting assets. This is examined in question 2.5, together with an explanation of how the chargeable gain can be reconciled with the apparent gain.

VALUATION AND TAXATION – QUESTIONS

2.1. Your client has £250 000 to invest and a choice of three property investments, each for sale at £250 000. Whichever investment is purchased, he intends to sell in 5 years' time.

Property A. A leasehold shop investment, with a fixed profit rent of £69 350 per annum for the next 5 years.

Property B. A freehold ground rent let on a lease with 998 years unexpired at £30 000 per annum.

Property C. A freehold property let at a fixed rent of £12 500 per annum for the next 5 years. It is estimated that the capital value in 5 years' time will be £361 450.

All three investments are considered to be of equal risk and each has an internal rate of return of 12 per cent.

Assuming your client pays tax at 30p in the £, calculate the positive net of tax return, where possible, of each investment in order to advise your client which investment he should purchase.

2.2. You have two clients, each with £750 000 to invest. Client A does not pay tax, Client B pays tax at 35p in the £.

The following two investments are each on the market for £750 000:

Investment 1   A freehold shop, let at £30 000 per annum, fixed for the next 10 years. The current full net rental value on the basis of 5 year reviews is estimated to be £80 000 per annum. Similar freehold properties are selling for yields of 7 per cent when let at current rental value on 5 year reviews and future rental growth is expected to be 5.5 per cent per annum.

Investment 2   A leasehold shop investment with 10 years unexpired at a fixed profit rent of £155 000 per annum.

Recommend to each of your clients which of the two investments they should purchase, giving your reasons.

2.3. (a) Explain how the sale of an individual's main private residence is treated for Capital Gains Tax purposes.

(b) The freehold interest in a shop investment was purchased in October 1958 for £35 000 and sold in April 1993 for £270 000. Improvements were carried out in January 1961 costing £6 000, in July 1973 costing £8 000 and in May 1989 costing £9 750.

The value of the property in March 1982 was estimated to be £130 000.

Calculate the chargeable gain for Capital Gains Tax purposes on the sale in 1993, assuming the taxpayer has not elected for a valuation at 1965.

The Retail Prices Index was 79.44 in March 1982, 115.0 in May 1989 and 141.2 in April 1993.

2.4. (a) In relation to Capital Gains Tax, explain how the chargeable gain is computed when only part of an interest in property is disposed of.

(b) A freehold property was purchased in 1970 for £30 000, including costs of £1 125.

Improvements costing £5 000 were carried out one year later and further improvements, costing £3 500, were carried out in June 1991.

Recently the owner sold part of the property for £67 000, the value of the part retained being £50 000. Costs of sale were £1 800.

Calculate the chargeable gain for Capital Gains Tax purposes as a result of the sale, assuming that the improvements in 1971 affected the value of the whole property, but those in 1991 affected only the value of the part sold.

The value of the whole property in March 1982 was £60 000.

The Retail Prices Index was 79.44 in March 1982, 134.1 in June 1991 and 139.6 at the date of sale.

2.5. Explain why the purchase price, or 1982 Market value, and any other allowable expenditure in respect of a short leasehold interest is amended by the Inland Revenue in calculating the chargeable gain for Capital Gains Tax purposes when the interest is sold.

Illustrate your answer with examples, including an example to reconcile the adjustment with the reasoning behind it.

2.6. The freehold interest in a shop was purchased in July 1983 for £400 000.

In January 1993, the freeholder granted a 20 year full repairing and insuring lease with 5 year reviews at a rent of £45 000 per annum, together with an initial premium of £90 000.

Calculate the chargeable gain for Capital Gains Tax purposes on the freeholder's receipt of the premium in January 1993.

The Retail Prices Index was 85.3 in July 1983 and 139.8 in January 1993.

VALUATION AND TAXATION – SUGGESTED ANSWERS

Question 2.1

The answer entails calculation of net of tax internal rates of return only, since the gross of tax internal rate of return of each investment is given as 12 per cent.

In each case, the income, which is assumed to be net of all outgoings apart from tax, must first of all be reduced to a net of tax figure appropriate to the particular client.

PROPERTY A

Fixed profit rent	£69 350 pa
less Income Tax at 30p in the £	£20 805 pa
net of tax income	£48 545 pa

£250 000, if invested in Property A, would be the purchase price of a fixed net of tax income of £48 545 per annum for the next 5 years. From this information, the Years' Purchase for 5 years can be calculated.

$$\text{Years' Purchase for 5 years} = \frac{£250\,000}{£\,48\,545} = 5.150$$

It is now necessary to discover the yield at which the Years' Purchase for 5 years is 5.150.

The Years' Purchase is greater than 5 and, since the Years' Purchase at 0 per cent is 5, then the net of tax return in this case must be *negative*. Reference to the 5 year line of the single rate Years' Purchase table will confirm this.

It is not necessary to proceed further, since the question requires only the calculation of *positive* net of tax returns. In any event, the fact that the return is negative should be sufficient information for the client to reject this investment.

PROPERTY B

As the ground rent is receivable for 998 years, this income may be considered as perpetual.

Income	£30 000 pa
less Income Tax at 30p in the £	£ 9 000 pa
net of tax income	£21 000 pa

The income is fixed and if it is assumed that yields remain unchanged in 5 years' time, there will be no capital gain (or loss) on the sale of this investment.

Since a perpetual income is involved, the net of tax yield can be obtained directly by expressing the net of tax income as a percentage of the proposed purchase price.

$$\text{net of tax yield} = \frac{£\,21\,000}{£250\,000} \times 100 = 8.4 \text{ per cent}$$

PROPERTY C

Income	£12 500 pa
less Income Tax at 30p in the £	£ 3 750 pa
net of tax income	£ 8 750 pa

£8 750 per annum will be the fixed net of tax income for the next 5 years.

The capital value in 5 years' time is estimated to be £361 450. Therefore, when the investment is sold, a capital gain will be realised, with consequent liability for Capital Gains Tax. The basis of charge to Capital Gains Tax will be the difference between the sale price and the purchase price, with an allowance for any gain caused by inflation over the 5 years of ownership. This allowance for inflation is normally calculated using the change in the Retail Prices Index as a yardstick (see question 2.3). Since we are looking forward 5 years in this instance, the Retail Prices Index at the date of sale cannot be known. Reference to past inflation rates and current trends would assist in producing an estimate of the figure. For the purpose of this example, an assumed inflation rate of 4 per cent per annum will be adopted. It will also be assumed that the estimated capital value in 5 years will be the sale price at that time.

Sale price in 5 years' time	£361 450
less current purchase price increased to allow for estimated inflation over the next 5 years £250 000 × (1.04)^5	£304 163
real gain in value in 5 years	£ 57 287

This real gain will be taxed at the investor's top slice rate of income tax.
Capital Gains Tax on sale (ignoring any exemptions or reliefs):

$$£57\,287 \text{ at } 30 \text{ per cent} = £17\,186$$

The amount received by the investor on disposal will be the sale price, reduced by the Capital Gains Tax paid.

Sale price	£361 450
less Capital Gains Tax	£ 17 186
net of tax sale price	£344 264

Property C would therefore produce a fixed net of tax income of £8 750 per annum for the next 5 years, plus a net of tax sale price at the end of 5 years, of £344 264.

The net of tax internal rate of return of this investment is now discovered by discounted cash flow analysis.

Trial rate 8 per cent

Years	Income £'s	PV of £1 at 8 per cent	Present value £
1	8 750	0.926	8 103
2	8 750	0.857	7 499
3	8 750	0.794	6 947
4	8 750	0.735	6 431
5	8 750	0.681	5 959
	344 264	0.681	234 444

present value of inflows	£269 383
less present value of outflows (purchase price)	£250 000
net present value at 8 per cent	+ £ 19 383

The positive net present value means that a net of tax return of more than 8 per cent is achieved. It is necessary to find the rate of return at which the net present value is nil, since this will be the internal rate of return of the investment. The net present value is calculated at two trial rates and the internal rate of return determined by interpolation.

It is evident that a higher trial rate needs to be tested and 10 per cent will be adopted.

Net of tax income		£ 8750 pa	
YP 5 years at 10 per cent [see note 1]		3.791	£ 33 171
net of tax sale price in 5 years' time		£344 264	
× PV of £1 in 5 years at 10 per cent		0.621	£213 788
present value of inflows			£246 959
less present value of outflows			£250 000
net present value at 10 per cent			− £ 3 041

Note

1: Where the income is constant over several years, the Years' Purchase may be applied to the income for the appropriate number of years, rather than discounting each year's income separately.

The negative net present value means that the investment does not achieve a 10 per cent return, and the net of tax internal rate of return must lie between 8 per cent and 10 per cent.

The actual return may be discovered using the principle of similar triangles.

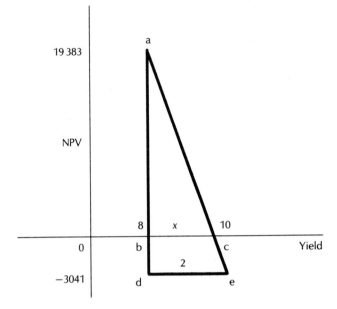

Triangles abc and ade are similar, therefore their base/height ratio will also be similar. It is the length of base bc that needs to be calculated in order to determine the required yield.

$$\frac{x}{19\,383} = \frac{2}{22\,424}$$

$$22\,424x = 38\,766$$

$$x = 1.73$$

net of tax internal rate of return $= 8$ per cent $+ 1.73$ per cent $= 9.73$ per cent.
Alternatively, the following formula may be adopted:

$$\text{internal rate of return} = \text{lower trial rate} + \left(\begin{array}{l} \text{net present value } at \\ \text{lower trial rate} \times \\ \text{difference in trial} \\ \text{rates} \div \text{sum of net} \\ \text{present values at the} \\ \text{two trial rates (ignoring} \\ \text{positive or negative} \\ \text{signs)} \end{array} \right)$$

$$= 8 \text{ per cent} + \frac{19\,383}{19\,383 + 3\,041} \times 2 = 9.73 \text{ per cent}$$

Summary of results:

Property A — leasehold investment, negative net of tax return
Property B — freehold ground rent, 8.4 per cent net of tax return
Property C — reversionary freehold, 9.73 per cent net of tax return

From the above results, advice to your client would be to invest in Property C, since it is least affected by the incidence of tax. For the first 5 years, the income from all three investments is fixed and that from Property C appears poor compared with either A or B. The important difference is that Property C achieves growth and an element of tax-free capital appreciation, which neither A nor B are able to do. The capital gain from Property C in 5 years' time more than compensates for its early poor performance. Even with the deduction of Capital Gains Tax from the future gain, Property C still proves to be the superior investment in terms of return.

Question 2.2

CLIENT A

Client A does not pay tax, therefore it is necessary, before giving advice, to calculate the internal rate of return gross of tax of the two investments. It is assumed that in both cases, the income is net of all outgoings apart from tax.

INVESTMENT 1: Freehold shop

The internal rate of return gross of tax for this investment is discovered by calculating its net present value at two trial rates, as described in question 2.1.

Trial rate 12 per cent

Net income		£ 30 000 pa	
YP 10 years at 12 per cent		5.650	£169 500
reversion to current net rental value		£ 80 000 pa	
× Amount of £1 in 10 years at			
5.5 per cent [see note 1]		1.708	
estimated rental value in 10 years		£136 640 pa	
YP in perpetuity at 7 per cent			
[see note 3]	14.286		
× PV of £1 in 10 years at			
12 per cent	0.322	4.600	£628 544
present value of inflows			£798 044
less present value of outflows [see note 3]			£750 000
net present value at 12 per cent			+ £ 48 044

Notes

1: Reversion in 10 years will be to full rental value at that time. The current rental value is compounded at the expected annual rate of rental growth over the next 10 years, in order to estimate the rental value on reversion.

2: All risks yield as given in the question. This yield is currently being accepted by investors purchasing similar rack rented freehold properties. It implies the future rate of rental growth anticipated by these investors to produce the required overall yield or internal rate of return.

3: Proposed purchase price of the investment.

The positive net present value indicates that this investment achieves more than a 12 per cent gross of tax return. A higher trial rate needs to be tested and 14 per cent will be adopted.

Trial rate 14 per cent			
Net income		£ 30 000 pa	
YP 10 years at 14 per cent		5.216	£156 480
estimated rental value in 10 years		£136 640 pa	
YP in perpetuity at 7 per cent	14.286		
× PV of £1 in 10 years at 14 per cent	0.270	3.857	£527 020
present value of inflows			£683 500

less present value of outflows	£750 000
net present value at 14 per cent	− £ 66 500

The negative net present value indicates that the return is lower than 14 per cent and the gross of tax internal rate of return must lie between 12 per cent and 14 per cent.

Using similar triangles (see question 2.1) to discover the actual return:

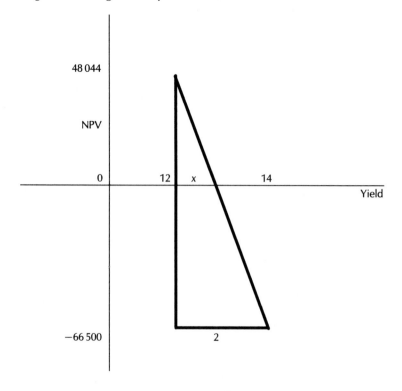

$$\frac{x}{48\ 044} = \frac{2}{114\ 544}$$

$$114\ 544x = 96\ 088$$

$$x = 0.84$$

gross of tax internal rate of return = 12 per cent + 0.84 per cent = 12.84 per cent

INVESTMENT 2: Leasehold shop

The profit rent of £155 000 per annum is fixed for 10 years.

Together with the proposed purchase price, this will enable the calculation of the Years' Purchase for 10 years.

$$\text{Years' purchase for 10 years} = \frac{\text{purchase price}}{\text{profit rent}}$$

$$= \frac{£750\,000}{£155\,000} = 4.839$$

It is now necessary to discover the yield at which 4.839 is the Years' Purchase for 10 years. This may be found by searching the 10 year line of the single rate Years' Purchase table, which reveals that the Years' Purchase for 10 years at 16 per cent is very close to this figure, at 4.833.

The gross of tax internal rate of return of Investment 2 is therefore 16 per cent.

Since Client A is concerned only with the return, gross of tax, he should be advised to purchase Investment 2, assuming it satisfies any other criteria he may have, since on this basis it outperforms Investment 1 by over 3 per cent.

CLIENT B

Client B pays tax at 35p in the £, therefore income and any capital gain from the investments will be reduced by 35 per cent. For Client B, the net of tax internal rate of return must be calculated.

INVESTMENT 1: Freehold shop

As for Client A, discounted cash flow analysis is used to discover the internal rate of return, but this time on a net of tax basis.

Trial rate 10 per cent

Net income	£	30 000 pa	
less Income Tax at 35p in the £	£	10 500 pa	
net of tax income	£	19 500 pa	
YP 10 years at 10 per cent		6.145	£119 828
reversion to current net rental value	£	80 000 pa	
× Amount of £1 in 10 years at 5.5 per cent [see note 1]		1.708	
estimated rental value in 10 years	£	136 640 pa	
less Income Tax at 35p in the £	£	47 824 pa	
net of tax income	£	88 816 pa	
YP in perpetuity at 4.55 per cent [see note 2]		21.978	

estimated capital value in 10 years	£1 951 998	
less £750 000 × $(1.055)^{10}$ [see note 3]	£1 281 108	
real gain in 10 years	£ 670 890	
This real gain is taxed at 35 per cent under Capital Gains Tax provisions		
£670 890 at 35 per cent =	£ 234 812 [see note 4]	

sale price net of tax: £1 951 998 − £234 812 = £1 717 186 [see note 5]

× PV of £1 in 10 years at 10 per cent	0.386	£662 834
present value of inflows		£782 662
less present value of outflows		£750 000
net present value at 10 per cent		+ £ 32 662

Notes

1: Reversion in 10 years' will be to full rental value at that time. The current rental value is compounded at the expected annual rate of rental growth over the next 10 years, in order to estimate the rental value on reversion.

2: All risks yield of 7 per cent reduced by 35 per cent to a net of tax yield.

3: Allowance to be set against the chargeable gain for Capital Gains Tax. The current purchase price is increased to allow for estimated inflation (in this case at 5.5 per cent per annum) over the next 10 years (see questions 2.1 and 2.3).

4: Capital Gains Tax exemptions and reliefs have been ignored.

5: Assuming that the estimated capital value in 10 years will be the sale price at that time.

The positive net present value indicates that the investment achieves a higher net of tax return than 10 per cent and a trial rate of 12 per cent will be tested. Fortunately, this calculation need not be as lengthy as the previous one, since the income net of tax and expected sale price in 10 years' time net of tax, have already been ascertained.

Net of tax income	£ 19 500 pa	
YP 10 years at 12 per cent	5.650	£110 175
sale price in 10 years net of tax	£1 717 186	
× PV of £1 in 10 years at 12 per cent	0.322	£552 934
present value of inflows		£663 109
less present value of outflows		£750 000
net present value at 12 per cent		− £ 86 891

A 12 per cent return is not achieved, therefore the internal rate of return net of tax lies between 10 per cent and 12 per cent.

Using similar triangles (see question 2.1) to discover the actual return:

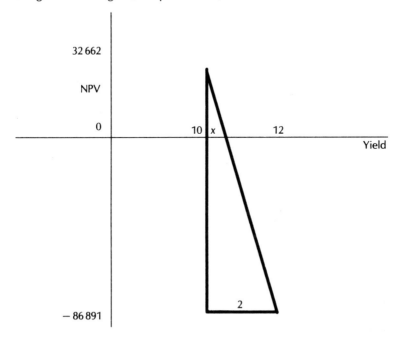

$$\frac{x}{32\,662} = \frac{2}{119\,553}$$

$$119\,553x = 65\,324$$

$$x = 0.55$$

net of tax internal rate of return = 10 per cent 0.55 per cent = 10.55 per cent

INVESTMENT 2: Leasehold shop

The fixed profit rent of £155 000 per annum must first be reduced to a net of tax basis.

Profit rent	£155 000 pa
less Income Tax at 35p in the £	£ 54 250 pa
income net of tax	£100 750 pa

The calculation may now proceed in the same way as that used to determine the gross of tax return for Client A.

$$\text{Years' Purchase for 10 years} = \frac{\text{purchase price}}{\text{income net of tax}}$$

$$= \frac{£750\,000}{£100\,750} = 7.444$$

7.444 is the Years' Purchase for 10 years at the net of tax yield.

Reference to the single rate Years' Purchase table reveals that the Years' Purchase for 10 years at 5.75 per cent is the closest to this figure, at 7.448.

The internal rate of return of Investment 2 net of tax is therefore 5.75 per cent, when tax is paid at 35p in the £.

Client B should be advised to purchase Investment 1, the freehold shop, since the incidence of tax only reduces the yield by 2.29 per cent. In contrast, the yield from the leasehold shop is drastically affected, falling by 10.25 per cent.

This illustrates very well the position of high rate tax payers, who are better advised to invest in reversionary freeholds, where the current income may be low, but there is the possibility of a considerable capital gain in the future. This holds true even when Capital Gains Tax on that future gain is taken into account. The fact that inflationary gains are now recognised, and deducted in computing Capital Gains Tax liability, is beneficial in this respect.

Question 2.3

(a) In answer to this part of the question, it should be explained that a person's principal private residence is exempt from Capital Gains Tax when sold, together with grounds of up to 0.5 hectare including the site of the residence. A greater area than this may be allowed if it is considered appropriate to the dwelling.

Total exemption depends upon the property being the principal residence during the whole period of ownership, or for the whole period of ownership except all or part of the last 36 months. Where this is not so, the *exempt* part of the gain is calculated as follows:

$$\text{total gain} \times \frac{\text{period of occupation} + \text{last 36 months of ownership}}{\text{total period of ownership}}$$

The period of 36 months is to assist those who purchase a 'new' house, but are then unable to sell their original one. This period was extended from 24 months by S.94(1) of the *Finance Act 1991*, because of the depressed state of the housing market. However, S.223(5) and (6) of the *Taxation of Chargeable*

Gains Act 1992, allows for the period of 24 months to be reinstated should the market improve, and then to vary between the 24 month period and the 36 month period, depending upon the housing market in the future. Where disposal is after 5 April 1988, the period of ownership does not now include any time before 31 March 1982 – this follows from the adoption of 31 March 1982 in the *Finance Act 1988* as the base date for the calculation of chargeable gains. For some reason, the restriction on the period of ownership to that since 31 March 1982, applies even though the taxpayer has not elected to have the gain calculated by reference to the market value at 31 March 1982.

The period of ownership for disposals on or before 5 April 1988, includes any time after 6 April 1965.

Under S.223(3) of the *Taxation of Chargeable Gains Act 1982,* the taxpayer is allowed to be absent from the property for certain periods without losing the exemption, and the allowable periods should be noted in the answer.

(i) Periods of up to 3 years for any purpose.
(ii) Periods of any length during which the taxpayer had to work outside the United Kingdom.
(iii) Periods of up to 4 years during which it was not possible to live in the house, due to the situation of the taxpayer's employment, or because of conditions imposed by the taxpayer's employer.

In addition to a person's own principal private residence, exemption is allowed for a residence occupied, rent free, by a dependent relative of the taxpayer.

Where more than one residence is owned, it is up to the taxpayer to elect which shall be regarded as his main residence, otherwise the Inland Revenue will decide from the facts in each individual case.

When part of the property has been let, exemption is extended to the tenanted part, but this must not exceed the exemption on the owner-occupied part and, in any event, is subject to a ceiling figure.

(b) *Computation of chargeable gain on the disposal in April 1993*
Since disposal of the freehold interest was after 5 April 1988, the calculation of the chargeable gain falls under the provisions of the *Finance Act 1988.* This Act changed the base date for Capital Gains Tax purposes from 6 April 1965 to 31 March 1982, that is, only gains occurring since 31 March 1982 are chargeable. It has to be assumed that assets were acquired on 31 March 1982 for their market value at that date – the difference between this value and the sale price is thus the gain in value since 31 March 1982. The cost of any improvements after 31 March 1982 are also deducted from the sale price and the total gain reduced by an allowance for inflation.

However, the *Finance Act 1988* also stated that this change of base date must not be allowed to disadvantage the taxpayer. If the gain calculated under the provisions in force prior to the *Finance Act 1988* is lower than that produced by the 1988 provisions, then the taxpayer is allowed to adopt the lower figure.

It is therefore necessary to carry out two calculations — one following the rules of the *Finance Act 1988* and the other following the rules prior to that Act.

Calculation of gain under the provisions of the Finance Act 1988

Sale price		£270 000 [see note 1]
less		
market value in March 1982		
[see note 2]	£130 000	
1989 improvements [see note 3]	£ 9 750	£139 750
total gain since 31 March 1982		£130 250

less indexation allowance [see note 4]

$$£130\,000 \times \frac{141.2 - 79.44}{79.44}$$

[see note 5] =	£101 067	

$$£   9\,750 \times \frac{141.2 - 115.0}{115.0}$$

[see note 6] =	£ 2 221	£103 288 [see note 7]
net gain from 31 March 1982	£ 26 962	

Notes

1: Incidental costs such as agents, legal fees, stamp duty and so on, incurred on sale, purchase, improvements and in ascertaining the March 1982 value, are ignored in the calculation, for simplicity. In fact, such costs are allowable expenditure and would be set against the chargeable gain.

2: The market value at 31 March 1982 is used in place of the actual purchase price. It has be to assumed that the freehold interest was acquired on 31 March 1982 for its market value at that time.

3: Only the cost of improvements in May 1989 is deducted. Because the property is assumed to have been purchased on 31 March 1982, any expenditure prior to that date must be ignored. The March 1982 market value will reflect any value attributable to the improvements in 1961 and 1973.

4: This is an allowance for any part of the capital gain caused purely by inflation since March 1982.

5: Any inflationary gains are measured by reference to the Retail Prices Index. Each item of allowable expenditure is multiplied by what is called the 'Relevant Fraction':

$$\text{Market Value in March 1982 or expenditure} \times \frac{RD - RI}{RI}$$

where RD = Retail Prices Index in month of disposal

RI = Retail Prices Index in March 1982 or the month of expenditure

In this part of the calculation in question, the market value in March 1982 is multiplied by the percentage rise in the Retail Prices Index from March 1982 to the date of sale. The result of this is that £101 067 of the total gain is assumed to have been caused by the inflation. In other words, a property costing £130 000 in March 1982 would cost £101 067 more in April 1993 solely because of the effects of inflation.

6: Allowance for the effects of inflation on the cost of the 1989 improvements. The expenditure is multiplied by the percentage rise in the Retail Prices Index between May 1989 and the month of disposal. The resultant figure of £2 221 means that improvements costing £9 750 in May 1989, would cost £2 221 more in April 1993 because of inflation.

7: The total gain since 31 March 1982 is £130 250, but £103 288 of this has been caused by inflation. This part of the gain is not taxable and is deducted from the total gain.

Calculation of gain under the provisions prior to the Finance Act 1988

Sale price		£270 000 [see note 1]
less purchase price	£35 000	
1961 improvements	£ 6 000	
1973 improvements	£ 8 000	
1989 improvements	£ 9 750	£ 58 750 [see note 2]
total gain		£211 250
less indexation allowance		
as previous calculation [see note 3]		£103 288
total net gain		£107 962
proportion of gain attributable to [see note 4]		

$$\text{purchase in 1958} \qquad £107\,962 \times \frac{£35\,000}{£58\,750} = £64\,318$$

1961 improvements	$£107\,962 \times \dfrac{£\,6\,000}{£58\,750}$	$= £11\,026$

1973 and 1989 improvements	$£107\,962 \times \dfrac{£17\,750}{£58\,750}$	$= £32\,618$

Time apportionment [see note 5]
purchase in 1958 $\qquad\qquad$ $£\,64\,318 \times \dfrac{28}{6.5 + 28} = £52\,200$

1961 improvements $\qquad\qquad$ $£\,11\,026 \times \dfrac{28}{4.25 + 28} = £\,9\,573$

1973 and 1989 improvement $\quad$ all gain chargeable
[see note 6] $\qquad\qquad\qquad\qquad\qquad\qquad\qquad$ £32 618

net gain from 6 April 1965 $\qquad\qquad\qquad\qquad\qquad$ £94 391

This is higher than the net gain calculated from 31 March 1982, therefore it is more beneficial for the taxpayer to adopt the latter figure.

Chargeable gain for Capital Gains Tax purposes = £26 962

Notes

1: Incidental costs incurred on sale, purchase or improvements have been ignored, but would be allowable expenditure.

2: In this calculation, actual expenditure on purchase and all improvements is set against the sale price.

3: See also notes 5–7 of *Finance Act 1988* calculation. In the calculation under consideration, the percentage increase in the Retail Prices Index from March 1982 to the date of disposal, is applied to the greater of (i) total expenditure up to 31 March 1982 or (ii) the market value of the interest at 31 March 1982. In this case, the value at March 1982 (£130 000) exceeds expenditure (£35 000 + £6 000 + £8 000), therefore the market value is adopted, and the indexation allowance is identical in both calculations.

4: The various items of expenditure have been incurred at different times. This means that any gains in value caused by the expenditures have accrued over varying lengths of time and so they must be separated in order to proceed with the time appointment calculation (see note 5). Since this would be virtually impossible to evaluate specifically, the separation is performed on a purely mathematical basis, using the formula:

$$\begin{array}{l} \text{part of gain attributable} \\ \text{to item of expenditure} \end{array} = \text{total gain} \times \dfrac{\text{item of expenditure}}{\text{total expenditure}}$$

In other words, the part of the total gain caused by an individual item of expenditure, is assumed to be in the same proportion as the individual expenditure is to the total expenditure. For example, 6 000/58 750 of the total expenditure was spent on the improvements in 1961, therefore 6 000/58 750 of the total gain is assumed to have been caused by these improvements.

5: The gain of £107 962 has accrued from 1958 and any gain prior to 6 April 1965 has to be excluded, since it is not chargeable to Capital Gains Tax. Using the time apportionment method, the capital gain from April 1965 is assumed to have occurred in the same proportion as the time after April 1965, compared with the total period of ownership (or the total period since a particular item of expenditure), both before and after 1965. The time apportionment formula is used for this calculation:

$$\text{gain attributable to item of expenditure} \times \frac{T}{P + T} = \text{chargeable part of gain}$$

where $T =$ time from 6 April 1965 to date of disposal

$P =$ time from date of expenditure to 6 April 1965

For example, 28/32.25 of the time since the 1961 improvements were carried out, is after 6 April 1965, therefore 28/32.25 of the gain caused by those improvements is also assumed to have occurred after 6 April 1965.

The Inland Revenue would normally carry out this apportionment on the basis of time in days, but, for convenience, whole years and months are adopted in this example.

6: Only gains accruing after 6 April 1965 are chargeable. Since these improvements were carried out in 1973 and 1989, any consequential gain in value arising from them must naturally have occurred after 6 April 1965, therefore it is all chargeable.

In a Capital Gains Tax calculation involving time apportionment, the indexation allowance has, since its introduction, always been deducted *before* applying the time apportionment formula to the gain. This followed the Inland Revenue Statement of Practice SP3/82. However, in *Smith v. Schofield*, this approach was challenged, the case being a test case funded by a consortium of accountancy firms and insurance companies. They argued that the indexation allowance should be deducted *after* time apportionment of the gain, otherwise the full benefit of the indexation allowance would not be achieved, resulting in a higher net gain.

Initially, the Special Commissioner found in favour of the taxpayer, but the Inland Revenue's appeal was allowed by the High Court. On 6 February 1992, the Court of Appeal reversed the decision once more, in favour of the taxpayer. The Inland Revenue again appealed and on 11 March 1993 this appeal was upheld when the House of Lords reversed the Court of Appeal's decision.

The Inland Revenue's argument centred on S.86 of the *Finance Act 1982* (as amended by the *Finance Act 1985*). This provided for the indexation allowance to be 'set against' the 'computed gain', and the Inland Revenue contended that indexation was part of the process of computing the gain – the purpose of time apportionment was to determine how much of the indexed gain should be chargeable to Capital Gains Tax.

This may seem a small point to pursue through the entire legal appeal system, and in *Smith v. Schofield* the amount of tax due was only in the region of £270. But this was a test case and the Inland Revenue estimated that in total, tax of 'substantially in excess of £50 000 000' was at stake.

In the above example, SP3/82 and the decision in *Smith v. Schofield* have been followed, the indexation allowance being deducted *before* applying the time apportionment formula.

Where an asset was acquired prior to 6 April 1965, the taxpayer has the right to elect to have the gain calculated, under the pre-*Finance Act 1988* provisions, using the value at April 1965 as a basis, rather than the time apportionment method. The approach is much the same as when the market value in March 1982 is used – the 1965 value being used in place of the acquisition price and 6 April 1965 as the assumed date of acquisition. When property is sold with development potential, the election is not available.

The question states that the taxpayer has not elected for this approach, which indicates that no attempt need be made to calculate the gain on this basis.

Question 2.4

(a) This question concentrates upon the part disposal of an interest in property. In this part of the question, the explanation should be directed at the method of dealing with expenditure.

When only part of an interest in property is disposed of, only an appropriate part of any allowable expenditure can be set against the disposal price in calculating the chargeable gain. Obviously only part of the purchase price, 1982 market value and improvement expenditure applicable to the entire property, can be attributed to the part being disposed of. On disposal, the allowable expenditure must be apportioned between the part sold and the part retained.

The method of achieving this apportionment is specified in S.42 of the *Taxation of Chargeable Gains Act 1992*. Before being deducted from the disposal price, each item of expenditure, and market value in March 1982 where applicable, in respect of the entire interest, is multiplied by

$$\frac{\text{net proceeds of part disposal}}{\substack{\text{net proceeds of} \\ \text{part disposal}} + \substack{\text{market value of} \\ \text{part retained}}}$$

In other words, at the time of purchase, or improvement or in March 1982, the value of the part being sold and the value of the entire property, are assumed to have been in the same proportion as at the date of disposal.

If any item of expenditure can be attributed *solely* to the part disposed of, or the part retained, then it will not be apportioned. For example, if certain improvements, carried out during the period of ownership, have clearly affected only the value of the part retained, then *none* of the expenditure on those improvements will be deducted from the disposal price. On the other hand, if such expenditure benefited only the part sold, then *all* of that expenditure is deducted from the disposal price (see part (b) of this question).

Section 242(1)–(3) of the *Taxation of Chargeable Gains Act 1992*, provides for the situation where the value of the part disposal is small, compared to the value of the entire interest prior to the part disposal. Where the value of the part disposal does not exceed 1/5 of the entirety value, or a maximum of £20 000, then the taxpayer may elect that the taxation of any gain may be postponed until the remainder of the interest is disposed of.

(b) *Calculation of chargeable gain using the provisions of the Finance Act 1988*

Sale price		£67 000
less costs of sale [see note 1]		£ 1 800
net proceeds of disposal		£65 200
less		
market value in March 1982		
$£60\,000 \times \dfrac{£65\,200}{£65\,200 + £50\,000} =$	£33 958	
	[see note 2]	
1991 improvements	£ 3 500	
	[see note 3] £37 458	
gain from March 1982		£27 742
less indexation allowance		
$£33\,958 \times \dfrac{139.6 - 79.44}{79.44} =$	£25 716	
[see note 4]		
$£3\,500 \times \dfrac{139.6 - 134.1}{134.1} =$	£ 144	£25 860
	net gain	£ 1 882

Notes

1: Incidental costs of £1 800 reduce the amount that the taxpayer receives on disposal and hence reduce the capital gain achieved. The costs are therefore considered to be allowable expenditure and are deducted from the sale price.

2: This is assumed to be the March 1982 market value of the part being disposed of. At the time of disposal, the value of this part is 65 200/115 200 of the value of the whole. The market value in March 1982 is assumed to have been in the same proportion.

3: These improvements enhanced only the value of the part sold, therefore the whole cost is allowable.

4: The allowance for inflation on the market value in March 1982 is based upon the market value of the part sold only.

Calculation of the chargeable gain using the provisions prior to the Finance Act 1988

Net proceeds of disposal		£65 200
less		
purchase price		
$£30\,000 \times \dfrac{£65\,200}{£65\,200 + £50\,000} =$	£16 979	
[see note 1]		
1970 improvements		
$£5\,000 \times \dfrac{£65\,200}{£65\,200 + £50\,000} =$	£ 2 830	
[see note 2]		
1991 improvements	£ 3 500	£23 309
gain from 1970		£41 891
less indexation allowance, as		
previous calculation [see note 3]		£25 860
net gain		£16 031

This net gain is greater than that calculated under the 1988 provisions, therefore the latter is adopted.

$$\text{Chargeable gain} = £1\ 882$$

Notes

1: £30 000 includes incidental costs of £1 125, so the actual purchase price of the entire interest would have been £28 875. However, the incidental costs are

allowable expenditure, since they increased the overall cost of acquiring the property and consequently reduce the capital gain obtained by the taxpayer. 2: Improvements in 1970 affected the value of the whole property. This expenditure must be apportioned to determine the amount attributable to the part sold.
3: The allowance for inflation from 31 March 1982 in this calculation, is based on the greater of market value at 31 March 1982 (£33 958) or expenditure up to that date (£19 809). Market value being the greater, the indexation allowance is the same as in the previous calculation.

Question 2.5

To begin with, a brief definition of a short leasehold interest should be given. At what point does a lease become a 'short' lease? For Capital Gains Tax purposes, a lease is regarded by the Inland Revenue as a short lease when it has 50 years or less unexpired. Such a lease is treated as a wasting asset.

On disposal of a short leasehold interest, the interest being sold is not the same as that originally purchased. If a lease is acquired with 25 years unexpired and sold 10 years later, the purchase and sale prices are not on the same basis. The purchase price was in respect of a 25 year lease, whereas the sale price is that achieved for a 15 year lease. In some way, the acquisition price must be adjusted to allow for the depreciation in value that is assumed to have occurred during the 10 years of ownership, so that acquisition and disposal prices may be reconciled.

The problem is that the passage of the same period of time has a different effect upon the value of leases with different unexpired terms. For example, the passage of 3 years will have little impact on the value of a 48 year lease, but it will make a great deal of difference to the value of a lease with 5 years unexpired.

The method of writing down expenditure incurred on a lease, is provided by *Schedule 8* of the *Taxation of Chargeable Gains Act, 1992*. In effect, determination of the depreciation in value is reduced to a formula, so that no subjective valuer judgement is involved and all leases are treated on the same basis.

Unlike other wasting assets, written down on a straight line basis, in the case of short leases curved line depreciation is assumed, with an accelerating rate of depreciation as the unexpired term becomes shorter.

A table in *Schedule 8* shows how a short lease is deemed to waste away. In this table, the value of an unexpired lease is expressed as a percentage of the value of a 50 year lease. With 50 years unexpired, the value of a lease is expressed as 100 per cent. A 49 year lease is assumed to be 99.657 per cent of

Applied Valuation

the value of a 50 year lease, a 48 year lease is 99.289 per cent of the value of a 50 year lease, and so on.

A few examples from the table will illustrate the curved-line nature of the depreciation.

Number of years unexpired	Value as percentage of 50 year lease	Number of years unexpired	Value as percentage of 50 year lease
50	100	20	72.770
49	99.657	19	70.791
48	99.289	18	68.697
47	98.902	17	66.470
46	98.490	16	64.116
45	98.059	15	61.617
30	87.330	5	26.722
29	86.226	4	21.983
28	85.053	3	16.959
27	83.816	2	11.629
26	82.496	1	5.983
25	81.100	0	0

Assumed depreciation from 50 years unexpired to 45 years, is only 1.941 per cent. During a similar period from 30 to 25 years unexpired, depreciation is 6.23 per cent and from 20 to 15 years is 11.153 per cent. Depreciation during the last 5 years of the lease is the most dramatic, at 26.722 per cent.

The figures in this table are based on the single rate Years' Purchase table at 6 per cent (a statutory figure, originally specified in the *Finance Act, 1965*). The Years' Purchase at 6 per cent for the unexpired term of a lease is expressed as a percentage of the Years' Purchase at 6 per cent for 50 years.

For example, if the unexpired term is 49 years:

$$\frac{\text{YP 6 per cent for 49 years}}{\text{YP 6 per cent for 50 years}} \times 100 = \frac{15.708}{15.762} \times 100 = 99.657 \text{ per cent}$$

If the unexpired term is 5 years:

$$\frac{\text{YP 6 per cent for 5 years}}{\text{YP 6 per cent for 50 years}} \times 100 = \frac{4.212}{15.762} \times 100 = 26.722 \text{ per cent}$$

On disposal of a short lease, the method of calculating the gain is to deduct the written down expenditure from the sale price.

Writing down of expenditure may be achieved by using either

(i) the percentages given in the table to *Schedule 8, Taxation of Chargeable Gains Act, 1992*, or

(ii) the single rate Years' Purchase table at 6 per cent.

(i) *Using percentages in the Schedule 8 table*
From the disposal price is deducted

Purchase price or market value in March 1982 —

$$\left[\text{Purchase price or market value in March 1982} \times \frac{P(1) - P(3)}{P(1)}\right]$$

where $P(1) =$ percentage applicable to the unexpired term of the lease at date of acquisition or 31 March 1982

$P(3) =$ percentage applicable to the unexpired term of the lease at date of disposal

If improvement expenditure has been incurred, the equation is:

$$\text{Cost of improvements} - \left[\text{Cost of improvements} \times \frac{P(2) - P(3)}{P(2)}\right]$$

where $P(2) =$ percentage applicable to the unexpired term of the lease at the date of expenditure

Example
A lease was purchased in May 1985 with 20 years unexpired, for £90 000. The premises were improved 5 years later, at a cost of £10 000. The lease was sold in May 1993 for £95 000.
   Any allowance for inflation will be ignored, to simplify the example.

Sale Price	£95 000
less	

$$£90\,000 - \left(£90\,000 \times \frac{72.770 \text{ [see note 1]} - 53.191 \text{ [see note 2]}}{72.770}\right)$$

$$= £65\,785 \text{ [see note 3]}$$

$$£10\,000 - \left(£10\,000 \times \frac{61.617 \text{ [see note 4]} - 53.191}{61.617}\right)$$

$$= £8\,633$$

	[see note 5]	£74 418
	gain	£20 582
		[see note 6]

Notes

1: Percentage applicable to 20 year lease – the unexpired term when it was purchased.

2: Percentage applicable to 12 year lease – the unexpired term on disposal.

3: Written down purchase price of lease.

4: Percentage applicable to 15 year lease – the unexpired term when improvements were carried out.

5: Written down cost of improvements.

6: From the total gain, an allowance for inflation would be deducted in the same way as explained in question 2.3. The 'relevant fractions' are applied to the written down items of expenditure.

(ii) *Using single rate Years' Purchase table at 6 per cent*

Since the percentages used in the above example are all based upon the single rate Years' Purchase table at 6 per cent, it is probably simpler for the valuer to use the Years' Purchase table directly.

In this case, the gain is calculated by deducting from the sale price:

purchase price
or market value ×
in March 1982

$\dfrac{\text{Years' Purchase at 6 per cent for the unexpired term of the lease on disposal}}{\text{Years' Purchase at 6 per cent for the unexpired term of the lease on acquisition or 31 March 1982}}$

The appropriate deduction for improvement expenditure is:

cost of
improvements ×

$\dfrac{\text{Years' Purchase at 6 per cent for the unexpired term of the lease on disposal}}{\text{Years' Purchase at 6 per cent for the unexpired term of the lease at date of expenditure}}$

Using the previous example:

Sale price	£95 000

less

$$£90\,000 \times \frac{\text{YP 12 years at 6 per cent}}{\text{YP 20 years at 6 per cent}}$$

$$= £90\,000 \times \frac{8.384}{11.470} = \qquad £65\,785$$

$$£10\,000 \times \frac{\text{YP 12 years at 6 per cent}}{\text{YP 15 years at 6 per cent}}$$

$$= £10\,000 \times \frac{8.384}{9.712} = \qquad £8\,633 \qquad £74\,418$$

gain £20 582

Reconciliation of the actual gain with the gain as calculated
In the above example, the taxpayer appears to have made a *loss* on disposal of
the lease.

Sale price		£ 95 000
less purchase price	£90 000	
improvement expenditure	£10 000	£100 000
loss		£ 5 000

Calculation under Inland Revenue assumptions results in a *gain* of £20 582
(prior to deduction of an allowance for inflation), which is £25 582 *more* than is
apparent.

The reason for this is that the writing down calculation is based upon the
single rate Years' Purchase at 6 per cent, which therefore incorporates the
assumption of an annual sinking fund, also at 6 per cent. This would enable
the leaseholder to sell his interest, prior to the expiration of the term, and
obtain, not only the sale price, but also the accumulations in the annual
sinking fund.

In answering this part of the question, an example should be constructed to
demonstrate that the reduction in purchase price, and any other expenditure,
caused by the writing down adjustment, is exactly equal to the notional
annual sinking fund accumulation between acquisition and disposal.

The example already constructed will be used here – such an approach
would also save time in an examination.

The calculated gain is £25 582 more than the apparent gain. If the assumed
annual sinking fund accumulation over the period of ownership is calculated,
it should be equal to £25 582.

Annual sinking fund instalment to recoup £90 000 over 20 years (the
unexpired term of the lease on acquisition) at an interest rate of 6 per cent:

£90 000 × Annual sinking fund for 20 years at 6 per cent

= £90 000 × 0.0271846 = £2 446.614 per annum.

total accumulation over period of ownership:

£2 446.614 × Amount of £1 per annum for 8 years at 6 per cent

= £2 446.614 × 9.8975 = £24 215.

A similar calculation is carried out in respect of improvement expenditure.

£10 000 × Annual sinking fund for 15 years at 6 per cent

= £10 000 × 0.0429628 = £429.628 per annum

total accumulation:

$£429.628 \times$ Amount of £1 per annum for 3 years at 6 per cent

$= £429.628 \times 3.1836 = £1\,367$

At the date of disposal, the total amount assumed to have accumulated in the annual sinking fund is

$$£24\,215 + £1\,367 = £25\,582$$

The taxpayer is assumed to receive:

Sale price		£ 95 000
plus annual sinking fund accumulations		£ 25 582
		£120 582
less purchase price	£90 000	
improvement expenditure	£10 000	£100 000
gain		£ 20 582

The figure reconciles with the gain as calculated.

Question 2.6

When a lease is granted subject to the payment of a premium because the premium is a capital sum received by the landlord, it is chargeable to Capital Gains Tax.

If the lease is a short lease, of 50 years or less (see question 2.5), the premium is also liable to a charge to Income Tax, under Schedule A – the premium is regarded partly as capital and partly as income.

However, Capital Gains Tax is only chargeable on the part of the premium that is *not* subject to Schedule A Income Tax. The granting of a lease is a part disposal of the freehold interest (see question 2.4), and the original purchase price of the interest, or its market value in March 1982, is apportioned using the part disposal formula (see question 2.4).

This calculation shows how much of the purchase price or market value in March 1982 is assumed to be attributable to the number of years now being let (20 years in this question). The apportionment is performed by:

purchase price of freehold interest or market value in March 1982	$\times$	part of premium not chargeable to Schedule A Income Tax
		net proceeds of disposal (the premium) + value of freeholder's retained interest

Thus, before calculation of the chargeable gain can proceed, it is necessary to calculate:

(i) the part of the premium *not* chargeable to Schedule A Income Tax, and
(ii) the value of the freeholder's retained interest.

(i) *Schedule A Income Tax*
To determine how much of the premium is chargeable to Schedule A Income Tax, it is discounted by two per cent for every year of the lease, except the first (in this case, 20 years − 1 = 19 years at 2 per cent). This is a statutory calculation and the resultant figure is the part of the premium regarded as income.

Premium	£90 000
less (20 − 1) × 2 per cent	
= 38 per cent	£34 200
amount of premium regarded as income	£55 800

£55 800 will be taxed under Schedule A Income Tax. The remainder of the premium, £34 200, is regarded as capital and is treated as the disposal price for Capital Gains Tax purposes.

(ii) *The value of the freeholder's retained interest*
First of all, the full rental value must be calculated.

$$\text{Annual equivalent of premium} = \frac{£90\,000}{\text{YP 5 years at 12 per cent}} \quad \text{[see note 1]}$$

$= \dfrac{90\,000}{3.605} =$		£24 965 pa
plus rent passing		£45 000 pa
full rental value		£69 965 pa
	say £70 000 pa [see note 2]	

Valuation

Net income	£ 45 000 pa	
YP 5 years at 12 per cent [see note 3]	3.605	£162 225
reversion to full net rental value	£ 70 000 pa	
YP in perpetuity deferred 5 years		
at 7 per cent [see note 4]	10.186	£713 020
capital value of freeholder's retained interest		£875 245
	say £875 000	

Notes

1: As the property has been let on the basis of 5 year reviews, it has been assumed that the premium was paid in respect of a reduction in rent for the first 5 years only, and at first review the rent will increase to full rental value. A high yield has been adopted in decapitalising the premium, to reflect the fixed income for 5 years.

2: It could be argued that full rental value should be calculated from both freeholder's and leaseholder's viewpoints, assuming a compromise between the two. However, since the freeholder is the taxpayer, the analysis has been carried out as if acting on the freeholder's behalf.

3: A fixed income for 5 years, therefore it has been valued at the equated yield.

4: As no information is given in the question, it has been assumed that the all risks yield for freehold properties of this type is 7 per cent. In practice, this yield would be obtained from transactions involving comparable properties.

Calculation of chargeable gain

Disposal price for Capital Gains Tax purposes   £34 200

$$\text{less } £400\,000 \times \frac{£34\,200 \text{ [see note 1]}}{£90\,000 + £875\,000} \qquad £14\,176 \text{ [see note 4]}$$

[see note 2]   [see note 3]

total gain   £20 024

less indexation allowance [see note 5]

$$£14\,176 \times \frac{139.8 - 85.3}{85.3} = \qquad\qquad £\ 9\,057$$

£10 967

chargeable gain =   £10 967 [see note 6]

Notes

1: The part of the premium not chargeable to Schedule A Income Tax – treated as the disposal price for the Capital Gains Tax computation.

2: Net proceeds of disposal – the total premium.

3: The value of the freeholder's retained interest following the granting of the lease. This, together with the premium of £90 000 is the value of the freehold interest.

4: The part of the freehold purchase price of £400 000 assumed to have been paid for the 20 years now being disposed of by way of a lease.

5: Allowance for inflationary gain in value from date of acquisition to date of disposal.

6: As the freehold interest was purchased after 31 March 1982 (in July 1983), only one calculation is necessary to determine the chargeable gain. The calculation based upon market value in March 1982 does not apply.

3 LANDLORD AND TENANT – BUSINESS PROPERTY

When valuing interests in business premises, although normal valuation concepts apply, the constraints of legislation, together with surrounding case law, must be borne in mind.

The main legislation affecting the valuation of interests in such property is embodied in three statutes – the *Landlord and Tenant Act 1927*, which deals with compensation for tenant's improvements, the *Landlord and Tenant Act 1954* and the *Law of Property Act 1969*, which make provision for security of tenure and compensation to the tenant for loss of this in the event of the landlord being able to gain possession of the premises.

How these may affect the valuation of interests in business property is explained in the answer to question 3.1. Also in this question, consideration is given to recent changes in the compensation provisions made by the *Landlord and Tenant Act 1954 (Appropriate Multiplier) Order 1990* and *Schedule 7* of the *Local Government and Housing Act 1989*.

An important point to remember in respect of improvements to business property, carried out by the tenant with the landlord's consent, is that the value of such improvements done within the present lease or the last 21 years, cannot be included in the rent (*Landlord and Tenant Act 1954* and *Law of Property Act 1969*). Part (c) of question 3.1 explains the valuation implications of this statutory constraint, but question 3.2 considers how the wording of a particular lease may complicate the issue.

Other problems dealt with in this section include the calculation of rent on surrender of a lease in return for a new lease and calculation of a premium which might be payable in such a situation – see questions 3.3, 3.5 and 3.6. Question 3.4 considers the analysis and use of comparable evidence, in first of all establishing the rental value of business premises and subsequently providing capital valuations of interests in the property.

LANDLORD AND TENANT – BUSINESS PROPERTY – QUESTIONS

3.1. With the aid of examples, discuss the possible effects that the following might have on the capital valuation of interests in business premises:

(a) compensation for loss of security of tenure under the *Landlord and Tenant Act 1954*

(b) compensation for tenant's improvements under the *Landlord and Tenant Act 1927*

(c) tenant's improvements and their effect on rent under the *Landlord and Tenant Act 1954* and the *Law of Property Act 1969.*

3.2. A shop was let 13 years ago on a 20 year lease with 5 year rent reviews and the current rent passing is £52 500 per annum on full repairing and insuring terms.

The tenant carried out substantial improvements to the property 2 years ago (without obligation to the landlord). Ignoring the effect of the improvements, which are estimated to add £8 000 per annum to the value of the premises, the present net rack rental value is £65 000 per annum on the basis of 5 year reviews. The rent review clause in the lease directs the new rent to be assessed to open market value, but is silent regarding the question of tenant's improvements.

Value the freehold interest, explaining fully each stage of your answer and any assumptions that you make.

3.3. Shop premises, situated in the main shopping area of a provincial town, are held on a 20 year internal repairing lease with 3 years unexpired. The present rent passing is £55 000 per annum exclusive.

The lessee wishes to surrender this lease and obtain a new one, in order to carry out improvements costing £40 000.

The current net rack rental value of the premises in their present state is £60 000 per annum on the basis of 5 year rent reviews, but the proposed improvements will increase this to £70 000 per annum. The freeholder is agreeable to the surrender and the proposed improvements, provided the new lease is on full repairing and insuring terms and the rent is reviewed every 5 years.

(a) Calculate the rent acceptable to both parties for the first 5 years of the new lease.

(b) As an alternative, the lessee is prepared to purchase the freehold interest in the premises. Advise him on the price he should offer.

3.4. (a) The head leaseholder of office premises, situated in the business area of a provincial town, has asked you to negotiate the rent for the first floor office space, which is vacant, with a prospective tenant.

The building is approximately 75 years old and was built originally as a large dwelling house. Major conversion work was carried out 15 years ago and the premises now comprise four office suites, each occupying one floor of the building. Access between the floors is by staircase only.

The head lessee holds on a 99 year lease with 20 years unexpired at a fixed ground rent of £100 per annum.

The schedule of tenancies is as follows:

Floor	Lettable area m^2	Present rent per annum	Tenancy details
Ground	90	£7 650	Let last month for 7 years with no rent reviews
First	84	–	Vacant
Second	84	£4 450	20 year lease with 5 year reviews, the last being one month ago
Third	78	£1 550	Let 5 years ago on a 7 year lease with no reviews

Tenants pay the rates and are responsible for internal repairs. The head lessee is responsible for external repairs and insurance.

In addition to the rent, each tenant pays a service charge, assessed annually, for central heating and maintenance of common parts. Assume the new lease for the first floor suite is for 7 years with no rent reviews. (b) Assuming that the rent assessed for the first floor suite in (a) is agreed at your figure, value the interests of the freeholder and head leaseholder.

3.5. The occupying lessee of a factory is considering the reorganisation of the manufacturing process carried out in the premises. This will involve expenditure in the region of £90 000 and, therefore, before committing himself to this, the lessee requires greater security of tenure.

His present lease, originally for 21 years, was granted 17 years ago, on full repairing and insuring terms, with provision for upwards only 7 year rent reviews. The present rent passing is £68 000 per annum and the current rental value of the property, on the same terms, is £80 000 per annum.

The freeholder is undecided whether to sell his interest to the lessee or to grant him a new lease.

You have been approached by both parties to assess:

(i) the value of the freehold interest
(ii) the premium to be paid for the surrender of the present lease and a renewal for 21 years on similar terms, including the present rent passing
(iii) the rent to be paid on renewal of the lease, assuming that no premium is paid and all other terms, except rent, are as in the existing lease.

3.6. The lessee of office premises has approached the freeholder to ascertain whether he is prepared to accept a surrender of the present lease and to grant a new 20 year lease, on full repairing and insuring terms, with 5 year rent reviews to open market value.

The present lease has 2 years unexpired at £29 500 per annum, on internal repairing terms. The current full rental value of the premises is £36 000 per annum on full repairing and insuring terms and on the basis of 5 year reviews.

Eight years ago, the lessee carried out certain improvements with the freeholder's consent at a cost of £14 000. It is estimated that these improvements have increased the current net rack rental value by £2 000 per annum and would cost £25 000 if carried out today.

(a) Assuming the freeholder is prepared to accept surrender of the present lease and grant a new lease on the terms proposed by the lessee, assess the rent for the first 5 years of the new lease which would be acceptable to both parties.

(b) If the freeholder does not accept the surrender, discuss his position, assuming that he requires the premises for his own occupation when the present lease expires.

LANDLORD AND TENANT – BUSINESS PROPERTY – SUGGESTED ANSWERS

Question 3.1

(a) The student should discuss the circumstances in which compensation is payable to a business tenant for loss of security of tenure, the possible amount of compensation and how it will affect the value of the landlord's and tenant's interests. Under S.24 of the *Landlord and Tenant Act 1954*, the tenant of business premises is entitled to continue in occupation and to be granted a new lease when the current lease ends. Should the landlord wish to obtain possession of the premises, he must serve a valid notice under S.25 of the Act, giving the tenant at least 6 months' notice. Alternatively, if the tenant has applied for a new lease under S.26, the landlord must serve a notice under S.26(6) opposing the tenant's application. The landlord must have valid grounds for seeking possession. These are set out in S.30 of the Act, the main ones being that the landlord requires the property for his own occupation or because he intends to demolish it.

If the landlord obtains possession, compensation for disturbance is payable to the tenant under S.37 of the 1954 Act, the amount of compensation being based upon the rateable value of the property on the date of service of the landlord's S.25 or S.26(6) Notice. Until the introduction of the Uniform Business Rate in 1990, there had not been a rating revaluation since 1973. Because of this, a multiplier was applied to the rateable value when assessing a tenant's compensation for disturbance, to allow for loss of value as the 1973 rateable value had become unrealistic. The appropriate multipliers were 3 times the rateable value (where the tenant had been in occupation for less than 14 years) and 6 times the rateable value (where the tenant had been in occupation for 14 years or more). In 1988, there was a general revaluation of business properties, prior to the introduction of the Uniform Business Rate on 1 April 1990, which meant that rateable values were brought up to date and consequently there was no longer any need for a multiplier to be used. Nevertheless, there are still circumstances in which tenant's compensation for disturbance may be based upon the 'old' (1973) rateable value rather than the 'new' (1990) rateable value. Under the *Landlord and Tenant Act 1954 (Appropriate Multiplier) Order 1990* and *Schedule 7* of the *Local Government and Housing Act 1989*, the situation is now as follows:

(1) When the landlord's S.25 or S.26(6) Notice was served *on or before 31 March 1990*, compensation will be
(a) 3 times the 'old' rateable value, where the tenant has been in occupation for less than 14 years
(b) 6 times the 'old' rateable value, where the tenant has been in occupation for 14 years or more.

(2) When the landlord's S.25 or S.26(6) Notice was served *on or after 1 April 1990*, compensation will be
(a) the 'new' rateable value, where the tenant has been in occupation for less than 14 years
(b) twice the 'new' rateable value, where the tenant has been in occupation for 14 years or more.

(3) When the landlord's S.25 or S.26(6) Notice was served *on or after 1 April 1990*, in respect *only* of business premises with a *domestic* element (*Busby and Another v. Co-operative Insurance Society Ltd., 1993*, a decision reached in Brentwood County Court) there are transitional arrangements which if applicable, mean that the date for fixing the rateable value will be taken as 31 March 1990, rather than the actual date on or after 1 April 1990 when the landlord's Notice was served. Four conditions must be satisfied for the transitional arrangements to apply and these are:
   (i) the lease was entered into before 1 April 1990, or was entered into on or after 1 April 1990 under a contract made before 1 April 1990
  (ii) the landlord's S.25 or S.26(6) Notice is served before 1 April 2000
 (iii) the tenant must serve notice on the landlord that he requires the special basis of compensation to apply. The tenant's notice must be not less than 2 nor more than 4 months after service of the landlord's S.25 or S.26(6) Notice
 (iv) there must have been a rateable value for the property shown in the Valuation List on 31 March 1990.

If these four conditions are met, the compensation will be

(a) 8 times the 'old' rateable value, where the tenant has been in occupation for less than 14 years

(b) 16 times the 'old' rateable value, where the tenant has been in occupation for 14 years or more.

In such circumstances, the tenant has a choice and needs to calculate whether the appropriate multiplier of the 'old' rateable value or that of the 'new' rateable value will provide the greater compensation. If it is the former, then the tenant must serve notice within the specified time limits (see earlier clause 3(iii)) to claim the higher amount.

Since it is the landlord who has to pay the tenant's compensation, the amount is deducted from the capital value of the landlord's interest and added to the capital value of the tenant's interest.

The student should construct a simple illustrative example.

Example

A shop with living accommodation above is let by the freeholder with 3 years unexpired at a rent of £60 000 per annum on full repairing and insuring terms. The current full rental value on the same terms is £67 500 per annum. The rateable value of the property on 31 March 1990 was £12 000 and on 1 April 1990 was £54 000. The tenant has been in occupation for 18 years and the landlord wishes to obtain possession for his own occupation at the end of the lease.

Value of freehold (landlord's) interest

Rent received	£60 000 pa	
YP 3 years at 12 per cent [see note 1]	2.402	£144 120
reversion to full net rental value	£67 500 pa	
YP in perpetuity deferred 3 years at		
7 per cent [see note 2]	11.661	£787 118
		£931 238
less compensation to tenant at end of lease		
either (i) 16 × £12 000 = £192 000		
or (ii) 2 × £54 000 = £108 000 [see note 3]		
adopt the higher figure	£192 000	
× PV of £1 in 3 years at 7 per cent		
[see note 4]	0.816	£156 672
Capital value		£774 566
	say £775 000	

Notes

1: Income fixed and inflation prone for 3 years therefore high yield adopted.
2: All risks yield of 7 per cent assumed appropriate for this type of property.
3: The tenant has been in occupation for more than 14 years so the higher multiplier is applicable in each case.
4: Payment of compensation is deferred until the end of the current lease.

Value of leasehold (tenant's) interest

Full net rental value	£ 67 500 pa	
less rent paid (net)	£ 60 000 pa	
profit rent	£ 7 500 pa	
YP 3 years at 8 per cent and 3 per cent		
(tax 35 per cent) [see note 1]	1.731	
	£ 12 983	
plus compensation received at		
the end of the lease	£156 672	
Capital value	£169 655	
say	£170 000	

Note

1: Traditional yield pattern. Remunerative yield 1 per cent above freehold all risks yield. Annual sinking fund assumed available at 3 per cent with tax at 35p in the £.

(b) Again, in this part of the answer, entitlement to compensation should be described, followed by quantification of the compensation and its effect upon the value of the landlord's and tenant's interests.

The tenant is entitled to compensation under S1(1) of the *Landlord and Tenant Act 1927*, provided proper notice was served on the landlord and his consent obtained, before carrying out the improvements. This compensation is payable if the tenant gives up the property on termination of the lease, or following service of notice to quit during the currency of the lease, either by the landlord or the tenant.

The improvements will probably have increased the value of the property and will therefore (usually) be of value to the landlord when the tenant leaves the property.

Compensation is the *lesser* of:

(i) the present reasonable cost of carrying out the improvements, less the amount needed to put the improvements into a reasonable state of repair
(ii) the net increase in value of the landlord's interest caused by the improvements.

So, if the landlord intends to demolish the property when he gains possession, the improvements are of no value to him and no compensation will be payable to the tenant. Additionally, there will be no compensation if the improvements were carried out as a condition of the lease.

The amount of compensation is deducted from the capital value of the landlord's interest and added to the capital value of the tenant's interest.

It should also be noted that the tenant will be entitled to disturbance compensation as described in part (a).

A simple example should be constructed to illustrate the effect of compensateable improvements.

Example

A shop is let by the freeholder with 3 years unexpired at a rent of £70 000 per annum on full repairing and insuring terms. The current full rental value on the same terms is £82 000 per annum, including £8 000 per annum attributable to improvements costing £40 000 carried out 5 years ago with the landlord's consent. The landlord wishes to obtain possession for his own occupation at the end of the current lease.

First of all, the amount of compensation is calculated.

(i) *Present cost of carrying out the improvements*

Information should be available in practice to estimate this fairly accurately, but, for the purposes of this example, it would be acceptable to assume a reasonable figure. For example, assuming that costs have risen by 7.5 per cent per annum over the 5 years since the improvements were done, the present cost will be:

£40 000 × $(1.075)^5$ =	£57 425
less cost of putting the improvements into a reasonable state of repair, say	£ 3 000
	£54 425

(ii) *Net increase in the value of the freehold interest caused by the improvements*

Value with the improvements		
rental value	£82 000 pa	
YP in perpetuity at 7 per cent	14.286	£1 171 452
Value without the improvements		
rental value	£74 000 pa	
YP in perpetuity at 7 per cent	14.286	£1 057 164
increase in value caused by the improvements		£114 288

The lower figure of £54 425 is adopted as the tenant's compensation for the improvements.

Value of freehold (landlord's) interest

Rent received	£	70 000 pa	
YP 3 years at 12 per cent [see note 1]		2.402	£ 168 140
reversion to full net rental value	£	82 000 pa	
YP in perpetuity deferred 3 years			
at 7 per cent [see note 2]		11.661	£ 956 202
			£1 124 342
less compensation to tenant for			
improvements	£	54 425	
× PV of £1 in 3 years at 6 per cent			
[see note 3]		0.840	£ 45 717
Capital value			£1 078 625
			[see note 4]

say   £1 078 000

Notes

1: Income fixed and inflation prone for 3 years, therefore high yield adopted.

2: All risks yield of 7 per cent assumed appropriate for this type of property.

3: Payment of compensation deferred until the end of the current lease. Yield of 6 per cent adopted, to allow for the possibility of costs increasing over the next 3 years.

4: The capital value would also be reduced by the appropriate amount of compensation for disturbance (see part (a) of this question).

Value of leasehold (tenant's) interest

Full net rental value	£82 000 pa
less rent paid (net)	£70 000 pa
profit rent	£12 000 pa
YP 3 years at 8 per cent and 3	
per cent (tax 35 per cent)	1.731
	£20 772
plus compensation for improvements,	
received at end of lease	£45 717
Capital value	£66 489 [see note 1]

say   £66 500

Note

1: The capital value would also be increased by the appropriate amount of compensation for disturbance.

(c) The student should refer to the '21 year rule' arising from the *Landlord and Tenant Act 1954* and the *Law of Property Act 1969*. On renewal of a lease, the value of tenant's improvements carried out during the current lease or the last 21 years, must be disregarded. This may not apply to rent reviews in the current lease unless expressly provided in the lease (see decision in *Ponsford v. HMS Aerosols Ltd. 1978*). Thus, the situation could arise where, on review, because the lease does not specify how tenant's improvements will be treated, the review is to a rent reflecting the value of the improvements, whereas when the lease in renewed, if 21 years have not elapsed since the improvements were done, the rent will exclude the value attributable to them. For an example illustrating this situation, see question 3.2. The effect of the '21 year rule' (assuming that a situation similar to the *Ponsford* case does *not* arise) is that the value of the improvements is reflected in the value of the tenant's interest at least 21 years before they may be reflected in the value of the landlord's interest.

A simple example will illustrate this.

Example

Assume the same conditions as the example in part (b), but that a new 15 year lease is granted at the end of the current lease.

Value of freehold interest

Rent received		£70 000 pa	
YP 3 years at 12 per cent		2.402	£ 168 140
reversion to full net rental value			
excluding improvements [see note 1]		£74 000 pa	
YP 15 years at 6 per cent [see note 2]	9.712		
× PV of £1 in 3 years at 6 per cent	0.840	8.158	£ 603 692
reversion to full net rental value			
including improvements [see note 3]		£82 000 pa	
YP in perpetuity deferred 18 years at			
7 per cent [see note 2]		4.227	£ 346 614
Capital value			£1 118 446

say   £1 120 000

Notes

1:   At this point, it is only 8 years since the improvements were carried out, therefore the value attributable to them cannot be reflected in the rent under the new lease.

2: All risks yield of 7 per cent assumed appropriate for this type of property. The rent under the new lease is valued at 6 per cent to reflect security of income – the tenant is certain of a profit rent, equal to the value of the improvements, for the duration of this lease.

3: It will be 23 years since the improvements were carried out and their value may now be reflected in the rent.

Value of leasehold interest

Full net rental value [see note 1]		£82 000 pa	
less rent paid (net)		£70 000 pa	
profit rent		£12 000 pa	
YP 3 years at 8 per cent and 3 per cent (tax 35 per cent) [see note 2]		1.731	£20 772
full net rental value		£82 000 pa	
less rent paid [see note 3]		£74 000 pa	
profit rent		£ 8 000 pa	
YP 15 years at 8 per cent and 3 per cent (tax 35 per cent) [see note 2]	6.146		
× PV of £1 in 3 years at 8 per cent	0.794	4.880	£39 040
Capital value			£59 812
		say	£60 000

Notes

1: The value attributable to the improvements is reflected immediately in the value of the tenant's interest. If the leaseholder were to sublet, he could do so at a rent including the value of the improvements.

2: Traditional yield pattern. Remunerative yield 1 per cent above freehold all risks yield. Annual sinking fund assumed available at 3 per cent with tax at 35p in the £.

3: The rent paid to the freeholder excludes the value attributable to the improvements.

Question 3.2

It is stated in the question that the improvements undertaken by the tenant were 'without obligation to the landlord'. This implies that carrying out the improvements was not a condition of the lease and therefore the provisions of the *Landlord and Tenant Acts 1927 and 1954* and the *Law of Property Act 1969* will apply to the improvements. It will be assumed in considering this question that the improvements were done after obtaining the consent of the landlord.

It is important to make these points before commencing the valuation since they affect the value of the freehold interest.

That the lease is silent regarding the question of tenant's improvements is also important to the valuation, since it determines the point at which the value of the improvements may be reflected in the rent, distorting somewhat the application of the '21 year rule'. This is explained in more detail in note 3 of the annotation to the valuation.

Valuation of freehold interest

Rent received		£ 52 500 pa	
YP 2 years [see note 1] at 12 per cent [see note 2]		1.690	£ 88 725
reversion to full net rental value including improvements [see note 3]		£ 73 000 pa	
YP 5 years at 12 per cent [see note 4]	3.605		
× PV of £1 in 2 years at 7 per cent [see note 5]	0.873	3.147	£229 731
reversion to full net rental value excluding improvements [see note 6]		£ 65 000 pa	
YP 15 years [see note 7] at 6 per cent [see note 5]	9.712		
× PV of £1 in 7 years at 6 per cent	0.665	6.458	£419 770
reversion to full net rental value including improvements [see note 8]		£ 73 000 pa	
YP in perpetuity deferred 22 years at 7 per cent [see note 5]		3.224	£235 352
Capital value			£973 578
	say	£975 000	

Notes

1: The shop was let 13 years ago on a 20 year lease with 5 year reviews, therefore the next rent review is in 2 years' time.

2: High yield adopted because income is fixed and inflation prone for 2 years.

3: Under the provisions of the *Law of Property Act 1969* the value of tenant's improvements, carried out during the current lease or the previous 21 years, must normally be disregarded in the rent. However, because in this case the lease is silent regarding how tenant's improvements shall be treated on review, the '21 year rule' will *not* apply to the remainder of the present lease. This follows the decision in *Ponsford v. HMS Aerosols Ltd. (1978)*. As a result, at the remaining review in the present lease, the value attributable to the improvements will be included in the open market rental value.

4: Although the £73 000 per annum is on the basis of 5 year reviews, it is received for 5 years only, until the end of the present lease. It will be fixed and inflation prone for those 5 years and a high yield has been adopted to reflect this.

5: In the absence of information, the all risks yield is assumed to be 7 per cent for this type of property. Where the term income is partially inflation proof (with rent reviews every 5 years) but excludes the value of the improvements, a yield of 6 per cent has been adopted, following a traditional yield pattern to reflect greater security of income.

6: At this point the present lease ends. It is assumed that the tenant is granted a new lease at the end of the present one. However, it is still only 9 years since the tenant carried out the improvements and the '21 year rule' comes into operation with the new lease. This means that the value attributable to the improvements must now be disregarded in the rent.

So, because the present lease is silent regarding the treatment of tenant's improvements, on review in the present lease the value of the improvements may be included in the rent but in the new lease this value must be excluded and the rent received by the landlord is reduced.

7: The agreement between landlord and tenant on the length of the new lease will depend upon the requirements of the two parties and their relative bargaining strengths. If the matter is referred to court, the maximum term that could be awarded is 14 years. As the present lease is on the basis of 5 year reviews, a new lease of 15 years would be reasonable. Alternatively 20 years is consistent with the length of the original lease. Whichever is adopted, the value of the improvements may be included in the rent at the same point.

8: At the end of the 15 year lease (or on review at year 15 in a 20 year lease) it will be 24 years since the tenant's improvements were carried out, and they can be reflected in the rental value.

This question requires that the valuation and any assumptions made in it are fully explained. Although the valuation is obviously important, the marks could well be weighted in favour of the explanation, which should be as thorough as possible.

Although the question does not require consideration of the leasehold interest, it is interesting to note how the treatment of tenant's improvements affects the value of this interest. At the next review in the current lease, the profit rent will 'disappear' only to be reinstated, albeit at a lower amount, when the new lease commences.

Full net rental value [see note 1]	£73 000 pa
less rent paid	£52 500 pa
profit rent	£20 500 pa

YP 2 years at 8 per cent and 3 per cent (tax 35 per cent) [see note 2]		1.194	£24 477
full net rental value	£73 000 pa		
less rent paid [see note 3]	£73 000 pa		
profit rent	nil		—
full net rental value	£73 000 pa		
less rent paid [see note 4]	£65 000 pa		
profit rent	£ 8 000 pa		
YP 15 years [see note 5] at 8 per cent and 3 per cent (tax 35 per cent) [see note 2]	6.146		
× PV of £1 in 7 years at 8 per cent	0.583	3.583	£28 664
Capital value			£53 141
		say	£53 000

Notes

1: The value of the improvements is included immediately in the value of the lessee's interest.

2: Traditional yield pattern. Remunerative yield 1 per cent above freehold all risks yield. Annual sinking fund assumed available at 3 per cent with tax at 35p in the £.

3: See note 3 of freehold interest. Because the lessee now has to pay the full net rental value including the value of the improvements, there will be no profit rent, and hence no capital value, for the last 5 years of the current lease.

4: See notes 6 and 7 of freehold interest. The lessee no longer has to pay the full rental value including the value of the improvements and is able to enjoy a profit rent for the next 15 years.

5: See note 7 of freehold interest.

Question 3.3

(a) In calculating the rent for the first 5 years of the new lease, the principle to be borne in mind is that neither party should be in any better or worse position than they were prior to surrender of the present lease and granting of the new one. The new arrangements must be equal in value to the present situation from both the landlord's and the tenant's point of view.

Initially, each interest is valued under the present lease arrangements. These values are then equated with the values under the proposed new lease.

Landlord's present interest

Rent received	£55 000 pa	
less external repairs and insurance [see note 1]	£ 4 500 pa	
net income	£50 500 pa	
YP 3 years at 12 per cent [see note 2]	2.402	£121 301
reversion to full net rental value	£60 000 pa	
YP in perpetuity deferred 3 years		
at 7 per cent [see note 3]	11.661	£699 660
Capital value		£820 961

Notes
1: The rent received is on internal repairing terms, therefore the cost of external repairs and insurance must be deducted from the landlord's income. In practice the valuer would have more precise knowledge of the cost, but, for the purpose of this example, 7.5 per cent of full net rental value has been assumed to be a reasonable amount.
2: Income fixed and inflation prone for 3 years, therefore high yield adopted.
3: In the absence of information, the all risks yield for this type of property is assumed to be 7 per cent.

Landlord's present interest – alternative approach
This alternative calculation is based upon the assumption that the landlord obtains possession at the end of the lease and carries out the improvements himself.

Net income (as before)	£50 500 pa	
YP 3 years at 12 per cent	2.402	£121 301
reversion to full net rental value [see note 1]	£70 000 pa	
YP in perpetuity deferred 3 years		
at 7 per cent	11.661	£816 270
		£937 571
less cost of improvements [see note 2]	£40 000	
× PV of £1 in 3 years at 7 per cent		
[see note 3]	0.816	£ 32 640
Capital value		£904 931

Notes
1: When the improvements have been done, the property may be let at a rent reflecting the increase in value attributable to them. In the valuation it

has been assumed that the improvements are carried out fairly quickly, therefore loss of rent is not appreciable and can be ignored.

2: The freeholder must pay for the cost of the improvements in order to enjoy the higher income of £70 000 per annum, so the cost is deducted from the capital value of his interest.

3: The cost of the improvements is deferred, because they cannot be carried out until the end of the lease in 3 years' time. A lower yield might be used to defer if it is considered that costs may increase over the next 3 years.

The alternative valuation is more beneficial to the landlord and will be adopted.

Landlord's proposed interest

Let the rent under the new lease =	£	x pa	
Rent received	£	x pa	
YP 5 years at 12 per cent [see note 1]	3.605		£3.605x
reversion to full net rental value			
[see note 2]	£70 000 pa		
YP in perpetuity deferred 5 years			
at 7 per cent	10.186	£713 020	
Capital value			£713 020 + 3.605x

Notes

1: The new lease is to be on the basis of 5 year reviews and the rent agreed will be fixed for the first 5 years.

2: Reversion is to full net rental value including the value of the improvements, which are not covered by the provisions of the *Landlord and Tenant Act 1954* and the *Law of Property Act 1969*, since they are a condition of the new lease.

The value of the landlord's present interest is now equated with the value of his proposed interest, to determine the value of £x.

Present interest	=	Proposed interest
£904 931	=	£713 020 + 3.605x
£191 911	=	3.605x
x	=	£53 235

The rent required by the landlord for the first 5 years of the new lease is £53 235 per annum.

Similar calculations must now be performed from the lessee's viewpoint.

Lessee's present interest

Full net rental value	£60 000 pa
plus external repairs and insurance [see note 1]	£ 4 500 pa
full rental value on internal repairing terms	£64 500 pa
less rent paid	£55 000 pa
profit rent	£ 9 500 pa
YP 3 years at 8 per cent and 3 per cent (tax 35 per cent) [see note 2]	1.731
Capital value	£16 445

Notes

1: To convert the current full rental value on to the same terms as the rent paid. See note 1 of landlord's present interest.

2: Traditional yield pattern. Remunerative yield 1 per cent higher than freehold all risks yield to reflect the extra risks perceived in investing in leaseholds. An annual sinking fund is assumed available at 3 per cent with tax at 35p in the £.

Lessee's proposed interest

Full net rental value	£ 70 000 pa
less rent paid	£ x pa
profit rent	£ 70 000 − x pa
YP 5 years at 8 per cent and 3 per cent (tax 35 per cent)	2.704
	£189 280 − 2.704x
less cost of improvements	£ 40 000
Capital value	£149 280 − 2.704x

Present interest	=	Proposed interest
£16 445	=	£149 280 − 2.704x
2.704x	=	£132 835
x	=	£ 49 125

The rent acceptable to the lessee for the first 5 years of the new lease is £49 125 per annum, whereas £53 235 per annum is the rent required by the freeholder. The parties will probably agree on a rent in the region of £51 200 per annum.

(b) *Purchase of freehold interest by the lessee*

If the lessee should purchase the freehold interest an element of marriage value will be involved. This arises from the merger of freehold and leasehold interests to produce the freehold with vacant possession. The present lessee could then continue to occupy the property as the new freeholder, or it would be available for immediate letting at full rental value.

Value of freehold in possession:		
Full net rental value		£ 70 000 pa
YP in perpetuity at 7 per cent		14.286
		£1 000 020
less cost of improvements		£ 40 000
		£ 960 020
less (i) value of freehold interest	£821 000	
(ii) value of leasehold interest	£ 16 445	£ 837 445
marriage gain		£ 122 575

On the assumption that this marriage gain is divided equally between the parties, the freeholder would have to be paid:

Value of freehold interest	£821 000
plus half share of marriage gain	£ 61 288
purchase price of freehold interest	£882 288
say £882 000	

However, the freeholder would probably attempt to negotiate for more than this, since the freehold interest contributes the greater part of the marriage gain. If the marriage gain were to be apportioned instead in the ratio of the respective values, the freeholder could argue that he ought to receive £941 000.

Marriage gain attributable to freehold interest:

$$£122\,575 \times \frac{£821\,000}{£837\,445} = £120\,168$$

Value of freehold interest	£821 000
plus apportioned part of marriage gain	£120 168
purchase price of freehold interest	£941 168
say £941 000	

In fact, the lessee can afford to pay anything up to £943 575 for the freehold interest:

		£1 000 020
Value of freehold in possession		£1 000 020
less value of leasehold interest	£16 445	
cost of improvements	£40 000	£ 56 445
		£ 943 575

The best advice to give the lessee is to initially offer £882 000, but be prepared to settle at a sum not exceeding £941 000.

Question 3.4

(a) The first step in answering this question is to analyse the information that is available. Reference to payment of a service charge by the tenants may be disregarded, since this payment is in addition to the rent paid for the accommodation. Similarly, payment of rates by the tenants may be ignored, as this is a normal occupier's liability. Only when rents are stated to be 'inclusive' (of rates) is the appropriate amount deducted from the landlord's income.

Ground floor
Because this suite was let last month, the rent of £7 650 per annum should represent the full rental value, on internal repairing terms, with 7 year rent reviews. There is no evidence in the schedule of tenancies to suggest that the suite was let at anything other than its full rental value. For example, a premium does not appear to have been paid.

The figure of £7 650 represents a rental value per square metre of:

$$\frac{£7\,650}{90\ m^2} = £85$$

Second floor
Since this rent was recently reviewed, £4 450 per annum should represent the full rental value of the suite, on internal repairing terms, with a 5 year rent review pattern.

The figure of £4 450 represents a rental value per square metre of:

$$\frac{£4\,450}{84\ m^2} = £52.98$$

Third floor
The rent of £1 550 per annum represents a rental value per square metre of:

$$\frac{£1\,550}{78\ m^2} = £19.87$$

However, this rent is 5 years old and consequently is of no assistance in determining the current rental value of the first floor accommodation. This information should be discarded.

It is a reasonable assumption that the rental value of the first floor will fall between that of the ground and second floors. An average of the rental values per square metre of these two floors is £68.99. However, the second floor suite is let on the basis of 5 year reviews, whereas it is required to determine the rental value of the first floor suite on the basis of 7 year reviews, which is comparable with the basis upon which the ground floor accommodation is let.

Because of this, rather than the average of ground and second floor rental values, a figure nearer to that of the ground floor suite will be adopted, at say £77.50 per square metre.

Since access between floors is by staircase only, this would tend to have a depressing effect upon the rentals for the upper two floors. This is a further reason for adopting a bias towards the ground floor rental information.

Estimated full rental value of first floor office suite, on internal repairing terms, for 7 years without review:

$$84 \text{ m}^2 \times £77.50 = £6\,510$$

$$\text{say} \quad £6\,500 \text{ per annum}$$

This is the rent at which you should seek agreement with the prospective tenant on behalf of your client.

(b) Before commencing the valuations, it is necessary to calculate the full rental value of the entire property from the rental values of the various suites. The information is already available for the ground, first and second floors, but the current rental value of the third floor needs to be ascertained.

It is anticipated that this suite will have the lowest rental value per square metre, again bearing in mind the staircase access. An attempt must be made to estimate the rental value per square metre from the available information. In the absence of evidence from other lettings of similar third floor accommodation, in an examination only a sensible estimate would be required by the examiner. For the purposes of this example, a figure of £45 per square metre will be adopted.

Estimated current full rental value of third floor accommodation, on internal repairing terms:

$$78 \text{ m}^2 \times £45 = £3\,510$$

$$\text{say} \quad £3\,500 \text{ per annum}$$

Estimated full rental value of the entire property on internal repairing terms:

ground floor	£ 7 650 pa
first floor	£ 6 500 pa
second floor	£ 4 450 pa
third floor	£ 3 500 pa
full rental value	£22 100 pa

Valuation of freehold interest

Rent received	£ 100 pa		
YP 20 years at 12 per cent [see note 1]	7.469	£	747
reversion to full rental value [see note 2]	£22 100 pa		
less external repairs and insurance [see note 3]	£ 1 540 pa		
Full rental value on full repairing and insuring terms	£20 560 pa		
YP in perpetuity deferred 20 years at 9 per cent [see note 4]	1.983	£40 770	
Capital value		£41 517	

say   £41 500

Notes

1: Low rent, fixed for 20 years. There is no growth potential, the income is inflation prone and so a high yield has been adopted.

2: Although this is mainly on 7 year reviews, the second floor is let on the basis of 5 year reviews. This can be assumed to be reflected in the all risks yield adopted.

3: The full rental value is on internal repairing terms and the cost of external repairs and insurance is deducted to convert on to full repairing and insuring terms. In the absence of information, 7.5 per cent of the full net rental value has been adopted as the estimated cost. This is calculated by

$$£22\,100 \times \frac{100}{107.5} = £20\,558$$

£20 558 at 7.5 per cent = £1 542 say £1 540 per annum

4: No information has been given in the question regarding the all risks yield and 9 per cent has been assumed reasonable for this type of property.

Valuation of head leasehold interest

Rent received		£ 20 150 pa [see note 1]	
less ground rent	£ 100		
external repairs and insurance [see note 2]	£1 540	£ 1 640 pa	
net income		£ 18 510 pa	

YP 2 years [see note 3] at 10 per cent
and 3 per cent (tax 35 per cent)
[see note 4]   1.166   £21 583

reversion to full rental value [see note 5]   £ 22 100 pa
less ground rent   £   100
external repairs and insurance   £1 540   £   1 640 pa

net income   £ 20 460 pa
YP 18 years at 10 per cent and 3 per
cent (tax 35 per cent) [see note 4]   6.035
× PV of £1 in 2 years at 10 per cent   0.826   4.985   £101 993

Capital value   £123 576

                                              say   £123 500

Notes
1: Total of income from the various floors – ground floor £7 650, first floor
£6 500, second floor £4 450, third floor £1 550.
2: External repairs and insurance are the responsibility of the head leaseholder
and the cost must be deducted from the rent received. For derivation of the
estimated cost, see note 3 to the valuation of the freehold interest.
3: The lease in respect of the third floor has 2 years unexpired. It can then be
let at full rental value.
4: Traditional yield pattern. Remunerative yield 1 per cent above freehold all
risks yield. An annual sinking fund is assumed available at 3 per cent with tax
at 35p in the £.
5: Full rental value is on internal repairing terms.

Question 3.5

(i) *Value of freehold interest*

Rent received [see note 1]   £68 000 pa
YP 4 years at 12 per cent
[see note 2]   3.037   £206 516

reversion to full net rental value   £80 000 pa
YP in perpetuity deferred 4 years
at 9 per cent [see note 3]   7.871   £629 680

Capital value   £836 196

                                              say   £840 000

Notes

1: Rent received is on full repairing and insuring terms.

2: Income is fixed and inflation prone for 4 years, until the end of the present lease, therefore a high yield is adopted.

3: In the absence of information, an all risks yield of 9 per cent has been assumed reasonable for this type of property.

The capital value of the freehold interest is estimated to be £840 000, but there will be an element of marriage gain if the lessee purchases the freehold interest. For this reason, the freeholder will most likely require more than £840 000 to persuade him to sell his interest (see answers to questions 1.1 and 3.3(b) for a consideration of marriage gain).

(ii) *Premium for surrender and renewal of lease*

If the present lease is surrendered and a new one granted, neither party should be in any better or worse position after the surrender and renewal than they were before. It is therefore necessary to equate values under the present lease with those under the proposed new lease (see also question 3.3(a)). The expenditure that the lessee is considering may be disregarded, since it is in respect of the manufacturing process and not improvements to the property itself.

Freeholder's present interest
From part (i) this is £836 196

Freeholder's proposed interest

Let premium = £x		
Rent received [see note 1]	£68 000 pa	
YP 7 years at 12 per cent [see note 2]	4.564	£310 352
reversion to full net rental		
value [see note 3]	£80 000 pa	
YP in perpetuity deferred		
7 years at 9 per cent	6.078	£486 240
		£796 592
plus premium [see note 4]		£ x
Capital value		£796 592 + x

Notes

1: The rent for the first 7 years of the new lease is to remain the same as the present rent passing under the current lease.

2: As the income will be fixed and inflation prone for 7 years, a high yield has been adopted.

3: The new lease is to be on similar terms to the present lease, including the review pattern of 7 yearly, upward only rent reviews. It is reasonable to assume that at first review the rent will increase to full net rental value.

4: The premium is paid by the lessee to compensate the freeholder for the rent being below full rental value for the first 7 years of the new lease. It therefore contributes to the capital value of the freehold interest under the proposed arrangements.

$$
\begin{aligned}
\text{Present interest} &= \text{Proposed interest} \\
£836\,196 &= £796\,592 + x \\
x &= £\ 39\,604
\end{aligned}
$$

Premium required by freeholder, say £39 600.

Similar calculations must now be performed from the lessee's point of view.

Lessee's present interest

Full net rental value	£80 000 pa
less rent paid (net)	£68 000 pa
profit rent	£12 000 pa
YP 4 years at 10 per cent and 3 per cent (tax 35 per cent) [see note 1]	2.138
Capital value	£25 656

Note:

1: Traditional yield pattern. Remunerative yield 1 per cent above freehold all risks yield. Annual sinking fund assumed available at 3 per cent with tax at 35p in the £.

Lessee's proposed interest

Full net rental value	£80 000 pa
less rent paid (net)	£68 000 pa
profit rent	£12 000 pa [see note 1]
YP 7 years at 10 per cent and 3 per cent (tax 35 per cent)	3.325
	£39 900
less premium	£ x [see note 2]
Capital value	£39 900 − x

Notes

1: The lessee will pay the same rent under the new lease as under the present lease, therefore the profit rent will also remain unchanged.

2: The lessee must pay the premium to the freeholder in order to retain a profit rent of £12 000 per annum for 7 years rather than 4 years, therefore the premium is deducted from the capital value of the lessee's interest.

$$
\begin{aligned}
\text{Present interest} &= \text{Proposed interest} \\
£25\,656 &= £39\,900 - x \\
x &= £14\,244
\end{aligned}
$$

Premium lessee is prepared to pay, say £14 250.

Compromise may be difficult in this situation, since the parties' positions are so far apart, the freeholder requiring a premium of £39 600. If agreement could be reached, it would probably be in the region of £27 000.

(iii) *Rent to be paid on renewal of lease assuming that no premium is paid*
   Let the new rent $= £x$ pa
Once again, the approach is to equate the respective values of the present interests with the values of the proposed interests.

Freeholder's present interest
From part (i) this is £836 196

Freeholder's proposed interest

	£	x pa
Net rent to be received		
YP 7 years at 12 per cent	4.564	£4.564x
reversion to full net rental value	£80 000 pa	
YP in perpetuity deferred 7 years		
at 9 per cent	6.078	£486 240
Capital value		£486 240 +4.564x

$$
\begin{aligned}
\text{Present interest} &= \text{Proposed interest} \\
£836\,196 &= £486\,240 + 4.564x \\
£349\,956 &= 4.564x \\
x &= £76\,677
\end{aligned}
$$

Rent required by freeholder on renewal of lease
say £76 650 per annum

Lessee's present interest
From part (ii) this is £25 656

Lessee's proposed interest

Full net rental value	£ 80 000 pa
less rent to be paid	£ x
profit rent	£ 80 000 − x pa
YP 7 years at 10 per cent and	
3 per cent (tax 35 per cent)	3.325
Capital value	£266 000 − 3.325x

$$
\begin{aligned}
\text{Present interest} &= \text{Proposed interest}\\
£25\,656 &= £266\,000 - 3.325x\\
3.325x &= £240\,344\\
x &= £\ 72\,284
\end{aligned}
$$

Rent that lessee is prepared to pay on renewal of lease, say £72 300 per annum.

The landlord and tenant would probably agree upon a rent in the region of £74 500 per annum.

Question 3.6

(a) In order to determine the rent for the first 5 years of the new lease, the value of each party's present interest must be equated with the value of their interest when the present lease is surrendered and a new lease granted (see also questions 3.3 and 3.5).

Freeholder's present interest

Rent received		£29 500 pa	
less external repairs and			
insurance [see note 1]		£ 2 700 pa	
net income		£26 800 pa	
YP 2 years at 12 per cent			
[see note 2]		1.690	£45 292
reversion to full net rental value			
excluding improvements [see note 3]		£34 000 pa	
YP 15 years [see note 4] at 7 per cent			
[see note 5]	9.108		
× PV of £1 in 2 years at 7 per cent	0.873	7.951	£270 334
reversion to full net rental value			
including improvements [see note 6]		£36 000 pa	

YP in perpetuity deferred 17 years at 8 per cent [see note 5]	3.378	£121 608
Capital value		£437 234

Notes

1: Income is on internal repairing terms, therefore external repairs and insurance are the freeholder's responsibility and the cost is deducted from the rent received. In the absence of information the cost has been estimated at 7.5 per cent of full net rental value.

2: Rent is fixed and inflation prone for 2 years therefore a high yield has been adopted.

3: It is only 10 years at this point since the tenant's improvements were carried out and the value attributable to them cannot yet be reflected in the value of the freehold interest ('21 year rule' under *Landlord and Tenant Act 1954* and *Law of Property Act 1969*).

4: It is assumed that the tenant will be granted a new lease at the end of the present one.

5: In the absence of information, the all risks yield for this type of property is assumed to be 8 per cent. A yield of 7 per cent has been adopted for the 15 years of the new lease when the value of the improvements is excluded, to reflect the increased security.

6: It will be 25 years since the tenant carried out the improvements and their value can be reflected in the rent.

Freeholder's proposed interest

Let rent for first 5 years of new lease =		£	x pa	
Rent received		£	x pa	
YP 5 years at 12 per cent		3.605		£3.605x
reversion to full net rental value excluding improvements [see note 1]		£34 000 pa		
YP 10 years at 7 per cent	7.024			
× PV of £1 in 5 years at 7 per cent	0.713	5.008	£170 272	
reversion to full net rental value including improvements [see note 2]		£36 000 pa		
YP in perpetuity deferred 15 years at 8 per cent		3.941	£141 876	
Capital value			£312 148 + 3.605x	

Notes

1: As it is only 13 years since the tenant's improvements were carried out, their value cannot be reflected in the rent on review (unless provided for in the lease, which is not stated in the question).

2: At this point, it will be 23 years since the improvements were carried out, therefore the value attributable to them can now be included in the rent.

The value of the freeholder's present interest is now equated with the value of his proposed interest to determine the value of £x.

Present interest	=	Proposed interest
£437 234	=	£312 148 + 3.605x
£125 086	=	3.605x
x	=	£34 698

Rent required by freeholder for first 5 years of the new lease, say £34 700 per annum.

The process is now repeated from the lessee's viewpoint.

Lessee's present interest

Full net rental value [see note 1]	£36 000 pa	
plus external repairs and insurance [see note 2]	£ 2 700 pa	
full rental value on internal repairing terms	£38 700 pa	
less rent paid [see note 3]	£29 500 pa	
profit rent	£ 9 200 pa	
YP 2 years at 8 per cent and 3 per cent (tax 35 per cent) [see note 4]	1.194	£10 985
reversion to full net rental value	£36 000 pa	
less rent paid [see note 5]	£34 000 pa	
profit rent	£ 2 000 pa	
YP 15 years [see note 6] at 9 per cent and 3 per cent (tax 35 per cent) [see note 4]	5.790	
× PV of £1 in 2 years at 9 per cent 0.842	4.875	£ 9 750
Capital value		£20 735

Notes

1: The lessee enjoys the value attributable to the improvements immediately.

2: Estimated cost of external repairs and insurance added to full net rental value, to convert this on to internal repairing terms. See note 1 of freeholder's present interest.

3: Rent paid is on internal repairing terms.

4: Traditional yield pattern. Remunerative yield 1 per cent above freehold yield. Annual sinking fund assumed available at 3 per cent with tax at 35p in the £.

5: See note 3 of freeholder's present interest.

6: It is assumed that the lessee will be granted a new lease at the end of the present one.

Lessee's proposed interest

Full net rental value	£36 000 pa		
less rent to be paid [see note 1]	£ x pa		
profit rent	£36 000 − x pa		
YP 5 years at 8 per cent and 3			
per cent (tax 35 per cent)	2.704	£ 97 344 − 2.704x	
reversion to full net rental value	£36 000 pa		
less rent paid [see note 2]	£34 000 pa		
profit rent	£ 2 000 pa		
YP 10 years [see note 3] at			
9 per cent and			
3 per cent			
(tax 35 per cent)	4.460		
× PV of £1 in 5 years at			
9 per cent	0.650	2.899	£ 5 798
Capital value			£103 142 − 2.704x

Notes

1: Rent to be paid and full rental value are both on full repairing and insuring terms.

2: See note 1 of freeholder's proposed interest.

3: At the third review in the new lease, it will be 23 years since the improvements were done and the value attributable to them can be reflected in the rent paid by the lessee.

Present interest	=	Proposed interest
£20 735	=	£103 142 − 2.704x
2.704x	=	£82 407
x	=	£30 476

Rent that lessee is prepared to pay for the first 5 years of the new lease, say £30 475 per annum.

As the freeholder requires £34700 per annum, the parties will probably agree upon a rent in the region of £32 500 per annum.

(b) *Freeholder requires the premises for his own occupation when the present lease expires.*

The answer should point out that if the freeholder requires possession for his own occupation at the end of the lease, the lessee must be given at least 6 month's notice.

The student should then note that, in the event of the freeholder obtaining possession, he will have to pay compensation for disturbance to the lessee, under *S.37 Landlord and Tenant Act 1954*. The amount of compensation will depend upon the length of time that the lessee has been in occupation and the rateable value of the premises. For a full consideration of this, together with an explanatory example, see question 3.1(a).

The freeholder's position in respect of improvements carried out by the lessee, should also be discussed. As these improvements were done with the freeholder's consent, he will have to pay compensation to the lessee for them under the *Landlord and Tenant Act 1927*.

The compensation will be the *lesser* of:

(i) the present cost of carrying out the improvements, less an amount to put the improvements into a reasonable state of repair
(ii) the net increase in value of the landlord's interest caused by the improvements.

(i) Present cost of improvements	£25 000	
less cost of putting the improvements into a reasonable state of repair, say	£ 1 250	
	£23 750	

Note that the actual cost of the improvements 8 years ago (£14 000) is irrelevant to the compensation payable. However, it may be used as a basis for estimating the present cost where this is unknown.

(ii) Rental value with improvements	£36 000 pa	
YP in perpetuity at 8 per cent	12.5	£450 000
rental value without improvements	£34 000 pa	
YP in perpetuity at 8 per cent	12.5	£425 000
increase in value of landlord's interest caused by the improvements		£ 25 000

The present cost is the lower figure and therefore the compensation payable by the freeholder to the lessee in respect of the improvements will be £23 750. (See question 3.1(b) for a fuller consideration of compensation for tenant's improvements).

4 LEASEHOLD ENFRANCHISEMENT

Legislation affecting the occupiers of houses held under long ground leases was introduced by the *Leasehold Reform Act 1967*. This act gave occupying leaseholders the right either to purchase the freehold interest or to have their present lease extended by a further 50 years, provided certain qualifying conditions were satisfied (see question 4.2(a)). The conferment of this right was based on the assumption that it is equitable to consider the freeholder to own the land and the leaseholder the buildings on the land.

Enfranchisement price calculations under the 1967 Act consist of the valuation of the freeholder's present interest, subject to the leaseholder's right to a 50 year lease extension. This 50 year extension, at a modern ground rent, is reviewable after 25 years, but since this is considered so remote, no attempt is now made to reflect this review explicitly in the valuation. The estimation of a modern ground rent is considered in question 4.3(a).

There have been various amendments to the 1967 Act by subsequent legislation, notably the *Housing Act 1974*, which introduced new valuation assumptions for properties with a rateable value between £500 and £750 (£1 000 and £1 500 in Greater London). In this case, the freeholder's interest is valued by capitalising the existing ground rent, as under the 1967 Act provisions, but then reversion is assumed to a fair rent rather than a modern ground rent. Additionally, following the decision in *Norfolk v. Trinity College, Cambridge (1976)*, the tenant's bid need not be excluded and a proportion of the gain caused by marriage of the freehold and leasehold interests may be included in the enfranchisement price. In valuations under the *Leasehold Reform Act 1967*, reflection of the tenant's bid is precluded by S.82 of the *Housing Act 1969* therefore any marriage gain is not considered in the calculation. This is discussed in question 4.1(a).

Students are likely to encounter one or more of four basic situations in examination questions. These are:

1. 1973 rateable value below £500 (£1 000 in Greater London), where the site has no redevelopment potential
2. 1973 rateable value below £500 (£1 000 in Greater London), where the site does have redevelopment potential

3. As 1, but the 1973 rateable value is between £500 and £750 (£1 000 and £1 500 in Greater London)
4. As 2, but the 1973 rateable value as in 3.

In the case of 1 and 2, the enfranchisement price is calculated under the provisions of the *Leasehold Reform Act 1967*, whereas in 3 and 4, the calculation will be governed by the *Housing Act 1974*. Examples of each one of these valuations are provided in question 4.4.

The abolition of domestic rating in 1990, presented difficulties in prescribing rateable value qualifications for properties where the ground lease was created after 1 April 1990, since these properties will have no rateable value. It was therefore necessary to substitute a qualifying condition as an alternative to rateable value and this was provided by the *Rating (Housing) Regulations 1990*, considered in question 4.5(b).

Leasehold enfranchisement legislation originally envisaged that a leaseholder would *either* obtain a 50 year lease extension *or* purchase the freehold interest in the property. However, nothing prevents the leaseholder from first securing an extended lease and then purchasing the freehold interest, but the anomaly that may emerge in such a situation became apparent from the case of *Mosley v. Hickman (1986)*. Leaseholders purchasing the freehold having obtained a 50 year extension were able to do so at a far lower price than those who did not first obtain the extension. This was rectified by S.23 of the *Housing and Planning Act 1986*, which is discussed in question 4.5(a).

Further reforms to the residential leasehold system were introduced by the *Leasehold Reform, Housing and Urban Development Act 1993*. This came into force on 1 November 1993 and gave most long leaseholders of flats the collective right to purchase the freehold of their building.

As this legislation is relatively new and has not yet been tested in the courts, a brief consideration only will be given here, so that students are aware of the main provisions.

The right of collective enfranchisement is given to 'qualifying tenants', who must have long leases (of 21 years or more) at a 'low rent'. A 'low rent' is defined as:

(i) Nil or
(ii) Where the lease was granted before 1 April 1963, the rent was less than two-thirds of the open market rent of the flat at the date of commencement of the lease, or
(iii) Where the lease was granted between 1 April 1963 and 31 March 1990 the rent at the commencement of the lease did not exceed
    (a) £1 000 per annum in Greater London
    (b) £250 per annum outside Greater London.

At least two-thirds of the flats in the building must be let to qualifying tenants and at least two-thirds of the qualifying tenants must give notice that they wish to purchase the freehold interest – these are then 'participating tenants'.

At least half of the participating tenants must have occupied their flats as their main residence for the last 12 months, or for 3 years out of the last 10 years.

The building must be self-contained and no more than 10 per cent of the floor area may be occupied for non-residential purposes.

Enfranchisement takes place through a 'nominee purchaser', which will probably be a company formed by the participating tenants.

If the freeholder wishes to prevent the collective purchase of his freehold interest, he must be able to show that
 (i) he intends to redevelop the building AND
(ii) the long leases in respect of two-thirds of the block are due to expire within 5 years.

The enfranchisement price will be made up of:
  (i) open market value of the freehold interest
 (ii) at least 50 per cent of the marriage gain
(iii) any depreciation in value of other property belonging to the freeholder and any other loss
(iv) the freeholder's costs.

The Leasehold Reform, Housing and Urban Development Act 1993 also provides for the following:
1. The right of individual qualifying tenants to extend the lease of their flat for a further 90 years from expiry of the current lease. They will pay an initial premium, followed by a peppercorn rent.
2. The right of qualifying lessees to acquire the freehold interest in higher value houses previously outside the scope of leasehold enfranchisement legislation.

LEASEHOLD ENFRANCHISEMENT – QUESTIONS

4.1. (a) Explain the reasons for the inclusion of a proportion of the marriage gain in certain calculations for leasehold enfranchisement.
(b) Discuss the 'adverse differential' and explain why it is no longer generally employed in leasehold enfranchisement calculations.
(c) Your client is ground lessee of a house in a provincial town, satisfying the qualifying conditions of the *Leasehold Reform Act 1967* and subsequent relevant legislation.

The lessee holds the property with 7 years unexpired at a ground rent of £35 per annum. The house has a vacant possession value of £68 000, a full net rental value of £5 450 per annum and a net fair rental value of £3 400 per annum. Advise your client of the likely enfranchisement price, assuming that the 1973 rateable value of the house was £435 and the site has redevelopment potential worth £180 000.

4.2. The lessee of a house outside the Greater London area has asked your advice regarding enfranchisement under the *Leasehold Reform Act 1967* and subsequent relevant legislation. He purchased the leasehold interest 4 years ago and has occupied the property ever since. He has undertaken substantial structural alterations, which have increased the vacant possession value of the house by £18 000 to the current estimated value of £90 000.

The 1973 rateable value of the house was £538 and the property is held on a 99 year ground lease with 18 years unexpired at a fixed rent of £21 per annum.

There have been no recent sales of comparable house plots in the area, but similar sized plots in a less attractive area sell for £22 500.

Advise the lessee:

(i) whether he qualifies for enfranchisement, giving full reasons for your decision, and

(ii) on the assumption that he does qualify (regardless of your advice in (i)), the likely enfranchisement price, fully annotating your calculation.

4.3. (a) Describe three possible methods of estimating a modern ground rent for the purposes of calculating the enfranchisement price under the provisions of leasehold reform legislation and state the circumstances in which each might be used.

(b) Your client is the ground lessee of a two storey, detached house in the provinces and he satisfies the qualifying conditions of the *Leasehold Reform Act 1967* and the *Housing Acts 1974 and 1980*. He has asked your advice regarding the enfranchisement price.

The house is let on ground lease with 6 years unexpired at a rent of £25 per annum. The 1973 rateable value of the house was £650 and the lessee occupies the upper floor as his main residence, this having a net rack rental value of £6 000 per annum.

The ground floor is sublet in two parts:

1. The front to an estate agent on internal repairing terms at £5 700 per annum with 4 years unexpired; the net rack rental value is £7 000 per annum.

2. The rear to an accountant on internal repairing terms at £4 700 per annum with 4 years unexpired; the net rack rental value is £6 000 per annum.

The site is capable of redevelopment and on this basis its value is estimated to be £250 000.

4.4. Your client is the leaseholder of a house in a Midlands town and qualifies for enfranchisement under the *Leasehold Reform Act 1967* and subsequent relevant legislation.

The lease has 8 years unexpired at a ground rent of £15 per annum and the vacant possession value of the property is £135 000.

(a) Making any reasonable assumptions you deem necessary, calculate the likely enfranchisement price, if the 1973 rateable value of the house was
 (i) £484 and
 (ii) £518

(b) Recalculate the likely enfranchisement price in (a)(i) and (ii) on the assumption that the property has redevelopment potential and its value with that potential is £300 000.

4.5. (a) Your client occupies a detached house in the provinces, held on a ground lease. One year ago, when the ground lease had 7 years unexpired at £125 per annum, your client obtained a 50 year extension at a modern ground rent of £2 250 per annum.

He has now served a valid notice to purchase the freehold interest and you are required to advise him regarding the likely enfranchisement price.

The vacant possession value of the house is estimated to be £125 000 and the 1973 rateable value was £510.

(b) A 50 year ground lease was created in a provincial town on 15 April 1990, for the building of one dwelling house. The initial rent of £225 per annum is on the basis of 5 year rent reviews and the lessee paid an initial premium of £75 000. The cost of building the house was £100 000. In September 1994, the lessee decides that he wishes to purchase the freehold interest.

Discuss whether or not he may do so, with particular reference to the property qualifications.

LEASEHOLD ENFRANCHISEMENT – SUGGESTED ANSWERS

Question 4.1

(a) In the answer to this part of the question, reference should be made to S.9(1) and S9(1A) of the *Leasehold Reform Act 1967*, S.82 of the *Housing Act 1969*, S.118 of the *Housing Act 1974* and the case of *Norfolk v. Trinity College, Cambridge (1976)*. Under S.82 of the *Housing Act 1969*, which amended the *Leasehold Reform Act 1967*, the existing leaseholder and members of his family must not be considered as being in the market for the property. In other words, the possibility of an extra bid by the existing leaseholder must be disregarded in the enfranchisement valuation.

It follows from this that calculations under the *Leasehold Reform Act 1967* provisions, (where the 1973 rateable value of the property was less than £1 000 in Greater London and less than £500 elsewhere) do *not* include any proportion of the marriage gain produced by merging the freehold and leasehold interests when enfranchisement takes place.

Section 82 of the *Housing Act 1969* refers only to S.9(1) of the 1967 Act and not to S.9(1A) which was added later by S.118 of the *Housing Act 1974*. Case law has established that, as a consequence, the existing leaseholder *can* be considered as being in the market for the house, in calculations involving the valuation method introduced by S.118 of the *Housing Act 1974* (properties in the higher 1973 rateable value band – see questions 4.2 and 4.4). A leading case is *Norfolk v. Trinity College, Cambridge (1976)*, in which it was established that a proportion of the marriage gain could be included in the enfranchisement price in 1974 Act calculations. In the Norfolk case, the marriage gain was divided equally between freeholder and leaseholder. Question 4.3(b) provides an example of a valuation including a proportion of the marriage gain, as does question 4.4(a)(ii) in which the approach in *Lloyd-Jones v. Church Commissioners for England (1981)* is also considered.

(b) Initially it should be explained that a modern ground rent for a 50 year lease extension under leasehold enfranchisement legislation, is calculated by decapitalising the site value of the house using a yield in the region of 6 per cent *(Farr v. Millersons Investments Limited (1971))*. In calculating the enfranchisement price, the modern ground rent is recapitalised (but deferred for the unexpired term of the existing ground lease), using the same yield.

The meaning of 'adverse differential' should then be explained. This was a device used by some valuers in early cases under leasehold enfranchisement legislation, in which site value was decapitalised at 6 per cent and the resulting modern ground rent was then recapitalised at 8 per cent. The adverse differential of 2 per cent resulted in a reduced enfranchisement price and was therefore beneficial to the lessee. A short explanation should give the arguments that have been presented in defence of the adverse differential. For instance, it has been argued that the use of the adverse differential allowed for the exclusion of the tenant's bid, as required by S.82 of the *Housing Act 1969*. *(Gajewski v. Anderton and Hershaw (1971))*.

A further contention was that the yield used to decapitalise the site value reflected market conditions, whereas valuation of the modern ground rent took place within the constraints of leasehold enfranchisement legislation.

Use of the adverse differential finally fell out of favour when it was rejected by the Court of Appeal in the case of *Official Custodian of Charities and others v. Godridge (1973)*.

A simple example may be constructed to demonstrate the adverse differential and its effect. A complete enfranchisement valuation is not necessary.

Example

Assume the capital value of the site is £30 000.

A (say) 6 per cent return on this provides the modern ground rent.

£30 000 at 6 per cent =	£ 1 800 pa
YP in perpetuity at 8 per cent	12.5
Capital value	£22 500

This seems to suggest that an investor requiring a 6 per cent return would purchase the site for £30 000, but would then be prepared to sell it for £22 500, making a loss of £7 500. (In a full enfranchisement calculation, the £22 500 would be deferred until the end of the existing ground lease – see questions 4.2 (ii) and 4.4.)

(c) The 1973 rateable value of the house was under £500 (£435), therefore the enfranchisement calculation falls under the provisions of the *Leasehold Reform Act 1967.*

As the site has redevelopment potential, the value of the freehold interest consists of the ground rent under the existing lease, plus reversion to the development value of the land when the existing lease ends. However, if the freeholder is to realise this development value, the leaseholder will be denied a 50 year extension to his lease at a modern ground rent and must be compensated for this by the freeholder. The amount of this compensation is therefore deducted from the value of the freehold interest, to determine the enfranchisement price.

Existing ground rent	£ 35 pa	
YP 7 years at 7 per cent [see note 1]	5.389	£ 189
reversion to development value [see note 2]	£180 000	
× PV of £1 in 7 years at 9 per cent [see note 3]	0.547	£98 460
		£98 649
less compensation to leaseholder for loss of 50 year lease extension [see note 4]		
net rack rental value [see note 5]	£ 5 450 pa	
less modern ground rent [see note 6]	£ 1 190 pa	
profit rent	£ 4 260 pa	

YP 50 years at 10 per cent and			
3 per cent (tax 30 per cent)	8.876		
× PV of £1 in 7 years at 10 per cent	0.513	4.553	£19 396
likely enfranchisement price			£79 253
		say	£79 250

Notes

1: Yield of 7 per cent, from Lands Tribunal decisions, for example, *Farr v. Millersons Investments Limited (1971)*. A yield of 6 per cent would be equally acceptable.

2: The freeholder is able to gain possession at the end of the existing lease if he wishes to redevelop the site and the leaseholder has asked only for a 50 year extension to his lease. If the leaseholder elects to purchase the freehold interest, the freeholder cannot prevent enfranchisement on the grounds that he wishes to redevelop.

3: Deferred for the length of the unexpired term of the existing ground lease, because the freeholder would be unable to gain possession until this lease expires.

4: In order to realise the redevelopment potential, the freeholder must pay compensation to the leaseholder for preventing the 50 year lease extension.

5: The leaseholder would be able to let the property at its full net rental value. This figure is given in the question, but would in practice be a point of negotiation between the parties. The net fair rent is also given in the question, but is not required in enfranchisement calculations under the 1967 Act.

6: This would be the rent paid by the leaseholder if he obtained a 50 year lease extension; a modern ground rent, as required by S.15 of the *Leasehold Reform Act 1967*. In this case, it has been calculated using the 'standing house' approach. The vacant possession value of the property comprises the value of the site together with the value of the buildings. The capital value of the site is estimated by taking a percentage of the vacant possession value, the percentage depending upon local land values. A percentage return on this site value produces the modern ground rent.

The modern ground rent of £1 190 per annum, was determined as follows:

vacant possession value = £68 000
site value at 25 per cent of vacant possession value = £17 000
modern ground rent at 7 per cent return on £17 000 = £1 190 per annum

For a further consideration of the estimation of a modern ground rent, see question 4.3.

Question 4.2

(i) In this part of the question, discussion of the qualifying conditions for enfranchisement is required. These are:

(a) The ground rent must be less than two-thirds of the rateable value of the house as at 23 March 1965, or, if later, the first day of the term.

(b) The ground lease must be for a term exceeding 21 years.

(c) The house (or part of it) must have been occupied as the leaseholder's main residence for the last 3 years or at least 3 out of the last 10 years (*Housing Act 1980*).

(d) The rateable value of the house must be within the limits set by the *Leasehold Reform Act 1967*, or the *Housing Act 1974*. These are:

1967 Act: Rateable value must not exceed £200 (£400 in Greater London) on the 'appropriate day', which is the later of 23 March 1965 or the date when the house was first entered in the Valuation List.

1974 Act: (i) Property in the Valuation List before 1 April 1973, the rateable value must not exceed £750 (£1 500 in Greater London).

(ii) Property entered in the Valuation List after 1 April 1973.

(a) Where the lease was created on or before 18 February 1966, the rateable value must not exceed £750 (£1 500 in Greater London).

(b) Where the lease was created after 18 February 1966, the rateable value must not exceed £500 (£1 000 in Greater London).

(e) Where the lease was created on or after 1 April 1990, the conditions set out in the *Rating (Housing) Regulations 1990* must be satisfied. These are:

(a) the rent must be less than £250 per annum (£1 000 in Greater London).

(b) *R* must not exceed £25 000 in the formula

$$R = \frac{P \times i}{1 - (1 + i)^{-T}}$$

where P = premium paid (if any)

T = term of years granted

$i = 0.06$, representing a yield of 6 per cent but may be varied by the Secretary of State

For a full consideration of the qualifying conditions under the *Rating (Housing) Regulations 1990*, see question 4.5(b).

Each of the qualifying conditions must be satisfied and should be considered in respect of the case in question, to determine whether or not the leaseholder qualifies to enfranchise.

(a) The ground rent of £21 per annum will almost certainly be less than two-thirds of the rateable value as at 23 March 1965 (the first day of the term would have been around 1912). Although this is not known, with a 1973 rateable value of £538, this condition appears to be satisfied.

(b) The original term of the ground lease exceeds 21 years – the lessee holds under a 99 year lease.

(c) The lessee satisfies the occupational requirements, since he has lived in the house for the last 4 years.

(d) The 1973 rateable value was £538. This falls within the rateable value limits specified in the *Housing Act 1974*. Whether the property was entered in the Valuation List before or after 1 April 1973 (it is more likely to be *before*), the lease was certainly created before 18 February 1966, therefore the rateable value limit is £750 as the house is situated outside the Greater London area.

The conditions are all satisfied and the client should be advised that he qualifies for enfranchisement.

(ii) Where the 1973 rateable value is over £500, the appropriate method of valuation is that introduced by the *Housing Act 1974* (see question 4.4). As the rateable value of the house in question is £538, at first sight it appears that this is the method of valuation that must be adopted.

However, the leaseholder has carried out substantial structural alterations to the house and under Schedule 8 of the 1974 Act, the rateable value may be notionally reduced in order to disregard the value of the improvements.

The notional adjustment of the rateable value may be achieved as follows:

$$\text{notional rateable value} = \frac{\text{rateable}}{\text{value}} \times \frac{\text{capital value excluding improvements}}{\text{capital value including improvements}}$$

In this case the notional rateable value is:

$$£538 \times \frac{£72\,000}{£90\,000} = £430$$

An alternative method of adjusting the rateable value would be to deduct the part of the rateable value attributable to the improvements from the total rateable value.

The rateable value is now notionally below £500 and the valuation can be carried out under the provisions of the *Leasehold Reform Act 1967*. This involves valuing the ground rent under the existing lease, with reversion to a modern ground rent.

Existing ground rent		£ 21 pa		
YP 18 years at 6 per cent [see note 1]		10.828	£ 227	

reversion to modern ground rent [see note 2]

(i) using cleared site approach [see note 3]

value of comparable site in less attractive area	£22 500	
plus 20 per cent [see note 4] for better location	£ 4 500	
capital value of site	£27 000	

(ii) using standing house approach [see note 3]

vacant possession value	£90 000		
site value at 30 per cent [see note 4]	£27 000		
Capital value of site	£27 000		
modern ground rent at 6 per cent return		£ 1 620 pa	
YP in perpetuity [see note 5] deferred 18 years at 6 per cent [see note 6]		5.839	£9 459
likely enfranchisement price			£9 686
		say	£9 700

Notes
1: A yield of 6 or 7 per cent is adopted to value the existing ground rent, following Lands Tribunal decisions, for example, *Farr v. Millersons Investments Ltd (1971)*.

2: As required by S.15 of the *Leasehold Reform Act 1967*. Reversion to a modern ground rent stems from the basic assumption of the legislation that only the land belongs to the freeholder and the buildings are already owned by the leaseholder. Therefore, in the enfranchisement price, the leaseholder pays the freeholder for the capitalised current income and expected future income, from the land only.

3: The answer should contain a brief consideration of which of these two methods might be preferable. From previous case decisions, it appears that the cleared site approach is preferred wherever possible, but since comparable plots are in a less attractive area and some subjective adjustment of the value has been made because of this, the standing house approach has been used as a check. For a more detailed consideration of the determination of a modern ground rent, see question 4.3.

4: The percentages used should ideally be obtained from market analysis, which will depend upon availability of information. This issue, particularly in the absence of market information, will be a matter of negotiation between the valuers for the two parties.

5: Leasehold enfranchisement legislation originally envisaged that the modern ground rent would be subject to a review after 25 years. However, remoteness was considered by the Lands Tribunal in early cases to be sufficient reason to ignore the review. The modern ground rent is simply valued into perpetuity, deferred for the unexpired term of the existing ground lease.

6: 6 per cent has been adopted to capitalise the modern ground rent, since 6 per cent was used in estimating this rent from the site value. The adverse differential has not been applied (see question 4.1(b)).

Question 4.3

(a) The answer should provide a brief description of three methods of calculating a modern ground rent, illustrating each with a simple example.

Estimation of a modern ground rent is necessary in determining the enfranchisement price under the provisions of the *Leasehold Reform Act 1967*, being specifically provided for in Section 15 of that Act. In the enfranchisement price, the leaseholder is paying the freeholder for the land only, it being assumed that he already owns the buildings on the land. The value of the freehold interest comprises the income under the current ground lease, together with reversion to the S.15 modern ground rent.

The three main methods of estimating the modern ground rent are:

1. *The cleared site approach*
This method has been preferred by the Lands Tribunal in past cases, such as *Farr v. Millersons Investments Ltd (1971)*. In this case, the Lands Tribunal also considered that the valuer, although adopting one method of calculating the modern ground rent, should preferably use an alternative method as a check.

The cleared site approach should be used in all cases where possible, but this is dependent upon the availability of comparable market evidence. It is particularly relevant when the subject property is nearing the end of its life.

The capital value of the site is first estimated by reference to recent sales of land for development or redevelopment for comparable uses. Having derived the capital value of the site, a percentage return on this will give the estimated modern ground rent. Yields adopted for this purpose are usually in the region of 6 or 7 per cent, based upon previous Lands Tribunal decisions. Leasehold valuation tribunals, introduced by the *Housing Act 1980*, appear to favour 7 per cent.

Example
Dimensions of site 10.5 m frontage by 12.25 m depth $= 128.625$ m^2
Assume market transactions reveal that comparable sites are selling for £175 per m^2
Site value $= 128.625$ m^2 at £175 $=$ £22 509
                        say   £22 500
Modern ground rent $=$ £22 500 at 7 per cent return $=$ £1 575 pa
Alternatively, sites may be compared on a length of frontage basis.
Assume market transactions reveal that comparable sites are selling for £2 145 per metre frontage
Site value $=$ 10.5 m at £2 145 $=$ £22 522
                        say   £22 500

2. *The standing house approach*
This method is mainly used where the subject house is likely to remain standing in the foreseeable future and the cleared site approach is not used due to the absence of market evidence. In this approach, the capital value of the site is assessed as a proportion of the vacant possession value of the house. Proportions generally applied are in the region of 25–30 per cent (outside London) but will vary with the locality. The extent of the buildings in relation to the size of the site will also affect the proportion adopted. Having derived the capital value of the site, the modern ground rent is determined in the same way as for the cleared site approach.

Example
    Vacant possession value of house £75 000
    Proportion attributable to land, say 30 per cent $=$ £22 500
    Modern ground rent $=$ £22 500 at 7 per cent return $=$ £1 575 pa

3. The 'new for old' approach
Using this method, an estimate is made of the value of the property if a new building were to be substituted for the existing building. From this figure, the present day cost of providing the new building is deducted, the residue being the value of the site. This approach is useful where the house in question has a limited life which is difficult to accurately predict (see *Gajewski v. Anderton (1971)*).

Example
    Capital value of property, but substituting a
        new structure for the old house, say   £90 000
    less estimated cost of providing the new structure   £67 500
                                                          ‾‾‾‾‾‾‾
    site value   £22 500
                                                          ‾‾‾‾‾‾‾
    modern ground rent $=$ £22 500 at 7 per cent return $=$ £ 1 575 pa

(b) The 1973 rateable value of the house is over £500, therefore calculation of the enfranchisement price is undertaken using the method introduced by the *Housing Act 1974* (see question 4.4).

The value of the freehold interest in this case comprises the ground rent for the unexpired term of the current ground lease, with reversion, not to a modern ground rent, but to a net fair rent. These tenancies still retain protection under the *Rent Act 1988* from Part I of the *Landlord and Tenant Act 1954*.

Existing ground rent		£ 25 pa		
YP 6 years at 7 per cent [see note 1]		4.767	£	119
reversion to net fair rent [see note 2]				
ground floor	£13 000 pa			
first floor, say	£ 5 000 pa	£18 000 pa [see note 3]		
YP in perpetuity deferred 6 years at 12 per cent	4.222		£ 75 996	
			£ 76 115	

plus half share of marriage gain [see note 4]						
value of freehold in possession				£250 000		
less (i) lessor's present interest			£76 115			
(ii) lessee's interest:						
rent received [see note 5]		£16 400 pa				
less external repairs						
and insurance						
[see note 6]	£975					
ground rent	£ 25	£ 1 000 pa				
profit rent		£15 400 pa				
YP 4 years at 12 per cent and						
3 per cent (tax 30 per cent)		2.167 £33 372				
reversion to full net rental						
value [see note 7]		£19 000 pa				
YP 2 years at 13 per cent						
and 3 per cent						
(tax 30 per cent)	1.199					
× PV of £1 in 4 years						
at 13 per cent	0.613	0.735 £13 965 £47 337 £123 452				
marriage gain				£126 548		
half share				£ 63 274		
likely enfranchisement price				£139 389		
			say	£140 000		

Notes

1: A yield of 6 or 7 per cent is adopted, following Lands Tribunal decisions, for example, *Farr v. Millersons Investments Limited (1971)*.

2: Valuation is under the provisions of the *Housing Act 1974*, therefore reversion is to a net fair rent, rather than to the modern ground rent required in valuations under the *Leasehold Reform Act 1967*.

3: This figure comprises the net rack rental value of the ground floor, together with an estimate of fair rent for the first floor. A figure £1 000 per annum less than rack rental value has been adopted as the fair rent, since it will invariably be less than full rental value. This is not the only approach that could be adopted and any reasonable method would be acceptable in the answer to an examination question. For example, a percentage of capital value might be adopted:

full net rental value (first floor)	£ 6 000 pa	
YP in perpetuity at 10 per cent	10	£ 60 000
full net rental value (ground floor)	£13 000 pa	
YP in perpetuity at 8 per cent	12.5	£162 500
capital value		£222 500

Say 8 per cent of this would represent a fair rent, which is £17 800 say £18 000 per annum.

4: Following the decision in *Norfolk v. Trinity College, Cambridge (1976)*, in which it was held that S.118 of the *Housing Act 1974* permits the present lessee to be considered as being in the market for the property. Thus, the possibility of an extra bid by the lessee because of the value released on merging the freehold and leasehold interests may be reflected in the enfranchisement price. In the Norfolk case, the marriage gain was equally divided between freeholder and leaseholder (see question 4.4).

5: This figure comprises the net rack rental value of the first floor, together with the rent received for the next 4 years in respect of the ground floor.

6: In the absence of information, the cost of external repairs and insurance has been estimated at 7.5 per cent of the net rack rental value, but of the ground floor only. The rack rental for the first floor is already expressed in net terms, therefore there is no need to make an adjustment for that element of the rent received or notionally received.

7: The present leases in respect of the ground floor expire in 4 years' time, when the leaseholder will be entitled to let the property at full rental value until his ground lease expires.

An alternative course of action for the leaseholder, should he wish to gain possession of the whole property for his own occupation or to redevelop, would be to buy out the tenants occupying the ground floor.

In total, it would still cost the leaseholder in the region of £140 000 to obtain the unencumbered freehold, but might simplify the enfranchisement negotiations with the freeholder.

The likely cost of buying out the occupiers of the ground floor is as follows:

Ground floor front

Full net rental value	£7 000 pa
plus external repairs and insurance [see note 1]	£ 525 pa
full rental value on internal repairing terms	£7 525 pa [see note 2]
less rent paid	£5 700 pa
profit rent	£1 825 pa
YP 4 years at 13 per cent and 3 per cent (tax 30 per cent)	2.121
Capital value	£3 871
Say	£3 900 [see note 3]

Ground floor rear

Full net rental value	£6 000 pa
plus external repairs and insurance [see note 1]	£ 450 pa
full rental value on internal repairing terms	£6 450 pa [see note 2]
less rent paid	£4 700 pa
profit rent	£1 750 pa
YP 4 years at 13 per cent and 3 per cent (tax 30 per cent)	2.121
Capital value	£3 712
Say	£3 700 [see note 3]

Notes

1: Cost of external repairs and insurance has been estimated at 7.5 per cent of full net rental value.

2: Full rental value is now on the same terms as the rent paid by the tenants.

3: The capital values of the tenants' interests are £3 900 and £3 700 respectively, but the actual prices paid by the leaseholder would be a matter for negotiation.

Assuming that the leaseholder does buy out the tenants of the ground floor, the enfranchisement calculation would be:

existing ground rent		£ 25 pa	
YP 6 years at 7 per cent		4.767	£ 119
reversion to net fair rent, say		£16 000 pa	
YP in perpetuity deferred 6 years at			
12 per cent		4.222	£ 67 552
			£ 67 671

plus half share of marriage gain

value of freehold in possession		£250 000	
less (i) lessor's present interest	£67 671		
(ii) lessee's interest:			
net rack rental value	£19 000 pa		
less ground rent	£ 25 pa		
profit rent	£18 975 pa		
YP 6 years at 12 per cent and			
3 per cent (tax 30 per cent) 2.934	£55 673	£123 344	
marriage gain		£126 656	
half share			£ 63 328
likely enfranchisement price			£130 999
			say £131 000

Question 4.4

This question entails the calculation of the likely enfranchisement price of a property both with and without redevelopment potential. Additionally, the calculations must be performed under the provisions of the *Leasehold Reform Act 1967* and the *Housing Act 1974*, depending upon the 1973 rateable values given in the question.

(a) (i) *1973 rateable value £484, site without redevelopment potential*

Since the 1973 rateable value is below £500, the calculation is carried out under the provisions of the *Leasehold Reform Act 1967*. This involves valuing the existing ground rent for the remainder of the current ground lease, with reversion to a modern ground rent. In other words, the leaseholder will pay the freeholder for the value of the land only. No element of the marriage value, resulting from the merger of the freehold and leasehold interests, is included in the enfranchisement price (an explanation of the reason for this is given in question 4.1(a)).

Existing ground rent	£ 15 pa		
YP 8 years at 6 per cent [see note 1]	6.210	£	93

reversion to modern ground rent [see note 2]			
vacant possession value £135 000 [see note 3]			
say site value is 30 per cent of this			
[see note 4] £40 500			
at 6 per cent return [see note 5]	£2 430 pa		
YP in perpetuity deferred 8 years			
at 6 per cent [see note 5]	10.457	£25 411	
likely enfranchisement price		£25 504	
	say	£25 500	

Notes

1: 6 per cent yield, from Lands Tribunal decisions such as *Farr v. Millersons Investments Limited (1971)*. It would be equally acceptable to adopt 7 per cent.

2: Reversion to a modern ground rent as required by S.15 of the *Leasehold Reform Act 1967*. For a consideration of the methods of estimating a modern ground rent, see question 4.3(a).

3: In the absence of further information, the modern ground rent has been calculated using the standing house approach (see question 4.3(a)).

4: The actual percentage of vacant possession value adopted will vary according to land values in the locality.

5: 6 per cent (or 7 per cent) from Lands Tribunal decisions. The adverse differential, now generally out of favour, has not been used (for an explanation of the adverse differential, see question 4.1(b)).

(a)(ii) *1973 rateable value £518, site without redevelopment potential*

Since the 1973 rateable value exceeded £500, the calculation is carried out using the method prescribed by the *Housing Act 1974*. Here, reversion at the end of the current ground lease is to a net fair rent rather than a modern ground rent, since the tenancy enjoys protection stemming from Part 1 of the *Landlord and Tenant Act 1954* (see question 4.3(b)).

Additionally, a proportion of the marriage gain, arising from the merger of freehold and leasehold interests, is included in the enfranchisement price (see note 4 to the valuation below).

Existing ground rent	£ 15 pa		
YP 8 years at 6 per cent [see note 1] 6.210		£	93
reversion to net fair rent [see note 2]			
say 7 per cent [see note 3] of vacant			
possession value	£9 450 pa		

YP in perpetuity deferred 8 years
    at 12 per cent   3.366   £31 809

                                                                £31 902

plus half share of marriage gain [see note 4]
value of freehold in possession   £135 000
less (i) lessor's present interest   £31 902
      (ii) lessee's interest:
net rack rental value
    [see note 5]   £10 800 pa
less ground rent   £   15 pa

profit rent   £10 785 pa
YP 8 years at 13 per cent
    and 3 per cent (tax
    30 per cent)   3.441   £37 111 £ 69 013

marriage gain   £ 65 987
half share   £32 993.5

likely enfranchisement price   £64 895.5

                                             say £65 000

Notes

1: Yield of 6 per cent (or 7 per cent) from Lands Tribunal decisions.

2: The valuation is governed by the provisions of S.118 of the *Housing Act 1974*, under which it is assumed that reversion is to a net fair rent under a protected tenancy.

3: The net fair rent has been assumed to be 7 per cent of the vacant possession value, but, in practice, the percentage adopted would be derived from market analysis, or, ideally, from evidence of actual fair rents determined for similar properties.

4: This follows the decision in *Norfolk v. Trinity College, Cambridge (1976)*, in which it was established that under S.118(4) of the *Housing Act 1974*, the leaseholder may be considered as being in the market for the property and the 'tenants' bid taken into account (an assumption excluded in valuations under the *Leasehold Reform Act 1967*). A more detailed consideration of this point is produced in question 4.1(a). In the Norfolk case, it was held that the freeholder was entitled to 50 per cent of the marriage gain, which has been adopted in this case.

5: The full net rental value of the property has been assumed to be 8 per cent of vacant possession value, but this percentage would be derived from comparable evidence, where possible, otherwise it would be a matter of negotiation.

A somewhat different approach to the method in valuations under the *Housing Act 1974* was accepted in *Lloyd-Jones v. Church Commissioners for England (1981)*. The freeholder argued that in the particular area in which the property was located, it was unlikely that a fair rent would be registered at the end of the current ground lease. The house was in an area of high value property and evidence was produced to support the freeholder's contention that, at the end of the lease, the likelihood was that the lessee would purchase the house at its full value. The case was decided in favour of the freeholder, even though it is contrary to the statutory requirement of reversion to a fair rent.

Although the circumstances of this case were unique and therefore not readily applicable to other situations, the approach adopted is shown below to demonstrate the method.

Existing ground rent		£ 15 pa	
YP 8 years at 6 per cent		6.210	£ 93
reversion:			
value of freehold with vacant possession			
[see note 1]		£135 000	
less 10 per cent [see note 2]		£ 13 500	
		£121 500	
× PV of £1 in 8 years at 6 per cent			
[see note 3]		0.627	£76 181
			£76 274
plus half share of marriage gain			
value of freehold in possession		£135 000	
less			
(i) lessor's present interest	£76 274		
(ii) lessee's interest [see note 4]	£37 111	£113 385	
marriage gain		£ 21 615	
half share			£10 807.5
likely enfranchisement price			£87 081.5
		say £87 000	
			[see note 5]

Notes

1: Reversion to vacant possession value of the house on the assumption that when the current ground lease expires the leaseholder will purchase the freehold at its full value.

2: A deduction for the risk of the tenant claiming a tenancy under Part 1 of the *Landlord and Tenant Act 1954*. Ten per cent was adopted in the Lloyd-Jones case.

3: Deferred at 6 per cent, the yield adopted in the Lloyd-Jones case.
4: Value of leasehold interest from previous valuation.
5: This approach is obviously beneficial to the freeholder and has increased the enfranchisement price by some £22 000.

(b)(i) *1973 rateable value £484, site with redevelopment potential*

The 1973 rateable value is below £500, therefore, as in part (a)(i) the calculation of the enfranchisement price is governed by the provisions of the *Leasehold Reform Act 1967*. Because the site has redevelopment potential, reversion after the current ground lease ends is to the value of the property with this potential, but allowance must be made for compensation due to the leaseholder. This is for the loss of a 50 year lease extension at a modern ground rent (see question 4.1(c)).

Existing ground rent		£ 15 pa	
YP 8 years at 6 per cent [see note 1]		6.210	£ 93
reversion to development value [see note 2]		£300 000	
× PV of £1 in 8 years at 9 per cent		0.502	£150 600
			£150 693
less			
compensation to leaseholder for loss of			
50 year extension [see note 3]			
net rack rental value [see note 4]		£ 10 800 pa	
less modern ground rent [see note 5]		£ 2 430 pa	
profit rent		£ 8 370 pa	
YP 50 years at 10 per cent and 3 per cent			
(tax 30 per cent)	8.876		
× PV of £1 in 8 years at 10 per cent	0.467	4.145	£ 34 694
likely enfranchisement price			£115 999
		say	£116 000

Notes

1: 6 per cent yield (or 7 per cent) from Lands Tribunal decisions.

2: The freeholder may gain possession at the end of the current ground lease, if he wishes to redevelop the site and the leaseholder has requested only a 50 year extension to his lease.

3: In order that the freeholder may realise the redevelopment potential of the site, he must pay compensation to the leaseholder for the loss of a 50 year lease extension. The value of this lies in the profit rent that would be available to the leaseholder for those 50 years.

4: Figure derived in part (a)(ii).

5: Although he would have the right to let the property at its full rental value during the 50 year lease extension, the leaseholder would have to pay the freeholder a modern ground rent for the site only. This figure was derived in part (a)(i).

(b)(ii) *1973 rateable value £518, site with redevelopment potential*

The 1973 rateable value is over £500 and, as in part (a)(ii), the enfranchisement price is calculated under the provisions of the *Housing Act 1974*. Even though the site has redevelopment potential, reversion after the current ground lease ends is to a net fair rent. The redevelopment potential is taken into account in calculating the marriage gain.

		£ 15 pa		
Existing ground rent				
YP 8 years at 6 per cent [see note 1]		6.210	£	93
reversion to net fair rent [see note 2]		£ 9 450 pa		
YP in perpetuity deferred 8 years at				
12 per cent		3.366	£ 31 809	
			£ 31 902	
plus half share of marriage gain [see note 3]				
value of freehold in possession [see note 4]		£300 000		
less				
(i) lessor's present interest	£31 902			
(ii) lessee's interest [see note 5]	£37 111	£ 69 013		
marriage gain		£230 987		
half share			£115 493.5	
likely enfranchisement price			£147 395.5	
	say	£147 500		

Notes

1: 6 per cent (or 7 per cent) from Lands Tribunal decisions.

2: Figure derived in part (a)(ii).

3: Following the decision in *Norfolk v. Trinity College, Cambridge (1976)*, when the marriage gain was divided equally between the parties. See note 4 of the valuation in part (a)(ii).

4: The value is with redevelopment potential and not vacant possession value in this case.

5: Figure derived in part (a)(ii).

Question 4.5

Calculation of the enfranchisement price in this case must follow the provisions of S.23 of the *Housing and Planning Act 1986*. This section provided an amendment to S.9(1A) of the *Leasehold Reform Act 1967*, following the case of *Mosley v. Hickman (1986)*.

The case concerned houses in London, falling in the higher rateable value bands. The occupiers first of all obtained 50 year lease extensions and then served valid notices to purchase the freehold interests.

Section 9(1A), before amendment by the 1986 Act, provided that the price payable for the freehold interest should be subject to certain assumptions, including an assumption that:

'the vendor was selling for an estate in fee simple, subject to the tenancy...'.

The 'tenancy' referred to was originally intended to mean the existing ground lease, but, in S.14(1) of the 1967 Act, it is stated that an extended lease is to be substituted for the existing lease. In the case of *Mosley v. Hickman (1986)* the original ground leases had 15 years unexpired when the 50 year extensions were obtained, therefore the extended leases were of 65 years duration. Because of the statement in S.14(1) of the 1967 Act, both the Lands Tribunal and the Court of Appeal held that the enfranchisement price should be calculated on the assumption that the freehold interest was subject to the extended lease of 65 years.

This drastically reduced the enfranchisement price. A leaseholder who first obtained a 50 year lease extension and then purchased the freehold interest would pay a far lower enfranchisement price than a leaseholder who purchased the freehold directly.

Section 23 of the *Housing and Planning Act 1986* was specifically enacted to remove the anomaly created by *Mosley v. Hickman,* so that the same enfranchisement price would be paid whether or not a 50 year lease extension had first been obtained. To achieve this, an amendment was made to S.9(1A) of the 1967 Act by S.23 of the 1986 Act. Under this amendment, the assumption that must be made in the enfranchisement calculation is that:

'...where the tenancy has been extended under this Part of this Act, that the tenancy will terminate on the original term date...'

This means that in the case in question, the enfranchisement price will be calculated as if the 50 year lease extension had *not* been obtained, and there are now 6 years of the original ground lease unexpired.

Existing ground rent	£ 125 pa		
YP 6 years [see note 1] at 6 per cent	4.917	£ 615	
reversion to net fair rent [see note 2]	£ 8 750 pa		
YP in perpetuity deferred 6 years at			
12 per cent	4.222	£36 943	
		£37 558	

plus half share of marriage gain [see note 3]				
value of freehold in possession		£125 000		
less				
(i) lessor's interest		£37 558		
(ii) lessee's interest				
net rack rental value [see note 4] £10 000 pa				
less ground rent	£ 125 pa			
profit rent	£ 9 875 pa			
YP 6 years at 13 per cent and				
3 per cent (tax 30 per cent)	2.850	£28 144	£ 65 702	
marriage gain			£ 59 298	
half share			£29 649	
likely enfranchisement price			£67 207	
		say	£67 200	

Notes

1: The unexpired term of the original ground lease. The 50 year lease extension is ignored.

2: Net fair rent estimated at 7 per cent of vacant possession value, but in practice would ideally be determined from comparable evidence. In the absence of this, it would be a matter for negotiation.

3: Following the decision in *Norfolk v. Trinity College, Cambridge (1976)*, when the marriage gain was divided equally between the parties. See questions 4.1(a) and 4.4(a)(iii).

4: Net rack rental value estimated at 8 per cent of vacant possession value. Again, this may be a point of negotiation and comparable evidence should be used to support the figure where possible.

(b) In answering this part of the question, the various qualifying conditions should be considered in turn, but paying particular attention to the property qualifications, as required in the question.

For a detailed consideration of the qualifying conditions see question 4.2(i).

(i) *Length of lease*

Under the *Leasehold Reform Act 1967*, the term of the ground lease must exceed 21 years. This condition is satisfied, the lease being of 50 years' duration.

(ii) *Period of Occupation*

Under the *Housing Act 1980* the house must have been occupied as the leaseholder's main residence for the last 3 years, or 3 years out of the last 10 years.

Whether or not this condition is satisfied will be a matter of fact, not made clear in the question. Although the ground lease was created some 4½ years prior to the leaseholder deciding that he wished to enfranchise, there is no indication of when he first occupied the house, or how long the house took to build. If the minimum period of occupation has not yet been satisfied, it would merely mean postponing the service of notice to enfranchise until the 3 years' occupation was achieved, which would probably be a relatively short period of time.

(iii) *Property qualifications*

Under the 1967 Act, the rent must be less than two-thirds of the rateable value of the property as at 23 March 1965, or, if later, the first day of the term. Additionally, there are rateable value limits that must not be exceeded, specified in the 1967 Act and in the *Housing Act 1974*.

The problem here is that because the lease was created after the 1 April 1990, the house would have no rateable value in the 1973 Valuation List. Neither could any rateable value qualifications be introduced for leases created on or after 1 April 1990, since, from this date, domestic rating was replaced by the Community Charge.

To overcome this difficulty, property qualifications in respect of leases created on or after 1 April 1990, were introduced by the *Rating (Housing) Regulations 1990*. Under these regulations:

1. The rent must be less than £250 per annum (£1 000 in Greater London).
2. R must not exceed £25 000 in the formula

$$R = \frac{P \times i}{1 - (1 + i)^{-T}}$$

where T = the term of years

      i = 0.06 representing a yield of 6 per cent (but may be varied by the Secretary of State)

      P = (i) the cost of building the house and premises, or

            (ii) the cost of acquiring the right to occupy the house subject to the lease, or

            (iii) the cash premium paid for the right to develop the land on a building lease, or

            (iv) the cash premium and the cost of building the house.

Where the value of R falls between £16 333 and £25 000, the enfranchisement price is calculated as if the house were in the higher rateable value band, that is, under the provisions of the *Housing Act 1974*.

In the case in question, (iv) above will provide the value of P:

initial premium	£ 75 000
plus cost of building the house	£100 000
P =	£175 000

Putting this figure into the equation:

$$R = \frac{£175\,000 \times 0.06}{1 - \dfrac{1}{(1.06)^{50}}}$$

$$= \frac{£10\,500}{1 - \dfrac{1}{18.420}} = \frac{10\,500}{0.9457}$$

$$R = £11\,103$$

In fact, the formula provides the annual equivalent of P at 6 per cent over the term of the lease, and it may be expressed in a form with which the valuer will be more familiar:

$$R = \frac{P}{YP \text{ for } T \text{ years at } i}$$

$$R = \frac{£175\,000}{YP \text{ 50 years at 6 per cent}}$$

$$= \frac{£175\,000}{15.7619}$$

$$R = £11\,103$$

The property qualifications provided by the *Rating (Housing) Regulations 1990* are therefore satisfied:

(i) The rent is less than £250 per annum (it is £225 per annum).
(ii) R does not exceed £25 000 (it is £11 103).

5 RATING

Rating can be a complicated topic area, as might be expected of a tax that has evolved over several hundred years, through a variety of statutes and volumes of case law.

Questions in this section cannot therefore be exhaustive, but rather are intended to demonstrate the approach in answering typical examination questions at this level. The areas considered cover the basic knowledge required when embarking upon a study of valuation for rating purposes – identification of the rateable occupier, the basis of assessment and an outline of the methods of valuation. In question 5.3(b), an introduction is given to the more specialised area of plant and machinery – its rateability, and the appropriate method of valuation.

Since 1990, there have been fundamental changes in the rating system, mainly affecting domestic property.

From the early 1970's the conservative party were committed to a reform of the system, which had fallen into disrepute, perhaps mainly because a revaluation was badly needed. The Community Charge, or 'poll tax', that replaced the rating of domestic property, fared much the same as its predecessor in 1377, very nearly producing a repeat of the peasant's revolt in 1381. The Community Charge was itself replaced in 1991 by the Council Tax, a system under which tax is charged upon domestic property according to its capital value. However, this capital value does not have to be determined precisely, there being 8 'bands' of value into which each domestic property has been placed.

These bands are as follows:

Valuation band	Range of values as at 1 April 1991
A	up to £ 40 000
B	£ 40 001 – £ 52 000
C	£ 52 001 – £ 68 000
D	£ 68 001 – £ 88 000
E	£ 88 001 – £120 000
F	£120 001 – £160 000
G	£160 001 – £320 000
H	over £320 000

The amount of tax charged on properties in each band is a proportion of the tax charged by a council on band D.

These proportions are as follows:

Valuation band	Proportion of Band D
A	6/9
B	7/9
C	8/9
D	One once
E	11/9
F	13/9
G	15/9
H	Two Twice

For example, the tax charged in respect of a property in Band A will be 6/9 of that charged in respect of a property in Band D and that charged on a property in Band H will be twice that charged on a property in Band D.

Non-domestic property remains within a rating system very much the same as that which existed prior to the changes in 1990, a system consolidated by the *General Rate Act 1967*. The relevant legislation now is the *Local Government Finance Act 1988* as amended by the *Local Government and Housing Act 1989*.

RATING – QUESTIONS

5.1. Discuss the ingredients essential in the determination of rateable occupation.

5.2. (a) Discuss the principles to be borne in mind when valuing a property for rating purposes.

(b) Identify and briefly explain five possible ways in which a typical lease rent may differ from the hypothetical lease rent envisaged in the *Local Government Finance Act, 1988*.

5.3. (a) Briefly describe the three main methods of valuation used in valuing property for rating purposes.

(b) Discuss how the rateability of an item of plant and machinery is determined and briefly consider how it would be valued.

RATING – SUGGESTED ANSWERS

Question 5.1

Before rates can be charged in respect of a business property, it is necessary for the property to be rateably occupied. Since rateable occupation is not defined by statute, the conditions necessary for it to exist have emerged from case law.

In answering this question, it should be noted that case law has established four *essential* ingredients of rateable occupation and *all* of these must be present.

To be rateable, an occupation must be actual, exclusive, beneficial and permanent. Each of these should be considered, together with supporting case law.

1. Actual occupation

The main points to discuss are:

(i) The property must be in actual use, no matter how minimal that use is (*R. v. St Pancras A.C. 1877*).

(ii) Intention to occupy the property at some time in the future does not establish actual occupation.

An illustrative case is *Associated Cinema Properties Ltd v. Hampstead B.C. (1944)*. The company, as a precaution, rented some empty houses, which they proposed to use as offices should their existing offices be destroyed by enemy bombing. They did nothing with the houses, which remained empty and unrepaired. It was held by the Court of Appeal that although there was obviously intention to occupy should the need arise, there was no *actual* occupation and so the premises were *not* rateable.

(iii) Past occupation, together with intention to occupy in the future, has been held to establish actual occupation.

Examples of this kind of situation can be seen at any coastal holiday resort and a case in point is *Southend on Sea v. White (1900)*. The proprietor of a shop closed it down during the winter, but with a definite intention to re-open when the holiday season commenced. Some items of fittings were left in the shop when closed, but no stock remained. It was held that actual occupation *did* exist. *Rex v. Melladew (1907)*, involved the owner of a warehouse who closed the property, removing chattels and disconnecting the water supply, when there was a reduction in demand for storage space. He intended to re-open the warehouse should demand increase and this intention, together with past occupation, was held to establish the existence of actual occupation.

2. Exclusive occupation

The major points to emerge should be:

(i) A person is in exclusive occupation if his use of the property excludes all others from the same use.

The case of *Peak (VO) v. Burley Golf Club (1960)* concerned a golf club using common land in the New Forest. They did this under licence, but the public were not excluded from the land and did not have to pay to use it. It was held that the golf club did not have exclusive occupation and was therefore not rateable.

(ii) Where there is more than one occupier, the person has exclusive occupation whose use of the property is *paramount* for a particular purpose.

This rule stems from the case of *Westminster Council v. Southern Railway Co Ltd (1936)*. The case concerned various properties, let to different occupiers by the Southern Railway Company, on Victoria Station in London. Properties included a bookstall, shops, kiosks and also sites used by coal merchants and builders' merchants. Each of the occupiers had a defined site, paid rent to the Southern Railway Company and had agreed to pay the rates should the properties be separately assessed. In addition, access to all of the properties was controlled by the Railway Company.

All of the tenants were held to be rateable occupiers, because theirs was in each case the paramount occupation.

(iii) It is possible for a trespasser to be in rateable occupation. In *Bruce v. Willis (1846)* a trespasser was held to be in rateable occupation because he, rather than the owner, was in physical control of the property.

3. Beneficial occupation

The main issues to consider are:

(i) The occupation must be of value to the occupier. However, value is not considered in financial terms and it is not necessary for the occupier to make any financial profit from the occupation. In essence, it means that the right to occupy the property is something for which a hypothetical tenant would be prepared to pay rent *(Jones v. Mersey Docks, 1865)*.

(ii) The rateability of bodies with statutory duties to provide properties for certain uses, such as schools, sewage works, fire stations and so on.

In the past, attempts have been made to argue that the occupation of such properties should not be rateable, because they are provided under a statutory duty and are of no benefit to the occupier.

A case in point is *West Bromwich School Board v. West Bromwich Overseers (1884)* in which the School Board were held to be in beneficial occupation. They could not make a profit from the school buildings, but were required by statute to provide them and if they did not, then they would have to rent them from some other source.

(iii) Land 'struck with sterility'

There are some properties, provided by statutory authorities, where neither the authority, nor any other person or body, can be said to be in beneficial occupation, because the properties are used by the general public, who cannot be rateable occupiers. These properties are said to be 'struck with sterility' since they are incapable of commanding a rent. A leading case is *Lambeth Overseers v. L.C.C. (1897)* – often referred to as the 'Brockwell Park Case'. This concerned a public park provided by the former London County Council (LCC) and the maintenance of it cost more than any proceeds. The park was required to remain open to the public throughout the year and it was held that there was no beneficial occupier, therefore the park was not rateable. In fact, this has since been formalised, originally by S.44 of the *General Rate Act 1967* and now by para. 15, Schedule 5 of the *Local Government Finance Act 1988*, public parks owned by local authorities are exempt from rateability.

4. *Permanent occupation*

The principal concern in this case is that there should be a likelihood of occupation continuing for a reasonable period of time.

It should be noted that there is no definite rule as to what is regarded as a 'reasonable' time, and the degree of transience must be considered in each individual case. Examples which could be used in illustration include:

(i) Contractors' huts

In *L.C.C. v. Wilkins (VO) 1954*, contractors' huts were held to be rateable after being in place for 12 months. A further example is provided by the case of *Sir Robert McAlpine and Sons v. Payne (1969)*.

(ii) Caravan sites

In *Field Place Caravan Park v. Harding (1966)* the Court of Appeal held that caravans on prepared sites were rateable after being in place for more than 12 months.

(iii) Travelling Shows

In *R. v. St Pancras A.C. 1877* sites occupied by travelling showmen were held not to be rateable, because their period of occupation was too transient.

Question 5.2 *Principles*

(a) The first step in answering this question, is to define what the valuer has to provide in the valuation of a property for rating purposes. This is the Rateable Value, which is defined in Schedule 6 of the *Local Government Finance Act 1988*:

'The Rateable Value of a non-domestic hereditament shall be taken to be an amount equal to the rent at which it is estimated the hereditament might reasonably be expected to let from year to year if the tenant undertook to pay all usual tenant's rates and taxes and to bear the cost of repairs and insurance and the other expenses (if any) necessary to maintain the hereditament in a state to command that rent'.

This is the same as the definition of Net Annual Value given in S.19 of the *General Rate Act 1967*. Under the 1967 Act, properties were valued either to Net Annual Value or Gross Value as specified in S.19. The assumption when valuing to Gross Value was that the *landlord* paid the costs of maintaining and insuring the property. Under the *Local Government Finance Act 1988* all rating assessments are on the basis of Rateable Value. This is a more realistic basis – the statutory definition is essentially a description of a rent on full repairing and insuring terms. One important difference is that the statutory definition envisages a tenancy from year to year, whereas a commercial lease will normally be for a term of years. This point is considered in part (b) of the question.

As it is the rental value of a property that is to be assessed, the first assumption to be made is that there is a hypothetical landlord and a hypothetical tenant.

Various points have been established by case law regarding this assumption and these should be discussed.

(i) The tenant includes *all* possible occupiers, including the actual occupier (even if he is the owner).
   (R. v. London School Board, 1886)

(ii) The tenancy is from year to year, with a reasonable expectation that it will continue.
   (R. v. South Staffordshire Waterworks Co., 1885)

(iii) The hypothetical tenant's ability to pay the hypothetical rent is immaterial, unless there is only one possible occupier.
   (Tomlinson (VO) v. Plymouth Argyle Football Club Ltd., 1960)

(iv) Both the hypothetical tenant and landlord are assumed to be reasonable people and of normal business capabilities.

(v) The hypothetical landlord is assumed to let the property to the highest bidder.

The valuation

The various principles that must be followed in producing a valuation for rating purposes should now be discussed.

(i) The property is assumed to be vacant and to let.

(ii) The property must be valued *rebus sic stantibus*. This means it is valued as it stands at the date of valuation. Schedule 6,2(3) of the *Local*

Government Finance Act 1988 defines the date of valuation as the day that the Rating List is compiled or a preceding day specified by the Secretary of State. For example, the Rating List that came into force on 1 April 1990 was 'compiled' on that date, but the valuation date was 1 April 1988 *(Rating Lists (Valuation Date) Order 1988 S1 No. 2146)*. The state of the property and its surroundings have to be taken at the date of compilation of the Rating List (Schedule 6,2(7), *Local Government Finance Act 1988*). This meant that values at 1988 had to be produced under circumstances that were expected to exist at 1 April 1990. For the 1995 revaluation, the date of compilation of the Rating List will be 1 April 1995 and the date of valuation 1 April 1993.

(iii) State of repair of the property.

As noted in (ii) above, the property has to be valued *rebus sic stantibus*, but it would be impractical to have to reflect the actual state of repair of every property in its individual assessment.

This problem is overcome by the statutory definition of Rateable Value, which assumes that the tenant keeps the property in a state of repair sufficient to maintain the rental value reflected by the rating assessment.

Whatever the actual state of repair, every hereditament is assumed to be in a satisfactory state of repair − unless it is so bad that a reasonable tenant would not be prepared to first bear the cost of putting it into a satisfactory state of repair. This follows from the cases of *Wexler v. Playle (1959)* and *Saunders v. Maltby (1976)*. When considering what is to be assumed as a 'satisfactory' state of repair, the valuer should have regard to the type of property, the neighbourhood and the age of the property.

(iv) The use of the property.

The hereditament is valued according to the mode or category of occupation. In *N & SW Railway Co., v. Brentford Union, (1888)* it was stated that

> 'the thing must be valued as it is for the purpose for which it is used'

The main issue for the valuer to consider is the use for which the hypothetical tenant is assumed to be paying rent. For example, where a shop in a parade was used as a house, with no structural alterations to convert it to a dwelling, the Lands Tribunal held that the property should be assessed as a shop *(Prince v. Baker (VO) and Widnes B.C., 1973)*. A tenant coming fresh to the scene would be prepared to pay rent reflecting use of the property as a shop.

(v) If the property is let, the actual rent passing may be good evidence of its rental value, but not necessarily the best evidence.

(vi) Although landlord and tenant are hypothetical, the rent that they are assumed to agree must reflect market conditions. Any benefits or disadvantages that might be expected to influence the hypothetical tenant's bid must be taken into consideration.

(vii) The tenant is assumed to come fresh upon the scene.

When familiar circumstances change, occupiers are sometimes aggrieved, mainly because they are able to compare the situation before and after the change. The hypothetical tenant is assumed to view the property and its situation with no prior knowledge that might prejudice his attitude.

(viii) Assessments of other comparable properties may be used as evidence in the absence of better evidence. 'Tone' of the list valuations in essence mean that properties must be valued at the valuation date of the Rating List. For instance, if a new property is entered into the 1990 Rating List, or an existing property is altered, the Rateable Value of the property will be based upon values in April 1988.

(b) The hypothetical lease rent envisaged in the *Local Government Finance Act, 1988*, is Rateable Value. Essentially, it is equivalent to a rent on full repairing and insuring terms – see part (a) of this question for the precise definition.

Possible ways in which a typical lease rent may differ from this statutory definition include the following (5 only are required):

(i) The property may be let on repairing and insuring terms that do not reconcile with the definition of Rateable Value. For example, the landlord may be responsible for external repairs and insurance, which, under rating hypothesis, would be the tenant's responsibility.

(ii) The property may be let at an inclusive rent, which means that out of the rent he receives, the landlord must pay the rates. Rates are part of 'usual tenant's rates and taxes' in the Rateable Value definition.

(iii) A service charge may be included in the rent paid. Such a charge is not part of the rent for the building, but for other services provided by the landlord, for example, heating, cleaning and lighting of the common parts in a building let to several tenants. It may not be easy to separate out that part of the rent attributable to the accommodation and that attributable to the services provided.

(*Bell Property Trust Ltd. v. Hampstead A.C. 1949*)

(iv) A property may be let at less than full rental value for a variety of reasons. For instance, the tenant may have paid a premium or carried out improvements as a condition of the lease, or there may be a special relationship between the landlord and tenant. It is possible that legislative interference has restricted the rent that may be charged (see Chapter 3).

The tenant may be enjoying the benefit of a reduced rent or a rent free period, familiar inducements to take the lease of a property in the early 1990s.

(v) Tenancies envisaged by the definition of Rateable Value are from year to year, whereas property is far more likely to be let for a term of years, with or without provision for rent review.

(vi) Rent under the lease may have been fixed at a different time from the date of valuation for rating purposes.

Question 5.3

(a) The three main methods of valuation for rating purposes are
1. Rental comparison
2. Profits or accounts method
3. Contractor's method.

The major points to discuss under these three headings are as follows:
1. Rental comparison

  (i) Since it is the rental value of the hereditament that is being assessed, it is the best method to use wherever possible.
      (*Robinson v. Chester-le-Street A.C. 1938*)
 (ii) The date of the evidence used must be as near as possible to the date of the valuation for rating purposes.
(iii) Evidence used must be of the same type of property that is being valued.
(iv) Rental evidence on different terms from the statutory definition of Rateable Value must be adjusted to comply with that definition (see question 5.2(b)).
 (v) Rental values are usually reduced to a unit price for comparison, such as £s per square metre, as would be done in any analysis of information to be used in a subsequent valuation. (For example, see questions 1.1 and 1.6.)

2. Profits or accounts method

  (i) The method is used only when there is no comparable rental evidence.
 (ii) It is often used where there is some element of monopoly, whether this be legal or factual, for example, when a particular use requires a licence, such as a public house. Other properties that might be valued by this method include cinemas, markets, petrol filling stations and caravan sites.
(iii) The basis of the method is that the profit earned by a hereditament will have a direct effect on the amount of rent that a hypothetical tenant can afford to pay.
(iv) Bearing in mind that the question requires only a *brief* consideration of the valuation methods, a simple outline illustration would suffice to aid the

description of this method. Gross receipts are ascertained and working expenses deducted, leaving a 'divisible balance'. From this balance is taken the 'tenant's share', leaving an amount available to pay rent and rates.

Gross receipts
less purchases   = gross profit
gross profit
less working expenses = net profit
net profit
less interest on
tenant's
capital   = divisible balance
divisible balance
less tenant's share   = rent and rates

Tenant's share, probably in the region of 40 or 50 per cent, is the tenant's remuneration for running the business. The amount required by the tenant will be affected by various things, including the type of business and the amount of risk.

3. Contractor's method *6% of CV = Rateable value*

(i) As with the profits method, it is only used when there is no comparable rental evidence.
(*Robinson Brothers (Brewers) Ltd. v. Boughton and Chester-le-Street, 1937*)

(ii) The basic assumption behind the method is that, as an alternative to renting the property, an occupier will buy the land and build the property himself.
Annual interest charged on this expenditure is taken to be equal to the rental value of the property.

(iii) Cost of erecting the building or a simple substitute is estimated, ignoring any unnecessary ornamentation since a tenant would pay no extra rent for this. An allowance for age and obsolescence is then deducted, the capital value of the site for its present use is added and the resultant figure is the effective capital value.

(iv) This capital figure is de-capitalised, using a yield of 6 per cent, as specified in the *Rating (Miscellaneous Provisions) (No 2) Regulations 1989, S1 No. 2303*, to produce the rental value of the property.

(v) An outline valuation would again clarify the explanation.

Estimated cost of replacing the building
less deduction for age
and obsolescence   = building costs
building costs
plus capital value of land   = effective capital value
6 per cent of effective capital value = rateable value

For more detailed examples of valuations for rating purposes, the student is referred to *Advanced Valuation* by Diane Butler and David Richmond (Macmillan, 1990).

(b) It should initially be explained that for plant and machinery to be rateable, it must belong to one of the classes listed in the *Valuation for Rating (Plant and Machinery) Regulations 1989*, which amended the *Plant and Machinery (Rating) Order 1960*.

Plant and machinery for these purposes is divided into 5 categories or classes and the student should outline the plant and machinery falling into each class.

Class 1A

This covers plant and machinery intended to be used mainly or exclusively for the generation, storage, primary transformation or main transmission of power in or on the hereditament.

Class 1B

Concerns plant and machinery used mainly or exclusively in connection with heating, cooling, ventilating, lighting, draining or supplying water to the hereditament.

Class 2

Passenger lifts and elevators.

Class 3

Railway and tramway lines and tracks within the curtilage of the hereditament.

Class 4

A list of rateable items is provided in Class 4. To be rateable under this class, the plant or machinery must be *named*. *All* items named will be rateable, with the exception of:

  (i) Any item that is *not* a building or structure nor in the nature of a building or structure,
 (ii) Any part of any item not forming an integral part of that item as a building or structure,
(iii) Any part or item that is moved or rotated by motive power as part of the process of manufacture.

    The Wood Committee which produced a report on the rating of plant and machinery in the Spring of 1993, declared that the distinction drawn between plant which moves or rotates as part of the process of manufacture and that which remains stationary is irrational, and should not be reflected in future regulations.

(iv) Any refractory or lining requiring renewal after normal use in under 50 weeks.
 (v) Any item where the external cubic capacity is less than 200 m^3 and which can easily be moved and re-erected elsewhere without substantial demolition of the item and its surrounding structure.

Class 5
Pipelines

Plant and machinery is a specialised area and a basic knowledge is usually sufficient at the stage envisaged by this text.

Identification of plant and machinery is sometimes difficult as is the decision regarding rateability. Some consideration of this aspect should be provided in answering this question.

For an item to be rateable, it must be *named* in the 1989 Regulations. Various cases have considered the meaning of 'named'. The following general conclusions have been reached:

(i) If the item has a technical name, with no suitable alternative in everyday use, the technical name must be listed for the item to be rateable.
(ii) If the item has an alternative name in everyday use, or a generic term that is included in the list, the item will be rateable.
(iii) Problems are more likely to be encountered in identifying larger items and establishing whether or not they are rateable.

Under Class 4 the item must be named and must *also* be in the nature of a building or structure.

Sometimes it is appropriate to consider a large item in terms of the smaller items of which it is comprised. If the smaller items are shown in the list, they may well be rateable even though the larger item considered in total, would not be.

Matters which may assist in deciding whether or not a building or structure is involved, include the manner of construction, the size and weight of the item, whether or not it is prefabricated, the degree of permanence and the extent to which the item is incorporated or attached to the hereditament. Guidance on these matters was provided in *Cardiff Rating Authority v. Guest, Keen, Baldwins, Iron and Steel Co. Ltd. (1949)*.

The Valuation of Plant and Machinery

This is a specialised area and the question requires only a brief consideration of the main points.

The first thing to note is that the building within which the plant and machinery is contained is valued by whatever method is appropriate for that building.

To the Rateable Value of the building is added the Rateable Value of the plant and machinery. The appropriate valuation method for the plant and machinery is the Contractors method.

The effective capital value may be obtained by:

(a) The actual cost of the plant and machinery, a satisfactory approach where it is fairly new,

or

(b) replacement cost

This will be more appropriate where advances in technology result in an item being superseded by a modern and cheaper replacement.

Prior to determining its annual equivalent deductions should be made from the effective capital value to allow for the following:

(i) Obsolescence
Consideration will need to be given to the extent to which technology has overtaken the item of plant and machinery.

(ii) Age and wear and tear
Deterioration may mean that the machinery breaks down more frequently, resulting in high maintenance costs.

(iii) Redundancy
This would result from decline in the particular trade or manufacturing process for which the plant and machinery are used.

6 COMPULSORY PURCHASE AND PLANNING COMPENSATION

Compensation for compulsory purchase is an extremely wide and complex area and, in examinations at the level envisaged by this text, a knowledge of basic principles is often tested. It is not intended to discuss all of these principles in detail, since they may be gleaned from a textbook specifically dealing with the subject. The emphasis here is upon the approach to answering examination questions, but specific points are expanded when necessary.

Compensation received by an owner when his interest in property is acquired compulsorily is intended to put the owner, in money terms, in the same position after the acquisition as he was before it *(Rickett v. Metropolitan Rail Co., 1867)*.

Over the years, there have been various statutes governing the acquisition of interests in land by authorities with powers of compulsory purchase and also providing a basis for compensation in such cases. Current legislation has evolved, via both case law and statutes, from the *Lands Clauses (Consolidation) Act, 1845*, the latest (at the time of writing) contributions to this development occurring in the *Town and Country Planning Act 1990* and the *Planning and Compensation Act 1991.*

In general, compensation for compulsory purchase may be quantified under various heads and it will aid the clarity of a student's answer, and probably crystallise the situation in the student's own mind, if items of compensation are considered in a similar way to the following:

(i) Compensation for the interest that is being acquired. There are six rules that govern the assessment of this compensation and these rules are contained in Section 5 of the *Land Compensation Act 1961.*

These rules have remained largely unchanged since their introduction in the *Acquisition of Land (Assessment of Compensation) Act, 1919*, and it will be assumed that the student is familiar with them. However, Rule 3 was amended by *Schedule 15,* para. 1, *Planning and Compensation Act 1991,* and is now as follows, the words in brackets having been *removed*:

'The special suitability or adaptability of the land for any purpose shall not be taken into account if that purpose is a purpose to which it could *be applied only in pursuance of statutory powers, or for which there is no market apart from [the special needs of a particular purchaser or] the requirements of any authority possessing compulsory purchase powers'.*

Thus special value to a purchaser, *other than* the authority acquiring the land with their powers of compulsory purchase, is *not now* to be disregarded.

(ii) Compensation for any injurious affection to land *not* acquired from the owner. There may also be a deduction from compensation for the land taken, where land retained is increased in value as a result of the acquiring authority's scheme.

If *no* land is taken, compensation is governed by S.10 of the *Land Compensation Act 1965*, which re-enacted S.68 of the *Lands Clauses (Consolidation) Act 1845*, together with the case of *Metropolitan Board of Works v. McCarthy, 1874*, which provided four rules to be followed in determining whether or not there is entitlement to compensation (see also question 6.2, *Advanced Valuation* by Diane Butler and David Richmond (Macmillan, 1990)). Further statutory authority for compensation when no land is taken, is provided by Part I of the *Land Compensation Act, 1973*. This allows compensation to be paid for depreciation caused by physical factors, such as noise, vibration, smell, fumes and smoke arising from the use of public works.

(iii) Compensation for disturbance, such as costs of finding alternative accommodation, removal expenses, adaptation of fixtures and fittings for the new accommodation and bridging finance for purchasing alternative accommodation. This compensation is provided for by rule 6 of S.5, *Land Compensation Act 1961*. It is payable provided that the loss is not too remote and can be shown to be a reasonable and natural consequence of the owner being dispossessed (*Harvey v. Crawley Development Corporation, 1957*).

(iv) The owner may be entitled to other payments, such as a home loss payment. Section 10 Schedule 2 of the *Land Compensation Act 1961* provided for owner-occupiers' supplements and well maintained payments, where site value compensation was appropriate for unfit houses under Ss 585–595 of the *Housing Act 1985*. These provisions have been repealed by Schedule 12 of the *Local Government and Housing Act 1989*. The payments are no longer necessary, since the basis of compensation is now open market value, which will reflect the actual physical condition of a property.

Home loss payments are still applicable and are considered in questions 6.1 and 6.3.

Surveyor's and legal fees in connection with the claim for compensation are also paid by the acquiring authority.

Serving a blight notice or a purchase notice are remedies available to the owner of an interest in land, the value of which is adversely affected, either by refusal of planning permission, or by the planning proposals of an authority having powers of compulsory purchase. In question 6.4, the differences between these two notices are considered, together with the circumstances in which they are appropriate.

For a further consideration of the topic areas covered in this section, the reader is referred to *Advanced Valuation* by Diane Butler and David Richmond (Macmillan, 1990), Chapter 6 (Compulsory Purchase Compensation) and Chapter 7 (Planning Compensation).

COMPULSORY PURCHASE AND PLANNING COMPENSATION – QUESTIONS

6.1. Notices to treat in respect of three houses were served six months ago under a Compulsory Purchase Order and entry is expected shortly.

Prepare simulated claims for compensation in respect of all interests in the three houses and detail the statutory payments that could be claimed by the various affected parties.

The estimated open market vacant possession value of each house is £35 000. The properties are in good condition and each had a rateable value of £160 on 31 March 1990.

No. 1 Freehold interest purchased 14 years ago by A, who has occupied the property ever since.

No. 3 Owned freehold by B and occupied by C for the past 12 years under a regulated tenancy. The registered rent is £130 per calendar month, exclusive.

No. 5 The freeholder is D, but E has a long leasehold interest with 15 years unexpired at a ground rent of £20 per annum. E had served a valid notice to enfranchise just before notice to treat was received.

Two furnished rooms on the first floor have been occupied by F for 12 months and F pays E £40 per week.

6.2. A detached, Victorian house, situated on the outskirts of a provincial town, was converted to offices some years ago. It is currently let with 4 years unexpired of a 21 year lease at a rent, on full repairing and insuring terms, of £17 500 per annum, fixed for the remainder of the term. The current rental value on full repairing and insuring terms is estimated to be £26 500 per annum.

In the development plan, the land is zoned for industrial use and, on this basis, is worth £350 000. However, the land is now required as part of the car park in the town's proposed park and ride scheme, and a Compulsory Purchase Order has recently been confirmed.

Prepare a compensation claim for the freeholder on the compulsory acquisition of his interest.

The rateable value of the premises on 1 April 1990 was £16 500.

6.3. Set out a claim for compensation on behalf of a tenant in respect of the imminent compulsory purchase of his grocery shop, together with living accommodation above. The tenant occupies under a 20 year lease with 3 years unexpired at a rent of £7 500 per annum. The estimated rack rental value of the property, disregarding the scheme, is £14 750 per annum.

The accounts show that the net pre-tax profits over the past three years were £21 500, £22 000 and £17 750, the recent fall in profits being attributable to the authority's scheme. An annual salary of £16 000 is drawn from the business by the tenant, who is a sole proprietor.

Stock is valued at £9 250, tenant's fixtures and fittings at £4 500 and capital of £4 000 is available for use in the business.

The tenant is 63 years old, intends to retire and has not sought alternative premises.

6.4. (a) Distinguish between a blight notice and a purchase notice, indicating the situations in which each may apply.

(b) A blight notice has been accepted in respect of a detached house which is to be acquired as a result of a proposed road scheme and you have been instructed to act for the owner-occupier. Explain how the case would be dealt with and set out a simulated claim for compensation on behalf of your client.

COMPULSORY PURCHASE AND PLANNING COMPENSATION – SUGGESTED ANSWERS

Question 6.1

Each property will be dealt with in turn, considering individual claims as appropriate.

No. 1
A (owner–occupier)
A's freehold interest is the only interest in respect of this property.
  (i) Compensation for land taken. A brief note should be made of the basis for this compensation.

Under S.5(2) of the *Land Compensation Act 1961* (rule 2), compensation will be the open market value of the freehold interest in the house, which is £35 000.

(ii) Costs of finding alternative accommodation. This would include travelling expenses incurred in searching for suitable alternative accommodation; also legal fees, surveyor's fees and stamp duty resulting from the purchase of alternative accommodation.

(iii) Removal expenses.

(iv) Costs of any bridging finance necessary for purchase of the alternative accommodation.

(v) Adaptation of fixtures and fittings for the new accommodation and any loss on forced sale.

(vi) Home loss payment. It would be appropriate here to provide an explanation of the qualification for, and the quantification of, a home loss payment. Entitlement to a home loss payment is provided for by the *Planning and Compensation Act 1991*, which repealed S1 1990 No. 776 and amended Ss 29 and 30 of the *Land Compensation Act 1973*. These amended provisions apply to displacements after 16 November 1990.

Section 29 as amended requires the owner to have been in occupation for a minimum of one year prior to displacement.

A clearly qualifies for this payment, having purchased the freehold interest 14 years ago and occupied the house ever since.

The amended S.30 specifies the amount of a home loss payment. In the case of an owner it is 10 per cent of the market value of the interest, subject to a maximum of £15 000 and a minimum of £1 500.

A's home loss payment = 10 per cent of £35 000
$$= £3\,500$$

(vii) Surveyor's and legal fees in connection with the claim for compensation.

No. 3

In this case, the house is occupied by a tenant and therefore the compensation to both freeholder and tenant must be considered.

B (freeholder)

(i) Compensation for land taken. Under S.5(2) of the *Land Compensation Act 1961* (rule 2), this is the open market value of the freehold interest in No. 3, subject to C's tenancy.

Value of B's interest

Rent received	£130 × 12 = £ 1 560 pa
less external repairs, say	£175
insurance, say	£ 75

management, 5 per cent of rent	£ 78	£	328 pa [see note 1]
net income		£ 1 232 pa	
YP in perpetuity at 9 per cent [see note 2]		11.11	
Capital value		£13 688	
Compensation for land taken,	say	£13 700	

Notes

1: Outgoings are estimated for the purposes of this example, but in practice the valuer would have more precise knowledge of the expenditure.

2: The yield adopted here would ideally be derived from market evidence.

(ii) Surveyor's and legal fees.

C (tenant)

No interest in the property is being acquired from C, therefore there will be no compensation for land taken. However, the payments for which C should claim are:

(i) Removal expenses.

(ii) Home loss payment.

 C has been in occupation for the past 12 years and so will be entitled to a home loss payment.

 Under S.30 of the *Land Compensation Act, 1973,* as amended by the *Planning and Compensation Act 1991,* because C is the occupier but not the owner of the house, the home loss payment will be restricted to £1 500 (see A's interest in No. 1).

(iii) It would be useful to note that, although C has no compensatable interest in the property, it is possible for the acquiring authority to make an *ex gratia* payment to cover expenses incurred in finding alternative accommodation.

(iv) Surveyor's and legal fees.

No. 5

D (freeholder)

(i) Compensation for land taken.

A valid notice to enfranchise existed at the date of notice to treat. It should be explained that under S.56(b) of the *Land Compensation Act 1961,* the notice to treat renders the notice to enfranchise ineffective. Nevertheless, D's compensation will be the price that E would have paid if enfranchisement had not been prevented by the compulsory acquisition (*Sharif v. Birmingham City Council, 1978).*

Enfranchisement price

		£	20 pa	
Existing ground rent		£	20 pa	
YP 15 years at 6 per cent [see note 1]		9.712		£ 194
Reversion to modern ground rent				
[see note 2]				
Vacant possession value	£35 000			
Site value, say 25 per cent				
[see note 3]	£ 8 750			
at 6 per cent return [see note 1]		£	525 pa	
YP in perpetuity deferred				
15 years at 6 per cent [see note 1]		6.954		£3 651
Enfranchisement price				£3 845
Compensation for land taken				£3 845

Notes

1: Yields adopted in previous Lands Tribunal decisions in respect of leasehold enfranchisement.

2: Rateable value of the house at 31 March 1990 was £160, therefore the valuation is governed by the provisions of the *Leasehold Reform Act 1967*.

3: Site value estimated using the standing house approach, described in question 4.3(a).

For a detailed consideration of leasehold enfranchisement, the reader should refer to Chapter 4.

(ii) Surveyor's and legal fees.

E (leaseholder)

(i) Compensation for land taken.

Because E had served a valid notice to enfranchise on D prior to service of notice to treat by the acquiring authority, in effect the compulsory acquisition has prevented E from becoming the freeholder.

Compensation under this heading will therefore be the value of the freehold in possession, reduced by the enfranchisement price that E would have paid to D that is:

$$£35\,000 - £3\,845 = £31\,155$$

(ii) Costs of finding alternative accommodation.

(iii) Removal expenses.

(iv) Home loss payment.

The question does not state how long E has been in occupation. However, the period must exceed the one year necessary to qualify for a home loss payment, since E qualifies for enfranchisement, which requires a minimum of 3 years occupation.

$$\text{Home loss payment} = 10 \text{ per cent of } £31\,155$$
$$= £3\,115$$

(v) Surveyor's and legal fees.

F (occupier of two furnished rooms)
F has no compensatable interest in the property, but the acquiring authority may make an *ex gratia* payment to cover expenses of finding alternative accommodation.

Question 6.2

Freeholder's claim
In preparing this claim, three valuations must be provided and compared, to establish that which is most beneficial to the claimant.

Under Ss 14–16 of the *Land Compensation Act 1961*, the value of the land is determined:

(i) for its existing use
(ii) for the purpose for which it is to be acquired, and
(iii) for any use for which it is reasonable to assume that, but for the scheme for which the land is to be acquired, planning permission would be granted.

The freeholder is then entitled to adopt the valuation that is most beneficial to him.

(i) *Existing use value*
This is the value of the freehold interest in the property as offices, subject to the current lease.

Income	£17 500 pa	
YP 4 years at 12 per cent [see note 1]	3.037	£ 53 148
reversion to	£26 500 pa	
YP in perpetuity deferred 4 years		
at 8 per cent [see note 2]	9.188	£243 482
Capital value		£296 630
	say	£295 000

Notes
1: High yield adopted because income is fixed and inflation prone for the next 4 years.

2: It is assumed that 8 per cent is a reasonable yield for this type of property. In practice, it would be obtained from market evidence.

(ii) *Value for the purpose for which the land is to be acquired*
Under S15(1) of the *Land Compensation Act, 1961*, it has to be assumed that planning permission would be granted for this use.

As this is for the construction of a car park, it is assumed that the value will be by far the lowest and that the freeholder will not adopt this basis.

(iii) *Value of the land for industrial use*
This is the use for which the land is zoned, and it is assumed that, but for the scheme, planning permission would be granted for industrial use. In producing this valuation, it is necessary to make certain assumptions, mainly in respect of compensation to the tenant. Assumptions made in the calculation that follows are:

(a) that the leaseholder has been in occupation since the commencement of the lease, that is, for 17 years
(b) that the landlord's S.25 notice requiring possession, is served *on or after* 1 April 1990

Income	£ 17 500 pa	
YP 4 years at 12 per cent	3.037	£ 53 148
reversion to site value for		
industrial use	£350 000	
× PV of £1 in 4 years at 10 per cent		
[see note 1]	0.683	£239 050
		£292 198
less compensation to tenant [see note 2]		
£16 500 × 2 = £33 000 [see note 3]	£ 33 000	
× PV of £1 in 4 years at 10 per cent	0.683	£ 22 539
Capital value		£269 659
	say	£270 000

Notes
1: It is assumed that 10 per cent is a reasonable yield for this type of property.
2: If the land were to be developed for industrial use, the freeholder would have to pay compensation to the tenant under S.37 of the *Landlord and Tenant Act 1954* for loss of security of tenure.
3: Rateable value at 1 April 1990 multiplied by two. The higher multiplier is appropriate because the tenant has been in occupation for more than 14 years.

For a detailed consideration of compensation to a business tenant for loss of security of tenure, see question 3.1(a).

Existing use value of £295 000 is the highest figure and the compensation claim for the freeholder will be this amount, together with surveyor's and legal fees.

Question 6.3

(i) Compensation for land taken.
Under Section 5(2) of the *Land Compensation Act 1961* (rule 2), compensation will be the value of the leasehold interest with 3 years unexpired.

Value of leasehold interest

Full rental value	£14 750 pa
less rent paid [see note 1]	£ 7 500 pa
profit rent	£ 7 250 pa
YP 3 years at 9 per cent and 3 per cent	
(tax 40 per cent) [see note 2]	1.589
Capital value	£11 520

Compensation for land taken, £11 520

Notes
1: It is assumed that the rent paid is on the same terms as full rental value, therefore no adjustments need be made.
2: 9 per cent is assumed a reasonable return for a leasehold interest in this type of property. Also that a sinking fund is available at 3 per cent, with tax being paid at 40 pence in the £.

The remainder of the claim will be for items of disturbance under S.5(6) of the *Land Compensation Act 1961*.

(ii) Permanent loss of profits.
   Initially it should be explained that since the occupier is over 60 years of age, under S.46 of the *Land Compensation Act 1973*, he may elect for total extinguishment of the business to be the basis of his claim for compensation. It is assumed that the occupier will make this election, because of his stated intention to retire and he has not sought alternative premises.
   Ideally, the claim would be based upon net pre-tax profits over the last three years and this information is actually available. However, the latest figure of

£17 750 shows a substantial reduction on the previous two years and this is stated to have been caused by the authority's scheme. This being the case, profits for the last year will be disregarded in quantifying compensation for permanent loss of profits.

		Year 1	Year 2
Pre-tax profits		£21 500	£22 000
less interest on capital:			
Stock	£ 9 250		
Fixtures and fittings	£ 4 500		
Capital	£ 4 000		
	£17 750 at 10 per cent [see note 1]	£ 1 775	£ 1 775
		£19 725	£20 225
less profit rent [see note 2]		£ 7 250	£ 7 250
Adjusted net profit [see note 3]		£12 475	£12 975
Average adjusted net profit	£12 725		
YP [see note 4] say	2		
Compensation for permanent loss of profits	£25 450		

Notes

1: This is capital tied up in the business and 10 per cent is assumed to be a reasonable rate of interest.

2: Profit rent is deducted since the loss of this has already been accounted for in the value of the leasehold interest.

3: The annual salary of the proprietor is £16 000 and this has been assumed to be adequate. If it appeared inadequate, a suitable further adjustment would have to be made to the net profit.

4: The Years' Purchase adopted will depend upon current business performance and future expectation. Comparable market information may be difficult to obtain, but guidance from past court decisions is available.

It has been assumed that the proprietor has no employees in the business, otherwise the compensation claim would include redundancy payments.

(iii) Forced sale losses.

Loss on forced sale of fixtures and fittings	
say 80 per cent of £4 500	£3 600
Loss on forced sale of stock	
say 30 per cent of £9 250	£2 775
[see note 1]	
Forced sale losses	£6 375

Notes

1: As this is a grocery business the stock will not be too difficult to dispose of.

(iv) Costs of finding alternative accommodation.
  This is in respect of the living accommodation. The question does not mention any subletting of this part of the property and it is assumed that the business proprietor lives on the premises.

(v) Removal expenses.

(vi) Home loss payment.
  On the assumption made in (iv) above. Section 29 of the *Land Compensation Act 1973*, as amended by the *Planning and Compensation Act 1991*, requires occupation for a minimum of one year prior to displacement (see question 6.1). It is a reasonable assumption, given the information in the question, that the claimant qualifies for a home loss payment. As the claimant is tenant and not owner of the property, the home loss payment will be the minimum of £1 500.

(vii) Surveyor's and legal fees in connection with the compensation claim.

Question 6.4

(a) The first point to note is that both a blight notice and a purchase notice are notices served by the owner of an interest in a property upon an authority possessing compulsory purchase powers, requiring that authority to purchase the interest.

  This should be followed by a more detailed consideration of both types of notice.

Blight notice

The main points to consider are as follows:

(i) A blight notice is served as a result of planning proposals. If it is proposed to acquire land at some future date for public use, for example by a government department, local authority or statutory undertaker, this may have a detrimental effect on the value of the land at the present time.

This effect is often called 'planning blight' and refers to the threat of compulsory acquisition, *not* the threat of the development for which the land is to be acquired. A blight notice requires the authority to acquire the property now rather than in the future.

Statutory provision for blight notices was introduced by the *Town and Country Planning Act 1959* and, after various amendments, consolidating legislation came in Ss 192–207 of the *Town and Country Planning Act 1971*. Amendments followed in the *Land Compensation Act 1973*, the *Highways Act 1990* and the *Local Government Act 1985* before consolidating legislation provided by the *Town and Country Planning Act 1990*. This was amended by the *Planning and Compensation Act 1991*. Under Ss 149–171 and Schedule 13 of the *Planning and Compensation Act 1991*, a blight notice may be served when a property is detrimentally affected by:

1. proposals included in development plans, structure plans and local plans (information in a local plan has precedence over that in a structure plan for the purposes of a blight notice),
2. a proposed compulsory purchase order,
3. a proposed highway order, and
4. being land within a slum clearance area.

(ii) A blight notice may be served in respect of a dwelling, agricultural property, or any property with an annual value not exceeding £18 000. There is no value limit in the case of owner-occupied dwellings. Annual value is defined as:

'(i) for non-domestic premises, the rateable value; (ii) for non-domestic premises which include domestic property (or property exempt from non-domestic rating) the sum of the rateable value and the 'appropriate value' which, in the case of domestic property is five per cent of the compulsory purchase value.'
(S.171 *Town and Country Planning Act 1990* and *Town and Country Planning (Blight Provisions) Order S1. 1990 No. 465*).

(iii) The notice may only be served by an owner–occupier. This includes the owner of a leasehold interest with at least 3 years unexpired and a mortgagee entitled to sell an interest in the property and to give immediate vacant possession.

Section 78 of the *Land Compensation Act 1973* enabled the personal representatives of a deceased person, who was owner-occupier at the date of death, to serve a blight notice. This was introduced to prevent a legatee, unable to satisfy the occupational requirements, from being left with a blighted property which they are unable to sell.

(iv) The required minimum period of occupation prior to serving the notice is 6 months, apart from personal representatives as noted in (iii) above.

(v) The person serving the notice must satisfy the authority that they have made sufficient effort to sell the property and that a sale is not possible, except at a price substantially less than would be the case if the property were not under the threat of being acquired. However, under the *Planning and Compensation Act 1991*, if a compulsory purchase order is *in force*, there is no necessity for the owner to prove that *any* attempt has been made to sell the interest.

(vi) On receiving a blight notice, the authority have two months within which to serve a counter notice. Disputes between the parties may be referred to the Lands Tribunal.

(vii) When a blight notice becomes effective, the parties are in the same position as they would be if the authority had served a notice to treat under a compulsory purchase order in respect of the property.

Purchase notice

The main points to consider are as follows:

(i) As with a blight notice, a purchase notice is also a notice that requires an authority with powers of compulsory acquisition to purchase an owner's interest in a property.

In this case the notice is served as a result of refusal of an application for planning permission, or the granting of permission subject to conditions. Service is under the provisions of S137 of the *Town and Country Planning Act 1990*.

A purchase notice may also be served as a result of a discontinuance order, a revocation order, a refusal of listed building consent, refusal of consent under a tree preservation order or Control of Advertisement Regulations.

(ii) The person serving the notice must satisfy the authority that the property as it exists is incapable of reasonably beneficial use and that it cannot be rendered capable of reasonably beneficial use if it is developed for the use for which planning permission *would* be granted, or which the local planning authority or Secretary of State have indicated would be granted.

If planning permission is granted subject to conditions, it is necessary to show that the conditions imposed render the land incapable of reasonably beneficial use.

(iii) The authority have three months in which to accept the notice, persuade another authority (for example, the County Council) to accept the notice, or to notify the Secretary of State that they do not accept the notice.

The Secretary of State may confirm the notice, confirm the authority's non-acceptance, grant the planning permission applied for, or grant planning permission for some other development.

(iv) If a purchase notice is accepted, confirmed, or deemed confirmed by the Secretary of State, then the authority is assumed to have served notice to treat upon the owner. Purchase by the authority will then proceed as if they were acquiring the interest using their powers of compulsory purchase.

In conclusion, it would be useful to underline the purpose of both a blight notice and a purchase notice, that is, to require an authority with powers of compulsory purchase to acquire an owner's interest in land. A blight notice results from planning proposals made by the authority whereas a purchase notice results from an adverse decision in respect of a planning proposal made by the owner of the interest.

(b) Because the blight notice has been accepted, the matter is dealt with in exactly the same way as if a compulsory purchase order exists and notice to treat has been served.

A compensation claim for your client would need to be prepared under the following heads:

(i) Compensation for land taken.

Under S5(2) of the *Land Compensation Act 1961*, compensation will be the open market value of the freehold interest in the house. In determining this value, any depreciation in value resulting from the road scheme must be ignored.

The acquiring authority might dispute any claim for disturbance compensation, because the owner is not being forced to move. If the authority did adopt this argument, as valuer acting for the owner-occupier, you would need to show that the move *is* forced, because it is inevitable that the property will eventually be acquired for the road scheme *(Prasad v. Wolverhampton Borough Council, 1983)*.

It will be assumed that the claim for compensation submitted on behalf of your client, will contain items relating to disturbance.

For a consideration of disturbance compensation and other supplementary payments, see question 6.1.

(ii) Costs of finding alternative accommodation.
(iii) Removal expenses.
(iv) Possible bridging finance.
(v) Adaptation of fixtures and fittings for the alternative accommodation.

(vi) Home loss payment.

Section 29(5) of the *Land Compensation Act 1973* prevented home loss payments where acquisition resulted from a blight notice. However, this section was repealed by the *Planning and Compensation Act 1991*. Provided that the owner satisfies the minimum occupation requirement, entitlement to a home loss payment is available as if the property were being acquired under a compulsory purchase order (see question 6.1, A's interest).

Assuming that your client qualifies for this payment, it will amount to 10 per cent of the market value of the freehold interest in the house, subject to a maximum of £15 000 and a minimum of £1 500.

(vii) Surveyor's and legal fees in connection with the claim.

7 VALUATION OF DEVELOPMENT PROPERTIES

In the valuation of property with development or redevelopment potential, the residual method of valuation may be used.

Although it is mainly employed to estimate the value of the land in question, it can be used to evaluate other variables. For example, given the asking price of a piece of land with the benefit of planning permission for a particular use, the residual method may be used to estimate the likely profit to be made by a developer.

Question 7.1 is used to demonstrate a straightforward calculation where the aim is to derive the value of the land. Question 7.2 shows a variation – the application of the residual method to determine the maximum building costs which a proposed development will be able to support.

A recognised problem with the residual method is that it is liable to error from various sources, which is the reason why it does not find favour with the Lands Tribunal, unless supported by an alternative valuation approach. Developments usually take months, perhaps even years to complete, and, during the development period, figures originally forecast may be subject to change. Relatively small changes in some of the variables may cause quite large changes in the valuation and if several variables are subject to alteration, the overall effect may be considerable. Sensitivity testing is a method of determining the variables that are particularly affected by changes and is dealt with in Chapter 3 of *Advanced Valuation* by Diane Butler and David Richmond (Macmillan, 1990).

As an alternative to the residual method, discounted cash flow techniques have gained favour over recent years. A discounted cash flow has greater versatility, enabling costs to be shown explicitly as they occur and changes to be easily incorporated should this be necessary. Two examples of discounted cash flow calculations are provided in this section, the first being question 7.3, where the technique is used to determine the minimum selling price of each property in a proposed development. Question 7.4 illustrates how a discounted cash flow approach is useful in the comparison of development schemes on the basis of their respective net present values and internal rates of return.

The final question in this section deals with life cycle costing, a technique which may be used in the preliminary stages of a development to assist in the

163

determination of, for example, the best materials or components or the best heating system to be incorporated in the development.

Each item is considered in terms of its initial cost, expected life and annual maintenance and operating costs.

VALUATION OF DEVELOPMENT PROPERTIES – QUESTIONS

7.1. A developer is considering the purchase of a site on which planning permission has been obtained for the erection of 55 detached houses.

The following information has been established:

Gross floor area of each house, 125 m^2
Costs of construction, £475 per m^2
Selling price of each house, £120 000
Development period, 2 years
Finance is available at 14 per cent per annum

Making any assumptions you consider necessary, carry out a residual valuation to determine the price that the developer can afford to pay for the site. The developer requires a pre-tax profit of 10 per cent of the total sale price.

7.2. Calculate the maximum building costs permissible for the following development to be viable.

The development comprises a block of shops, in total 110 m frontage by 25 m depth (gross), with first floor offices 110 m by 25 m (gross).

The following information is also available:

Building period,	2 years	
Anticipated rents per m^2 (net):		
Shops	Zone A	£520 (5 m depth)
Offices		£230
Yield required,	8.5 per cent	
Developer's profit,	15 per cent of gross development value	
Purchase price of land	£4 000 000	

Acquisition costs, 4 per cent of purchase price.
Finance is available at 16 per cent per annum.

Maximum building costs should be expressed as £s per m^2 (gross) on the assumption that the offices will cost 40 per cent more per m^2 than the shops.

7.3. A developer wishes to purchase freehold land for £1 500 000 to build 110 bungalows. The scheme would take one year to complete and 30 bungalows could be sold after 6 months, a further 50 after 9 months and 30 on completion.

The following information has been established:

Incidental costs of land acquisition, 4 per cent of purchase price

Gross floor area of each bungalow, 82 m^2

Building costs (including site works and contingencies), £550 per m^2 (assume an even distribution over the building period).

Quantity surveyor's and architect's fees, 10 per cent of building costs.

(60 per cent to be paid at commencement and 40 per cent on completion).

Estate agency, legal fees etc., 4 per cent of sale price.

Cost of financing, 1 per cent per month.

Prepare a monthly discounted cash flow to establish the minimum selling price of each bungalow if the developer requires a pre-tax profit of £750 000.

7.4. Your client has just purchased the freehold interest in development land. He has obtained planning permission to build 75 houses on the site and you are aware of the following information:

Purchase price of the land, £2 350 000

Incidental costs of acquisition, £94 000

Building period, 1 year

Gross floor area of each house, 115 m^2

Building costs, £465 per m^2

(5 per cent evenly distributed over the first 3 months, 90 per cent evenly distributed over the following 6 months and 5 per cent evenly distributed over the last 3 months).

Contingencies, 10 per cent of building costs.

Architect's and quantity surveyor's fees, 10 per cent of building costs and contingencies.

(50 per cent payable on commencement of the development and 50 per cent on completion).

Anticipated sale price of each house, £105 000.

Estate agent's and legal fees, 3 per cent of sales proceeds.

Finance will cost 1 per cent per month.

Using a monthly discounted cash flow, calculate

(i) the net present value of the scheme, and
(ii) the internal rate of return of the scheme.

Assume that 25 houses will be sold after 4 months, 40 houses after 8 months and 10 houses on completion.

7.5. Explain the relevance of a life cycle costing calculation to a proposed development and discuss the inadequacies in such an analysis.

VALUATION OF DEVELOPMENT PROPERTIES – SUGGESTED ANSWERS

Question 7.1

The approach adopted in the residual method, is firstly to determine the value of the site when developed. This is called the gross development value. Costs of achieving this value, including developer's profit, are then deducted from it, the residual figure being the amount available to purchase the site.

The layout shown below is illustrative of the approach required.

Gross development value £120 000 × 55 [see note 1]			£6 600 000 [see note 2]
Less [see note 3]			
(i)	Building costs, 55 × 125 m² × £475	£3 265 625	
(ii)	Contingencies [see note 4] say	£ 150 000	
(iii)	Architect's and quantity surveyor's fees say 10 per cent of building costs and contingencies	£ 341 563	
(iv)	Finance on building costs and contingencies at 14 per cent for 12 months [see note 5]	£ 511 661	
(v)	Finance on fees at 14 per cent for 12 months [see note 5]	£ 51 166	
(vi)	Estate agent's and legal fees say 3 per cent of sale price [see note 6]	£ 198 000	
(vii)	Promotion [see note 7] say	£ 2 500	
(viii)	Developer's profit, 10 per cent of gross development value [see note 8]	£ 660 000	£5 180 515
			£1 419 485 [see note 9]
	× PV of £1 in 2 years at 14 per cent		0.769
			£1 091 584
	less acquisition costs at say 4 per cent [see note 10]		£ 43 663
	Price developer can afford to pay for the site		£1 047 921
		say	£1 050 000

Notes

1: It is stated in the question that the 55 houses are expected to sell for £120 000 each.

2: This is the value of the development when completed. The gross development value is not deferred, because at this stage the approach is to simply divide this value into its constituent parts.

3: From the value of the completed development, the costs of achieving that value are deducted. Any residue will then be available for the developer to acquire the site.

4: This is an allowance for unforeseen expenditure.

5: The money is not all borrowed at the same time. Costs will be incurred in differing amounts at various times over the building period and it is generally accepted that this is roughly equivalent to borrowing all the money for half the building period. There are various ways to estimate the costs of finance and in this case, the approach adopted is to calculate 14 per cent interest for the whole construction period of 2 years, then to halve the resultant amount. Thus

Building costs and contingencies	£3 415 625
× Amount of £1 in 2 years at 14 per cent	1.2996
Amount borrowed plus interest at 14 per cent for 2 years	£4 438 946.2
less amount borrowed	£3 415 625
Interest for 2 years	£1 023 321.2

$$\text{Interest for one year} = \frac{£1\,023\,321.2}{2}$$
$$= £511\,661$$

6: Sale price is the gross development value.

7: Allowance for costs of advertising and marketing the development.

8: The amount required by the developer for risk and remuneration.

9: The residual amount, available to purchase the land.

10: Acquisition costs will include estate agent's fees, legal fees and stamp duty.

Although the above is probably the method usually adopted in practice, an alternative and more correct approach to the final stage of the calculation is as follows:

Total amount available to purchase the land £1 419 485

	£	x
Let acquisition price =		x
Then acquisition costs will be		0.04x
Finance for 2 years at 14 per cent on 1.04x		
Amount borrowed		1.04x
× Amount of £1 in 2 years at 14 per cent		1.2996
Amount borrowed plus interest at 14 per cent for 2 years (total cost of land acquisition)		1.352x
Therefore, £1 419 485 =		1.352x
and x =		£1 049 915
Price the developer can afford to pay, say		£1 050 000

Question 7.2

The rental value of the completed development must first be calculated, in order to determine the gross development value.

Rental information given in the question is based upon net floor areas, whereas the dimensions of the shops and offices are quoted in terms of gross floor areas.

Before commencing the calculations, it is necessary to state the assumptions made in respect of the relativity of gross and net areas. Any reasonable adjustment would be acceptable.

Shops

In the calculations that follow, it is assumed that the net floor area of the shop is 90 per cent of gross floor area.

Using 5 m zones and halving back:

Zone A $= 110$ m $\times$ 5 m $= 550$ m^2 $- 10$ per cent
$\qquad\qquad\qquad\qquad = 495$m^2 at £520 $\qquad = £257\,400$

Zone B $= 110$ m $\times$ 5 m $= 550$ m^2 $- 10$ per cent
$\qquad\qquad\qquad\qquad = 495$ m^2 at £260 $\qquad = £128\,700$

Remainder $= 110$ m $\times$ 15 m $= 1\,650$ m^2 $- 10$ per cent
$\qquad\qquad\qquad\qquad\quad = 1\,485$ m^2 at £130 $\qquad = £193\,050$

$\qquad\qquad\qquad$ Rental value of shops $\qquad\qquad$ £579\,150 pa

Offices

It is assumed that the net floor area of the offices is 80 per cent of gross floor area.

$$110 \text{ m} \times 25 \text{ m} = 2\,750 \text{ m}^2 - 20 \text{ per cent}$$
$$= 2\,200 \text{ m}^2$$

Rental value of offices 2\,200 m^2 at £230 $= $ £506\,000 pa
Rental value of completed development:

Shops	£ 579\,150 pa
Offices	£ 506\,000 pa
Total rental value	£1\,085\,150 pa

The gross development value of the completed development may now be calculated. The question states that a yield of 8.5 per cent is required, therefore the rental value is capitalised at this yield.

Total rental value	£ 1 085 150 pa
YP in perpetuity at 8.5 per cent	11.765
Gross development value	£12 766 789

The next step is to calculate the total costs of development. A large part of these costs, the building costs, are unknown, therefore let the maximum permissible building costs of the shops be £x per m^2 (gross). It is stated in the question that building costs in respect of the offices will be 40 per cent more than the building costs of the shops, therefore the maximum permissible building costs of the offices will be £1.4x per m^2 (gross).

The total costs are then as follows:

(i) Building costs

Shops $X \times 110$ m $\times$ 25 m =	2 750X	
Offices $1.4X \times 110$ m $\times$ 25 m =	3 850X	6 600X

(ii)	Site preparation, say	£	25 000
(iii)	Contingencies [see note 1], say 7.5 per cent of building costs and site preparation	£	1 875	495X
(iv)	Architect's and quantity surveyor's fees, say 10 per cent of building costs, site preparation and contingencies [see note 2]	£	2 688 + 709.5X
(v)	Finance on building costs, site preparation and contingencies at 16 per cent for 12 months [see note 3]	£	4 644 + 1 226X
(vi)	Finance on fees at 16 per cent for 12 months [see note 3]	£	464 + 123X
(vii)	Estate agent's and legal fees say 3 per cent of gross development value	£	383 004
(viii)	Promotion [see note 4] say	£	10 000
(ix)	Purchase of site [see note 5]	£4 000 000	
(x)	Costs of purchase at 4 per cent of purchase price of the land [see note 6]	£	160 000
(xi)	Finance on purchase and costs of purchase at 16 per cent for 2 years [see note 7]	£1 437 696	
(xii)	Developer's profit 15 per cent of gross development value	£1 915 018	
	Total costs	£7 940 389 + 9 153.5X	

This will be equal to the gross development value, thus:

$$£12\,766\,789 = £7\,940\,389 + 9\,153.5X$$

$$£4\,826\,400 = 9\,153.5X$$

$$X = \frac{£4\,826\,400}{9\,153.5} = £527.27$$

The maximum building costs permissible for the development to be viable are:

Shops £527 per m^2 of gross floor area

Offices £527 × 1.4 = say £738 per m^2 of gross floor area

Notes
1: An allowance for unforeseen expenditure.
2: This may also include engineer's fees if site preparation is complex.
3: Total costs are assumed to be borrowed for half the building period, in this case calculated by halving the full 16 per cent interest over the total development period of 2 years. See note 5 of question 7.1.
4: This is the cost of advertising and marketing the development.
5: Very often, a residual valuation is used to estimate the likely purchase price of the land. In this case, the purchase price has already been established.
6: These costs include estate agent's and legal fees and stamp duty.
7: Purchase of the site is at the commencement, therefore finance is needed for the whole of the building period.

In the above calculations, value added tax (VAT) has not been shown, because it has been assumed to be recoverable by the developer. If it were not recoverable then VAT would increase building costs and professional fees and consequently the finance required for these amounts. Even though VAT *is* recoverable, it may well affect the cash flow at various times, but this would not be obvious from a residual valuation.

Question 7.3

Before the discounted cash flow can be prepared, it is necessary to carry out preliminary calculations, as follows:

Building costs

The total cost of building the 110 bungalows will be

$$110 \times 82 \text{ m}^2 \times £550 = £4\,961\,000$$

The question states that this may be assumed to be evenly distributed over the building period (although this is unlikely to be the case in practice, as building costs are lower during the earlier and later parts of the contract). Therefore, the monthly building cost is

$$\frac{£4\,961\,000}{12} = £413\,417.$$

Architect's and quantity surveyor's fees

Total fees are 10 per cent of building costs = £496 100
60 per cent is payable on commencement = £297 660
40 per cent is payable on completion   = £198 440

Proceeds of sale of bungalows

This is unknown, since it is the minimum sale price that is required to be determined.
Let total proceeds of 110 bungalows = £X
After 6 months, sales proceeds =

$$\frac{30}{110} \times X = 0.273X$$

Estate agents and legal fees at 4 per cent of sales proceeds = 0.011x
After 9 months, sales proceeds =

$$\frac{50}{110} \times X$$

$$= 0.455X$$

Estate agents and legal fees at 4 per cent = 0.018X
After 12 months, sales proceeds are the same as those at 6 months, that is, 0.273X, together with estate agent's and legal fees of 0.011X.

Costs of acquisition

These are incidental costs, including surveyor's fees, legal fees and stamp duty.

$$4 \text{ per cent of } £1\,500\,000 = £60\,000$$

All of the information is now in a form that may be incorporated in a discounted cash flow calculation.

END OF MONTH

	immediate	1	2	3	4	5	6	7	8	9	10	11	12
Land purchase	−1 500 000												
Costs of purchase	−60 000												
Building costs		−413 417	−413 417	−413 417	−413 417	−413 417	−413 417	−413 417	−413 417	−413 417	−413 417	−413 417	−413 417
Architect's and QS fees	−297 660												−198 440
Sales proceeds							+0.273x			+0.455x			+0.273x
Estate agent's and legal fees							−0.011x			−0.018x			−0.011x
Total	−1 857 660	−413 417	−413 417	−413 417	−413 417	−413 417	0.262x −413 417	−413 417	−413 417	0.437x −413 417	−413 417	−413 417	0.262x −611 857
Discounted at 1 per cent per month	1	0.990	0.980	0.971	0.961	0.951	0.942	0.933	0.923	0.914	0.905	0.896	0.887
Total flow	−1 857 660	−409 283	−405 149	−401 428	−397 294	−393 160	0.247x −389 439	−385 718	−381 584	0.399x −377 863	−374 142	−370 422	0.232x −542 717

Total flow = 0.878x − £6 685 859

Since the developer requires a pre-tax profit of £750 000, this must be equal to the total flow — it is the net present value of the development.

$$£750\,000 = 0.878X - £6\,685\,859$$

$$£7\,435\,859 = 0.878X$$

$$X = \frac{£7\,435\,859}{0.878} = £8\,469\,087.6$$

The minimum selling price of 110 bungalows = £8 469 088

Minimum selling price of each bungalow = £76 992

say   £77 000

Question 7.4

Various preliminary calculations are necessary before commencing the discounted cash flow calculation.

Building costs

Total cost of building the 75 houses:

$$75 \times 115 \text{ m}^2 \times £465 = £4\,010\,625$$

Distribution of building costs over the building period:

5 per cent evenly distributed over the first 3 months:
5 per cent of £4 010 625 = £200 531
Cost per month = £66 844

90 per cent evenly distributed over the following 6 months:
90 per cent of £4 010 625 = £3 609 563
Cost per month = £601 594

5 per cent evenly distributed over the last 3 months:
Cost per month = £66 844

Contingencies

This is an allowance for unforeseen expenditure, and is stated to be 10 per cent of building costs. It would be reasonable in answering this question to assume that distribution follows the same pattern as building costs.

First 3 months, cost per month   = £ 6 684
Following 6 months, cost per month = £60 159
Last 3 months, cost per month   = £ 6 684

Architect's and quantity surveyor's fees

These are said to be 10 per cent of building costs and contingencies.

Building costs	£4 010 625
plus Contingencies	£ 401 063
Building costs and contingencies	£4 411 688

£4 411 688 at 10 per cent = £441 169

50 per cent payable on commencement = £220 585
50 per cent payable on completion   = £220 584

Sales proceeds

After   4 months, 25 × £105 000 = £2 625 000
After   8 months, 40 × £105 000 = £4 200 000
After 12 months, 10 × £105 000 = £1 050 000

Estate agent's and legal fees

At 3 per cent of sales proceeds, the amounts involved are:

After   4 months, 3 per cent of £2 625 000 = £   8 750
After   8 months, 3 per cent of £4 200 000 = £126 000
After 12 months, 3 per cent of £1 050 000 = £ 31 500

The information may now be used to provide the required discounted cash flow, in order to determine the net present value and internal rate of return of the scheme.

(i) *Net present value*

The calculation on page 175 is set out in a similar way to that used in question 7.3, except that a different 'unknown' is involved.

The net present value of + 114 827 means that if finance is available at one per cent per month, the developer will achieve a pre-tax profit of £114 827.

(ii) *Internal rate of return*

The internal rate of return is the actual return achieved by the scheme. It is the yield at which the net present value is nil. To discover the internal rate of return, the net present value is calculated at two different discount rates and the internal rate of return is determined by interpolation or extrapolation.

In this case, the net present value at one per cent per month, of + 114 827 calculated in part (i) will be used, and the net present value will be tested at another

END OF MONTH	immediate	1	2	3	4	5	6	7	8	9	10	11	12
Land purchase	−2 350 000												
Costs of purchase	−94 000												
Building costs		−66 844	−66 844	−66 844	−601 594	−601 594	−601 594	−601 594	−601 594	−601 594	−66 844	−66 844	−66 844
Contingencies		−6 684	−6 684	−6 684	−60 159	−60 159	−60 159	−60 159	−60 159	−60 159	−6 684	−6 684	−6 684
Architect's and QS fees	−220 585												−220 584
Estate Agent's and legal fees					−78 750				−126 000				−31 500
House Sales					+2 625 000				+4 200 000				+1 050 000
Total	−2 664 585	−73 528	−73 528	−73 528	+1 884 497	−661 753	−661 753	−661 753	+3 412 247	−661 753	−73 528	−73 528	+724 388
Discounted at 1 per cent per month	1	0.990	0.980	0.971	0.961	0.951	0.942	0.933	0.923	0.914	0.905	0.896	0.887
Total flow	−2 664 585	−72 793	−72 057	−71 396	+1 811 002	−629 327	−623 371	−617 416	+3 149 504	−604 842	−66 543	−65 881	+642 532

Net present value = 5 603 038 − 5 488 211
= + 114 827

discount rate. A higher rate will be used, since the positive net present value indicates that the internal rate of return is greater than one per cent per month.

A discount rate of 2 per cent will be tested. Calculation of the net present value is not as cumbersome as that in part (i), since the total flow has already been determined.

End of month	Flow	Discounted at 2 per cent per month	Discounted flow
Immediate	−2 664 585	1	−2 664 585
1	−73 528	0.980	−72 057
2	−73 528	0.961	−70 660
3	−73 528	0.942	−69 263
4	+1 884 497	0.924	+1 741 275
5	−661 753	0.906	−599 548
6	−661 753	0.888	−587 637
7	−661 753	0.871	−576 387
8	+3 412 247	0.853	+2 910 647
9	−661 753	0.837	−553 887
10	−73 528	0.820	−60 293
11	−73 528	0.804	−59 117
12	+724 388	0.788	+570 818

$$\text{Net present value} = 5\,222\,740 - 5\,313\,434$$
$$= -90\,694$$

The internal rate of return lies between 1 per cent and 2 per cent per month and may be found by using the principle of similar triangles (see question 2.1).

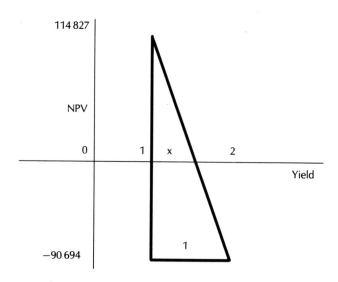

$$\frac{x}{114\,827} = \frac{1}{205\,521}$$

$$205\,521x = 114\,827$$

$$x = \frac{114\,827}{205\,521} = 0.56$$

Internal rate of return $= 1$ per cent $+ 0.56$ per cent
$$= 1.56 \text{ per cent per month}$$

The rate of financing is 1 per cent per month and the internal rate of return is 1.56 per cent per month — the scheme will be profitable so long as financing is below 1.56 per cent per month.

Internal rate of return is often used to compare the financial attractiveness of development schemes.

Comparison using net present value will reveal whether or not a scheme is profitable at a particular discount rate, and also that one scheme appears more profitable than another. However, calculation of the internal rate of return reveals the actual return from a scheme, and may be a more satisfactory basis upon which to compare schemes.

Question 7.5

Life cycle costing is a technique used to compare the financial implications of the use of different materials, components or systems in a building over its effective life.

Initial, annual and periodic costs are reduced either to an annual equivalent or an initial capital equivalent (present value) to make this comparison, taking time differences into account.

A simple example will enhance the explanation.

Example
A building will cost £1 750 000 to construct. Some components and services will require renewal every 10 years at a cost of £10 000 and others every 20 years at a cost of £35 000. It is estimated that the building itself has a life of 50 years. Annual maintenance costs are expected to be £5 000.

Assuming an interest rate of 10 per cent:

(i) *Initial capital equivalent*

Initial cost		£1 750 000
Renewals in 10 years	£10 000	
× PV of £1 in 10 years at 10 per cent	0.386	£ 3 860
Renewals in 20 years	£45 000	

× PV of £1 in 20 years at 10 per cent	0.149	£	6 705
Renewals in 30 years	£10 000		
× PV of £1 in 30 years at 10 per cent	0.057	£	570
Renewals in 40 years	£45 000		
× PV of £1 in 40 years at 10 per cent	0.022	£	990
Annual maintenance costs	£ 5 000		
YP 50 years at 10 per cent	9.915	£	49 575
Initial capital equivalent			£1 811 700

(ii) *Annual equivalent*

Initial cost	£1 750 000
Initial capital equivalent of renewals	
in 10, 20, 30 and 40 years [from (i)]	£ 12 125
	£1 762 125

$$\text{Annual equivalent} = \frac{£1\,762\,125}{\text{YP 50 years at 10 per cent}}$$

$$= \frac{£1\,762\,125}{9.915} = £177\,723$$

plus annual maintenance costs	£ 5 000
Total annual equivalent costs	£182 723

This information may be used in a comparison with the costs of providing alternative components and services which have varying lives, initial costs and replacement costs.

In the discussion required by this question, the following are the main points to consider:

(i) Problems associated with reconciling the different lives of the components of a building, such as the roof, heating system and electrical system.

(ii) Many different types of materials are available and all vary in terms of the years of service they give and the maintenance they require.

(iii) Different mixtures of materials/components result in different lives and annual maintenance costs.

(iv) The life expectancy of materials and components is estimated. This may be difficult when materials or components are newly developed, since some may not last as long as anticipated whilst others may last longer and manufacturers' claims are often excessive.

(v) The difficulty of accounting for the effects of inflation and increases in costs. This is virtually impossible to forecast over the life of a building.

(vi) The effect of taxation must be borne in mind and the impact of possible exemptions, reliefs or allowances. All of these may change at various times over the life of a building.

(vii) Life cycle costing considers the physical life of materials and components, but the physical life of a building may not coincide with its economic life.

(viii) The choice of interest rates, used in calculating the annual or capital equivalent of costs, is difficult over the long periods of time involved.

(ix) Different users may treat property differently or use it for a purpose which may affect the annual maintenance and operating costs and periodic costs.

(x) A developer who intends to sell the property will mainly be interested in his initial profit. He will not wish to incur increased costs at the outset for components, in order to reduce maintenance costs for some future owner of the building.

(xi) Life cycle costing considers only financial implications. Convenience, utility and aesthetic qualities are not taken into account.

(xii) The calculation does not produce a conclusive answer, but it does help to reconcile initial and long-term financial considerations.

8 MORTGAGES

Valuation for mortgage purposes is very often an important part of the work of a surveyor in general practice. It is also an area in which legal precedent has now extended the circle of those who may depend upon the valuation produced.

Question 8.1 therefore considers the important aspect of the approach to such a valuation and the factors which the valuer should take into account. The valuer is aided in this respect by *Valuation Guidance Notes 1 and 2*, produced by the Royal Institution of Chartered Surveyors. The recommendations of these *Guidance Notes* are highlighted in question 8.1. Reference is also made in this question to the problems of providing mortgage valuation advice in a difficult economic climate. Additionally, consideration is given to case law that the valuer cannot afford to ignore – that which has extended the duty of care beyond the valuer's client to the purchaser of the property.

The remaining questions test a student's knowledge of the mortgage instalment table and the ability to manipulate this in changing circumstances, particularly changes in interest rates. This involves calculation of the loan outstanding at the appropriate time and determination of the revised annual or monthly repayments, or the revised length of the mortgage term.

In question 8.2, the effect of relief from income tax on interest repayments is also considered.

MORTGAGES – QUESTIONS

8.1. You are required to carry out a mortgage valuation of a dwelling house on behalf of a Building Society.

Discuss your approach to the valuation, making reference to the recommendations made by the Royal Institution of Chartered Surveyors.

8.2. (a) A mortgage advance of £37 500 is to be repaid over 20 years at an interest rate of 10 per cent per annum.

Calculate the gross of tax annual instalments required to repay the mortgage and, without the use of either valuation tables or formulae, show how much of the loan would remain outstanding at the end of the fourth year.

   (b) Discuss the effect of the MIRAS provisions for tax relief on mortgage interest repayments.

8.3. (a) Explain how the monthly instalment shown in the Mortgage Instalment Table fulfils both payment of interest and repayment of capital.

   (b) Five years ago, a mortgagor borrowed £30 000 to be repaid over 20 years at 13 per cent per annum. The rate of interest has now been reduced to 8 per cent.

     Calculate the new monthly instalment, gross of tax.

   (c) Calculate how long it will take to repay the original loan if, when the interest rate changes to 8 per cent, the monthly instalments remain unchanged.

MORTGAGES – SUGGESTED ANSWERS

Question 8.1

In carrying out a mortgage valuation, it should be explained that a valuer will apply normal valuation principles, but must also consider the position of the mortgagee (the lender) should the mortgagor default. If this occurs, and the property has to be sold, the sale price needs to be sufficient to cover the outstanding debt, with perhaps a margin for any arrears.

The property is valued at the date of inspection, but bearing in mind the future – will the value be maintained and easily realisable? Any possibility of an increase in value is not reflected in the valuation, but a possible diminution in value cannot be ignored.

In the economic climate of the early 1990s, falling values became a common feature of the property market generally and house prices fell throughout the country. There were large numbers of repossessions, as mortgagors defaulted, unable to maintain repayments, at increasing rates of interest (although by 1993 interest rates were reduced significantly), in respect of mortgages entered into when house prices were high. As house prices fell during the recession, many mortgagors found themselves in the unfortunate position of having outstanding loans in excess of the value of their homes.

Valuers have become increasingly conservative, some more than others, because of the difficult market conditions within which they have been required to provide mortgage valuations.

Additionally, case law has established that the valuer's duty of care, when inspecting a property for mortgage purposes, is not only to his client, the lender, but extends to the prospective purchaser of the house, who may base his decision to purchase upon the valuer's report. The case that established this principle was *Yianni v. Edwin Evans and Sons (1982)*, but others have followed this, including *Smith v. Eric S Bush (1989)* and *Harris v. Wyre Forest D.C. 1989*. In the case of *Lloyd v. Butler (1990)* it was stated in the judgement that valuation reports, even though prepared for the mortgagee, 'should alert *purchasers* to substantial defects which the purchaser should be aware of; because purchasers will rely on these reports, first, to decide whether to investigate further; second, to decide whether to negotiate further; and ultimately to decide whether to complete...'.

Thus, the valuer producing a mortgage valuation faces the possibility of being sued for negligence not only by his client, but also by the purchaser. Valuers must therefore ensure a thorough inspection of the property, but, in the case of *Gibbs v. Arnold Son and Hockley (1989)*, it was held that purchasers were not entitled to expect the same information as that contained in a structural survey. The judgement expressed there to be 'a world of difference between a valuation survey and a structural survey'.

Reference should be made in the answer to *Valuation Guidance Note VGN 1* relating to sale, purchase, mortgage and miscellaneous valuations and *Valuation Guidance Note VGN 2a* relating specifically to the valuation of residential properties for mortgage purposes. These *Guidance Notes* were prepared by the Valuation and Rating Committee of the Royal Institution of Chartered Surveyors.

Guidance Note VGN 2a, paragraph 1.1.1 notes that the valuer is to advise the lender as to the open market value of the property. Open market value is defined in paragraph 4.4 as:

> 'the best price at which the sale of an interest in the property might reasonably be expected to have been completed unconditionally for cash consideration at the date of the valuation'.

The date of valuation is the date of inspection and there are various assumptions that should be made in assessing the open market value. These are:

1. A willing seller.
2. Prior to the date of valuation, a reasonable period has been allowed for marketing the interest in the property, agreeing the price and terms and completing the sale.
3. All the circumstances, including levels of value and the state of the market, were the same at the date of valuation as at any earlier assumed date of completion.
4. No account is to be taken of any additional bid that might be made by a special purchaser.

Mention should also be made of the main items which the *Guidance Notes* recommend should be taken into account by the valuer, including:

1. The character of the locality and availability of communications and other facilities affecting value.
2. The age, description, size and use of the property and its accommodation, construction, installations, amenities and services.
3. The apparent state of repair and condition.
4. Site stability, including the effects of mining and quarrying and any liability to flooding.
5. The nature of the interest in the property and details of any lettings and other occupants.
6. Any development potential should be disregarded, unless the valuer has instructions to the contrary.
7. The results of any planning, highway or similar enquiries should be taken into account as should the apparent contravention of any statutory requirements or any outstanding statutory notices.
8. Any furnishings or removable fittings to be included in the sale should be disregarded in the valuation.
9. Details of comparable market transactions and general market conditions and trends. The valuer is advised in the *Guidance Notes* to keep a record of the comparable transactions that have been used in preparing the valuation.

It is noted in paragraph 1.1.3 of *Valuation Guidance Note 2a* that the valuer may also be requested to provide an estimate of the current reinstatement cost of the property for insurance purposes. In assessing this, the valuer is advised in paragraph 5 to have regard to the Building Costs Information Service *House Rebuilding Cost Index*.

When producing a mortgage valuation, the valuer should not make any recommendations regarding the amount of the loan or the length of the mortgage term.

The contents of the *RICS Guidance Notes* have recently come under scrutiny in several court cases. These cases have usually involved alleged professional negligence by valuers, as those who had previously provided loans with property as security, sought to blame valuers for their losses following the collapse of the commercial property market in 1989/90.

In *Allied Trust Bank Limited v. Edward Symmons and Partners (1993)* the defendant valuers supplied a valuation for the purpose of funding the proposed redevelopment of a stately home. The case resulted from the developer going bankrupt and the property subsequently being sold for less than both the original valuation and the amount of the loan.

After considering the *RICS Guidance Notes*, the judge found in favour of the valuer, holding that it was correct:

(i) to use open market value as the basis of valuation when the property was to be security for a loan, and

(ii) unless specifically instructed otherwise, to reflect the value of alternative uses as long as they are realistically achievable – in this case, planning permission was expected to be granted for redevelopment of the property as apartments and terraced houses.

Another relevant case is *Craneheath Securities Limited* v. *York Montague Limited (1993)*. In this case, the judge similarly concluded that the RICS *Guidance Notes* made it quite clear that open market value was the correct basis to adopt when a property was being valued in order to provide security for a loan. He also went on to state that

'a valuation is not a guarantee of the figure reached...'

and that it was the responsibility of the lender *not* the valuer

'to assess the risk involved and express his assessment in fixing the terms of the loan, such as the percentage of value to be advanced'.

Question 8.2

(a) *Calculation of annual instalments*

The annual instalments in respect of a mortgage loan must provide both for repayment of the capital advanced and for interest on that capital. This is provided by the formula:

$$\text{annual instalment} = i + sf$$

where i = rate of interest on capital (expressed as a decimal)
sf = annual sinking fund to provide for repayment of capital.

Incorporating the formula for the annual sinking fund in the above formula produces:

$$\text{annual instalment to repay £1 in } n \text{ years} = i + \frac{i}{(1+i)^n - 1}$$

In the question $i = 10$ per cent
$n = 20$ years

$$\text{annual instalment} = 0.1 + \frac{0.1}{(1.1)^{20} - 1}$$

$$= 0.1 + \frac{0.1}{5.7275} = 0.1175$$

The annual instalment to repay £1 over 20 years at 10 per cent is £0.1175. The annual instalment to repay £37 500 over 20 years at 10 per cent is:

$$£37\,500 \times £0.1175 = £4\,406.25$$

Amount of loan outstanding at the end of the fourth year

It is required to show this without using either tables or formulae. In other words, the student has to demonstrate an awareness of how the mortgage instalment table works. In fact, this is quite simple. Interest is added to the outstanding loan at the beginning of each year, the annual repayment is then deducted revealing the amount outstanding at the end of the year.

This may be shown as follows:

Amount of mortgage loan	£37 500
plus interest at 10 per cent	£ 3 750
	£41 250
less annual instalment	£ 4 406.25
Amount outstanding at end of year 1	£36 843.75
plus interest at 10 per cent	£ 3 684.38
	£40 528.13
less annual instalment	£ 4 406.25
Amount outstanding at end of year 2	£36 121.88
plus interest at 10 per cent	£ 3 612.19
	£39 734.07
less annual instalment	£ 4 406.25
Amount outstanding at end of year 3	£35 327.82
plus interest at 10 per cent	£ 3 532.78
	£38 860.60
less annual instalment	£ 4 406.25
Amount outstanding at end of year 4	£34 454.35

(b) When the MIRAS (Mortgage Interest Relief at Source) system was introduced, the greatest effect was in the case of the annuity loan. Under the previous system, income tax relief was given separately on the interest element included within the total annual repayment. Mortgage repayments were calculated gross of tax and the Building Society then notified the Inland Revenue of the amount of interest paid in each year. This amount was then taken into account in calculating the mortgagor's allowances against income tax and his Pay As You Earn (PAYE) tax was reduced accordingly.

A short example could be used in the answer to illustrate this.

Example
Loan of £10 000 repayable over 25 years at 12 per cent.
Repayments would be £106.25 per month

Interest element in first year = £10 000 at 12 per cent
$$= £\ 1\,200 \text{ per annum}$$
$$= £\qquad 100 \text{ per month}$$

Assuming that income tax was paid at 25p in the £, the borrower would obtain tax relief of £25 per month. Thus, although £106.25 was actually paid to the Building Society, tax relief on PAYE meant that, in effect, the mortgagor was only paying £81.25 per month.

Each year, the proportion of the repayments attributable to interest were reduced, therefore tax relief was also reduced.

Under the MIRAS system, the borrower pays the net of tax amount to the Building Society. Monthly repayments for annuity loans have a higher content of capital for low rates of interest than for high, therefore net of tax payments mean that capital is repaid more quickly. Under the old system, borrowers paid a constant amount, which only changed when the rate of interest changed. However, because the amount of interest fell each year, so also did income tax relief resulting in increased net repayments. Under the MIRAS system net repayments remain constant.

Tax relief on mortgage interest payments has generally been considered as an incentive to encourage owner-occupation of dwellings, but it seemed probable that progressive abolition of this relief was the aim of the current Conservative Government in 1993/95.

Relief is restricted to interest charged on the first £30 000 of a mortgage loan. Until April 1994, relief was available at the basic rate of tax (25 per cent) on the interest payments. In the 1993 Budgets, it was announced that from 6 April 1994 the rate would fall to 20 per cent and from 6 April 1995 it would fall to 15 per cent.

These changes would appear to be the first stages of the phasing out of this relief.

Question 8.3

(a) The answer to this part of the question should first set out the formula for the mortgage instalment table, which is

$$\frac{i + \dfrac{i}{(1+i)^n - 1}}{12} \times 100$$

$$\text{or} \quad \frac{i + asf}{12} \times 100$$

This provides the monthly instalments for each £100 borrowed, giving interest on capital together with an annual sinking fund to repay the capital.

Example
From the Mortgage Instalment Table in *Parry's Valuation and Investment Tables*, the monthly instalment to redeem £100 borrowed over 20 years at 9 per cent is £0.9129.
This may also be derived using the formula:

$$\text{Monthly instalment} = \frac{i + \dfrac{i}{(1+i)^n - 1}}{12} \times 100$$

$$\text{Monthly instalment} = \frac{0.09 + \dfrac{0.09}{(1.09)^{20} - 1}}{12} \times 100$$

$$= \frac{0.09 + \dfrac{0.09}{4.60441}}{12} \times 100$$

$$= 0.9129$$

Assuming that £10 000 is borrowed, the annual instalment will be:

$$£0.9129 \times 100 \times 12 = £1\,095.48$$

The instalment of £1 095.48 may be divided between the interest element and that required to repay capital:

Interest	*Repayment of capital*
9 per cent of £10 000 = £900 pa	£1 095.48 − £900 = £195.48 pa

If £195.48 per annum is invested each year for 20 years at 9 per cent interest, the original £10 000 capital will be recouped.

	£195.48 pa
× Amount of £1 pa in 20 years at 9 per cent	51.1601
Capital recouped	£10 000

The annual mortgage instalment has achieved both payment of interest on the capital and repayment of the capital.
(b) First of all, the original mortgage instalment must be calculated in order to determine the amount of the loan now outstanding, to be repaid at the revised rate of interest.

$$\text{annual instalment} = (i + asf) \times £30\,000$$

$$= 0.13 + \frac{0.13}{(1.13)^{20} - 1} \times £30\,000$$

$$= 0.13 + \frac{0.13}{10.5231} \times £30\,000$$

$$= 0.1423537 \times £30\,000 = £4\,270.61 \text{ pa}$$

The Years' Purchase table may now be used to calculate how much of the loan remains to be repaid over the next 15 years. In other words, the annual instalment multiplied by the Years' Purchase for 15 years will provide the capital value of those annual payments over that time.

If the formulae for the two are compared, it will be noted that the Years' Purchase is the reciprocal of the mortgage instalment table:

$$\text{Annual mortgage instalment} = i + asf$$

$$\text{Years' Purchase} = \frac{1}{i + asf}$$

Annual instalment	£ 4 270.61 pa
YP 15 years at 13 per cent	6.4624
Amount outstanding after 5 years	£27 598.39

As the wording of the question does not preclude the use of valuation tables, it would be acceptable to calculate the amount outstanding using the Years' Purchase table. However, the calculation could alternatively be carried out as demonstrated in the answer to question 8.2(a):

Amount of mortgage loan	£30 000
plus interest at 13 per cent	£ 3 900
	£33 900
less annual instalment	£ 4 270.61
Amount outstanding at end of year 1	£29 629.39
plus interest at 13 per cent	£ 3 851.82
	£33 481.21
less annual instalment	£ 4 270.61
Amount outstanding at end of year 2	£29 210.60

plus interest at 13 per cent	£ 3 797.38
	£33 007.98
less annual instalment	£ 4 270.61
Amount outstanding at end of year 3	£28 737.37
plus interest at 13 per cent	£ 3 735.86
	£32 473.23
less annual instalment	£ 4 270.61
Amount outstanding at end of year 4	£28 202.62
plus interest at 13 per cent	£ 3 666.34
	£31 868.96
less annual instalment	£ 4 270.61
Amount outstanding at end of year 5	£27 598.35

The rate of interest has now been reduced to 8 per cent, therefore the revised instalments will have to repay £27 598.39 over 15 years at 8 per cent.

Using the formula:

$$\frac{i + asf}{12} \times £27\,598.39$$

the new monthly instalment will be:

$$\frac{0.08 + \dfrac{0.08}{(1.08)^{15} - 1}}{12} \times £27\,598.39$$

$$= \frac{0.08 + \dfrac{0.08}{(2.1722)}}{12} \times £27\,598.39$$

$$= \frac{0.116829}{12} \times £27\,598.39$$

$$= £268.69$$

(c) To calculate how long it will take to repay the original loan if the monthly repayments remain unchanged when the rate of interest changes to 8 per cent, it is again necessary to know the amount of the loan outstanding at the end of 5 years.

This was determined in part (b) and is £27 598.39.

The capital outstanding, divided by the annual repayments will produce the Years' Purchase for the number of years (n) that it will now take to repay the loan.

$$\frac{£27\,598.39}{£4\,270.61} = \text{YP } n \text{ years at 8 per cent}$$

$$= 6.4624$$

The number of years can be found from *Parry's Valuation and Investment Tables*, by referring to the Years' Purchase single rate table at 8 per cent. By searching down the 8 per cent column, the multiplier of 6.4624, or the closest figure to it, is located. The figures to the extreme left or right of this multiplier will reveal the appropriate number of years. In this case some interpolation is required, because an exact number of years does not emerge. The Years' Purchase at 8 per cent for 9 years is 6.2469 and for 10 years is 6.7101. From this it can be deduced that it will take approximately 9½ years to repay the mortgage at the reduced rate of interest.

9 LIFE INTERESTS

Life interests in property are rarely encountered by the majority of valuers, but because the necessity to value such interests does occasionally arise, students are usually expected to have some knowledge of the approach to these situations.

As the name implies, the duration of a life interest is dependent upon the length of someone's life. When they die, the property reverts either to the freeholder (known as the reversioner) or to the leaseholder (known as the remainderman).

Normal Years' Purchase tables cannot be used in the valuation of a life interest – see question 9.1(a) – since the duration of the interest is as uncertain as the life to which it is linked. Single rate Years' Purchase tables are adapted to take account of this uncertainty, and how this is achieved is described in the answer to question 9.1(b).

Strictly speaking, a life interest ought to be valued using a dual rate Years' Purchase, since it is for a limited term. It is possible to construct dual rate capitalisation figures for the valuation of these interests, but they are rarely used. In constructing the appropriate figures, the sinking fund element of the Years' Purchase is linked to life assurance premiums for the life involved, and allowance has to be made for the premium having been paid in the year of death, before receipt of rental income. Such calculations can become quite complicated, and the uncertainty introduced by the fact that the continuing receipt of income depends upon the continuing existence of life, means that such a rigorous approach has little justification. The extra risks involved in a life interest are generally allowed for by applying a single rate Years' Purchase and adopting a yield some two or more per cent higher that than used in the valuation of freehold or leasehold interests in similar properties.

All Years' Purchase figures used in the examples that follow are taken from the Eleventh Edition of *Parry's Valuation and Investment Tables*. They are based on the English Life Tables No. 14, prepared by the Government Actuary for the Registrar General. There are separate tables of Years' Purchase for males and females, since their life expectancies differ.

Although the life expectancy of both men and women has improved considerably over this century, the author of *Parry's Valuation and Investment Tables* cautions the valuer that the continuation of such improvement cannot be taken for granted. In particular, the problem of AIDS is highlighted, and the possible effect that the spread of this virus might have on mortality rates in the future.

Additionally, although the valuation of a life interest may initially be performed mathematically, the *actual* life involved must be taken into account. The general health of that person should be considered, along with other factors, including where they live, their occupation and life style, all of which will assist in the valuer's judgement of whether or not the individual's life expectation can be anticipated to conform to the general expectation.

The basic valuation situations likely to be encountered are:

1. The interest of a single tenant for life, either male or female, in freehold or leasehold property (see questions 9.2 and 9.3)
2. An interest involving two tenants for life of either freehold or leasehold property.

   The Years' Purchase will vary according to whether the tenants for life are:

   (i) both male,
   (ii) both female,
   (iii) male and female, the male being the older of the two,
   (iv) male and female, the female being the older of the two.

When two tenants for life are involved, the life interest may be for the longer of two lives (see question 9.4(a)) or for the joint continuation of two lives (see question 9.4(b)).

Situations involving more than two tenants for life are beyond the scope of this book.

3. The interest of a reversioner (see questions 9.2 and 9.4).
4. The interest of a remainderman (see question 9.3).

LIFE INTERESTS – QUESTIONS

9.1. (a) According to the English Life Tables No. 14 in *Parry's Valuation and Investment Tables*, a man aged 33 is expected to live another 40 years. Demonstrate why it is wrong to use the Years' Purchase for 40 years in the valuation of the life interest of a man aged 33.

   (b) Calculate the Years' Purchase for a female life aged 105, at 7 per cent.

9.2. A man aged 50 is tenant for life of a freehold shop let with 15 years unexpired at a fixed rent of £15 000 per annum on internal repairing terms. The current rental value of the property on full repairing and insuring terms is £55 000 per annum.

Similar rack rented freehold properties are currently selling for yields of 7 per cent.

Value the interests of

(i) the tenant for life
(ii) the reversioner and
(iii) the lessee.

9.3. A man aged 55 is tenant for life of leasehold office premises. The lease has 45 years unexpired at a ground rent of £50 per annum. The current rental value of the offices on full repairing and insuring terms, on the basis of 5 year reviews, is £65 000 per annum, but they are currently let with 10 years unexpired at a fixed rent of £37 000 per annum, the tenant being responsible for internal repairs.

Value the interests of

(i) the tenant for life
(ii) the remainderman and
(iii) the sub-lessee.

9.4. A man aged 45 and a woman aged 40 have a life interest in freehold shop property for so long as either of them remains alive. The shop is let by them with 8 years unexpired at a fixed rent of £10 000 per annum on full repairing and insuring terms. The current rental value on the same terms and on the basis of 5 year reviews is £45 000 per annum.

(a) Value the interests of

(i) the tenants for life and
(ii) the reversioner.

(b) Demonstrate what difference it would make to your valuations in (a) if the life interest were for so long as *both* the man and woman remain alive.

LIFE INTERESTS – SUGGESTED ANSWERS

Question 9.1

(a) The 40 years that the man of 33 is expected to live is given in the Mean Expectation of Life table. Forty years is an average, obtained from a considerable number of lives and therefore includes those who live only a few more years and those who live many more.

To demonstrate that it is wrong to use the Years' Purchase for the average life expectation to value the life interest of a man aged 33, we can use two assumed lives. Let us assume that one man aged 33 lives another 25 years and the other lives another 55 years — that is, an average of 40 years. The first man loses 15 years from the average and the second man gains 15 years.

It will also be assumed that each receives an income of £10 000 per annum and that a 10 per cent return is required.
Thus:

First man		*Second man*	
Loss is 15 years' income		Gain is 15 years' income	
Income	£10 000 pa	Income	£10 000 pa
YP 15 years at		YP 15 years at	
10 per cent	7.6061	10 per cent	7.6061
Loss	£76 061	Gain	£76 061

It would appear that the loss to the first man is equal to the gain of the second man. However, the loss does not commence for 25 years, when the first man dies, and the gain does not commence for 40 years when, according to the average, the second man would be expected to die. The present value of the loss is not therefore equal to the present value of the gain.

Loss	£76 061	Gain	£76 061
× PV of £1 in 25		× PV of £1 in 40	
years at 10 per cent	0.0923	years at 10 per cent	0.0221
Present value of loss	£ 7 020	Present value of gain	£ 1 680

a difference of £5 340

An alternative method of demonstrating this is to compare the difference in capital values of the income received for the differing time periods.

First man

Income	£10 000 pa
YP 25 years at 10 per cent	9.0770
Capital value	£90 770

Second man

Income	£10 000 pa
YP 55 years at 10 per cent	9.9471
Capital value	£99 471

Average man

Income	£10 000 pa
YP 40 years at 10 per cent	9.7791
Capital value	£97 791

Difference between the capital value of the income received by the first man and the average man −£7 021.

Difference between the capital value of the income received by the second man and the average man +£1 680.

(b) *Years' Purchase for a female life aged 105, at 7 per cent*
This is calculated as follows:

$$\text{Present value of £1 in 1 year at 7 per cent} \times \frac{\text{number of females alive at 106}}{\text{number of females alive at 105}}$$

plus

$$\text{Present value of £1 in 2 years at 7 per cent} \times \frac{\text{number of females alive at 107}}{\text{number of females alive at 105}}$$

plus

$$\text{Present value of £1 in 3 years at 7 per cent} \times \frac{\text{number of females alive at 108}}{\text{number of females alive at 105}}$$

plus

$$\text{Present value of £1 in 4 years at 7 per cent} \times \frac{\text{number of females alive at 109}}{\text{number of females alive at 105}}$$

plus

$$\text{Present value of £1 in 5 years at 7 per cent} \times \frac{\text{number of females alive at 110}}{\text{number of females alive at 105}}$$

Thus

$$0.9346 \times \frac{43}{83} = 0.4842$$

plus

$$0.8734 \times \frac{21}{83} = 0.2210$$

plus

$$0.8163 \times \frac{9}{83} = 0.0885$$

plus

$$0.7629 \times \frac{4}{83} = 0.0368$$

plus

$$0.7130 \times \frac{1}{83} = 0.0086$$

$$\overline{0.8391}$$

YP for female life aged 105, at 7 per cent $= 0.8391$

Income receivable for life is uncertain and, as each year goes by, there is a gradual reduction in the probability of receiving the income for that year and the years that follow. The probability of receiving future income payments reduces more significantly each year when the life interest involves a person who has reached a great age.

Years' Purchase single rate for a life incorporates the basic single rate Years' Purchase – that is, the total of the present values for the number of years for which the income is expected to be received.

According to the sample of female lives on which the English Life Tables No. 14 are based, the one who lives the longest attains 110 years. Therefore, the longest that the woman of 105 can be anticipated to live is five years. Thus, the Present Values of £1 for one to five years are added together in the normal way, giving the Years' Purchase single rate for 5 years at 7 per cent. However, of the 83 women of the original sample who are still alive at 105, some die each year, so each Present Value is modified to allow for the decreasing expectation of life continuing for another year.

The modification is carried out using the Probability Factor, which is made up of:

$$\frac{\text{the number of females alive at the greater age}}{\text{the number of females alive at the lesser age}}$$

At 105, there are 83 women alive, whereas at 106, only 43 are alive. Therefore, at 105, the woman has 43/83 or a 52 per cent chance of living to 106. At 106, the probability of living a further year reduces to 21/83 or 25 per cent, at 107 it is 9/83 or 11 per cent and so on.

The need to carry out such a calculation is probably fairly remote, but would arise when valuing a life interest involving anyone aged over 100, since the Years' Purchase figures in *Parry's Valuation and Investment Tables* terminate at 100 years.

Question 9.2

(i) *The tenant for life*
The tenant for life will receive income from the property for as long as he lives. Firstly, the valuer has to estimate whether or not the tenant for life will survive long enough to receive the income for the next 15 years. Secondly, if survival is expected to be longer than 15 years, the capital value of the income that the tenant for life is expected to receive after reversion to full rental value, must be estimated.

Rent received		£15 000 pa	
less external repairs and insurance [see note 1]		£ 4 125 pa	
net income		£10 875 pa	
compare YP life (male) age 50 at 14 per cent [see note 2]	6.371		
with YP 15 years at 14 per cent	6.142		
adopt the lower YP [see note 3]		6.142	£ 66 794
reversion to full net rental value		£55 000 pa	
YP life (male) aged 50 at 9 per cent [see note 4]	8.982		
less YP 15 years at 9 per cent [see note 5]	8.061	0.921	£ 50 655
Capital value			£117 449
		say	£115 000 [see note 6]

Notes
1: The rent received is on internal repairing terms, therefore the landlord is responsible for external repairs and insurance of the property. In the absence of any other information, the cost of these has been estimated at 7 ½ per cent of full net rental value.
2: Similar rack rented freehold properties yield 7 per cent. Adopting an uplift of 2 per cent for the extra risks involved in a life interest produces a yield of 9 per cent for the reversion. Since the term income is fixed for 15 years and is therefore inflation prone, a high yield of 14 per cent has been adopted. This is on the assumption that for freehold interests, unencumbered by a life interest, the yield expected would be 12 per cent.

3: The two Years' Purchase are compared in order to estimate which is likely to expire first — the 15 years or the life. In this case, the Years' Purchase for life is greater than the Years' Purchase for 15 years, indicating that the tenant for life will probably live beyond 15 years and is likely to receive all the income from the property for the duration of the unexpired term. Having made this assumption, the lower Years' Purchase is nevertheless adopted to allow for the fact that there can be no absolute certainty in the expectation of the man surviving for the full 15 years.

4: This is the Years' Purchase for the total period during which the man is expected to receive income from the property — the anticipated length of his life.

5: Receipt of full rental value is deferred for 15 years. This is carried out using the approach of deducting Years' Purchase from Years' Purchase, rather than Years' Purchase multiplied by the Present Value of £1. The Years' Purchase for 15 years must be deducted from the Years' Purchase for life, since 15 years of the life will have expired at this point. The resultant figure is the Years' Purchase for the length of time during which the tenant for life can be expected to enjoy receipt of the full rental value.

6: This figure might be rounded down more to further allow for the uncertainty of life.

(ii) *The reversioner*

When the tenant for life dies, the freehold interest in the property will pass to the reversioner.

In dealing with the term income, the valuer has to estimate whether or not the reversioner will receive any of it. To do this, a similar calculation is employed as that adopted to value the term income in the case of the tenant for life — the valuer estimates the probability of the tenant for life surviving longer than 15 years.

In the second stage of the valuation, the full rental value is capitalised into perpetuity. If it appears likely that the tenant for life will survive to receive the higher income, the Years' Purchase in perpetuity is reduced by the Years' Purchase for life, and the resultant figure will be the capital value of the income after the tenant for life has died — only when this life expires, is the reversioner entitled to receipt of the income.

Rent received		£15 000 pa
less external repairs and insurance		
[see note 1]		£ 4 125 pa
net income		£10 875 pa
YP 15 years at 14 per cent	6.142	
[see note 2]		

less YP life (male) aged 50 at 14 per cent [see note 3]	6.371	− 0.229	NIL
reversion to full net rental value		£55 000 pa	
YP in perpetuity at 9 per cent [see note 4]	11.111		

less YP life (male) aged 50
   deferred 15 years
   at 9 per cent
   [see note 5]
	0.921	10.19	£560 450

Capital value			£560 450
		say	£560 000 [see note 6]

Notes

1: Estimated at 7½ per cent of full net rental value.

2: Yield adjusted because a life interest is involved. See note 2 of tenant for life's interest.

3: The difference between these two figures is the Years' Purchase for the number of years for which the reversioner is expected to receive income from the property during the first 15 years. The minus figure indicates the probability of the tenant for life living beyond 15 years and, consequently, the reversioner receiving no income during this period. Although this could have been deduced from the valuation of the tenant for life's interest, the calculation is shown here to demonstrate the method.

4: After the tenant for life dies, the interest of the reversioner will be the freehold in perpetuity.

5: Receipt of full rental value by the reversioner is deferred for however long the tenant for life survives. The Years' Purchase for life deferred 15 years was calculated in the valuation of the tenant for life's interest − see note 5 of annotation to that calculation.

6: This figure might be further rounded down to allow for the eventuality of the tenant for life surviving longer than expected.

(iii) *The lessee*

The lessee's interest is valued in the same way as any other lessee's interest. It is immaterial to the lessee that his present landlord only has a life interest in the property; if the tenant for life dies, rent will be payable instead to the reversioner.

Full net rental value	£ 55 000 pa
plus external repairs and insurance [see note 1]	£ 4 125 pa

full rental value on internal repairing terms	£ 59 125 pa
less rent paid	£ 15 000 pa
profit rent	£ 44 125 pa
YP 15 years at 8 per cent and 3 per cent	
(tax 35 per cent) [see note 2]	6.146
Capital value	£271 192
	say £270 000

Notes

1: The estimated cost of external repairs and insurance is added to the full rental value on full repairing and insuring terms, to convert it to the same terms as the rent paid by the lessee.

2: Although the question does not reveal whether or not the full rental value quoted is on the basis of a particular review pattern, it is assumed that the most commonly adopted 5 year reviews will apply. Consequently, the profit rent will not be fixed for 15 years. The all risks yield from similar rack rented freeholds is 7 per cent and a traditional risk adjustment of one per cent has been adopted in valuing the lessee's interest.

Question 9.3

(i) *The tenant for life*

The technique involved is similar to that used in the valuation of a tenant for life's interest in freehold property (see question 9.2). The valuer must estimate whether or not there is a likelihood of the tenant for life surviving to receive income from the property for the remaining 10 years of the sub-lease. If it appears probable, this element of the income is included in the valuation.

The tenant for life will then go on to receive the full rental value from the property for as long as he lives, or until the leasehold interest expires, and an estimate is made of which is more likely to expire first. This is done by comparing the Years' Purchase for the life involved, with the Years' Purchase for the unexpired term of the lease.

Rent received		£37 000 pa
less ground rent	£ 50 pa	
external repairs and insurance		
[see note 1]	£ 4 875 pa	£ 4 925 pa
net income		£32 075 pa
compare YP 10 years at 16 per cent		
[see note 2]	4.833	

with YP life (male) aged 55				
at 16 per cent	5.409			
adopt the lower YP				
[see note 3]			4.833	£155 018
reversion to full net				
rental value			£65 000 pa	
less ground rent			£ 50 pa	
net income			£64 950 pa	
compare the YP for life				
with the YP for the				
unexpired term				
of the lease				
YP life [see note 4] (male)				
aged 55 at				
9 per cent [see note 5]	8.277			
less YP 10 years				
[see note 6]				
at 9 per cent	6.418	1.859		
YP 35 years [see note 7]				
at 9 per cent	10.567			
× PV of £1 in 10 years				
at 9 per cent	0.422	4.459		
adopt the lower YP				
[see note 8]			1.859	£120 742
Capital value				£275 760
			say	£275 000

Notes

1: The rent received is on internal repairing terms, therefore the landlord is responsible for external repairs and insurance. In the absence of other information, the cost of these has been estimated at 7 ½ per cent of full net rental value.

2: Since the net income from the leasehold interest is fixed for the next 10 years, it is inflation prone and so a high yield of 16 per cent has been adopted.

3: Comparing the Years' Purchase for life with the Years' Purchase for 10 years, the former is greater than the latter. This indicates that the tenant for life will probably live beyond 10 years and so is likely to receive the income from the property for the whole of that period. Having made this assumption,

the lower Years' Purchase is nevertheless adopted, since there can be no absolute certainty in the expectation of the man surviving for the full 10 years.
4: This is the Years' Purchase for the total period during which the man is expected to receive income from the property, unless the leasehold interest ends before his life does.
5: Assuming yields for leasehold interests in this type of property are 7 per cent, with an uplift of 2 per cent for the extra risks attaching to life interests. A lower yield than that used in the term valuation is adopted at this point, since the profit rent will not be fixed, the full rental value being on the basis of 5 year reviews.
6: This is the period before reversion to full rental value. Deferment is carried out using the technique of deducting the Years' Purchase for the deferment period from the Years' Purchase for life. The resultant figure is the Years' Purchase for the length of time during which the tenant for life can be expected to enjoy receipt of the full rental value.
7: This is the Years' Purchase for the unexpired term of the leasehold interest in 10 years' time. At that time, 35 years will be the maximum period for which the tenant for life can receive income from the property.
8: The Years' Purchase for life is less than the Years' Purchase for the remainder of the lease, indicating that the tenant for life will probably die before the lease expires.

(ii) The remainderman

When the tenant for life dies, the leasehold interest in the property will pass to the remainderman for the unexpired term of the head lease.

In dealing with the income for the next 10 years, the valuer has to estimate whether or not the remainderman is likely to receive any of it. This is achieved in much the same way as a reversioner's interest in freehold property (see question 9.2). It is evident from the valuation of the tenant for life's interest that the remainderman has little chance of receiving any income for the next 10 years – the tenant for life is expected to live beyond this. Any value to the remainderman will therefore be in the reversion. In the valuation of the reversion, the full rental value is capitalised for the unexpired term of the leasehold interest at that point. This is deferred by deducting the Years' Purchase for life from the Years' Purchase for the unexpired term. The resultant figure is the Years' Purchase for the period after the tenant for life has died, when the remainderman will be entitled to the income for the property.

Full net rental value	£65 000 pa
less ground rent	£ 50 pa
net income	£64 950 pa

YP 35 years [see note 1] at 9 per cent		10.567	
less YP life (male) aged 55 at 9 per cent	8.277		
less YP 10 years at at 9 per cent	6.418	1.859	8.708
[see note 2]			£565 585
Capital value say			£565 000

Notes

1: The unexpired term of the leasehold interest is the maximum possible time for which income can be received from the property.

2: This is the Years' Purchase for the unexpired term of the head lease after the tenant for life has died. This is the period of time for which the remainderman will be in receipt of the net income.

(iii) *The sub-lessee*

In valuing the sub-lessee's interest, the existence of the life interest is ignored. It is of no consequence to the sub-lessee whether he pays rent to the tenant for life or the remainderman.

Full net rental value	£ 65 000 pa	
plus external repairs and insurance [see note 1]	£ 4 875 pa	
full rental value on internal repairing terms	£ 69 875 pa	
less rent paid	£ 37 000 pa	
profit rent	£ 32 875 pa	
YP 10 years at 8 per cent and 3 per cent (tax 35 per cent)	4.669	
[see note 2]	£153 493	
Capital value	say	£155 000

Notes

1: The estimated costs of external repairs and insurance are added to the full rental value on full repairing and insuring terms, to convert it to the same terms as the rent paid by the sub-lessee.

2: Assuming yields for leasehold interests in this type of property are 7 per cent. As this is the sub-lessee's interest, the yield has been increased slightly. The profit rent is not fixed for 10 years, since the full rental value is on the basis of 5 year reviews.

Question 9.4

(a)(i) *The tenants for life*
The situation here involves a life interest that will exist for the longer of two
lives – the freehold interest in the property will not pass to the reversioner
until the man and the woman are *both* dead.

The approach, as with a single tenant for life, is to estimate the likelihood of
the tenants for life receiving income during the entire unexpired term, then to
value the reversionary income they are likely to receive, if the probability is
that their survival will extend beyond 8 years.

Rent received		£10 000 pa	
YP life (male) aged 45 at			
14 per cent [see note 1]	6.635		
plus YP life (female)			
aged 40 at 14 per cent	6.933		
[see note 2]	13.568		
less YP for the joint continuation			
of two lives aged 45 (male)			
and 40 (female) at 14 per cent			
[see note 3]	6.501		
YP for the longer of two lives			
at 14 per cent [see note 4]	7.067		
Compare this with			
YP 8 years at 14 per cent	4.639		
adopt the lower YP [see note 5]		4.639	£ 46 390
reversion to full net rental value		£45 000 pa	
YP life (male) aged 45 at			
9 per cent [see note 6]	9.559		
plus YP life (female) aged			
40 at 9 per cent	10.344		
	19.903		
less YP for the joint continuation			
of two lives aged 45 (male)			
and 40 (female) at 9 per cent	9.250		
YP for the longer of two			
lives at 9 per cent [see note 7]	10.653		
less YP 8 years at 9 per cent			
[see note 8]	5.535	5.118	£230 310

Capital value   £276 700

                                  say   £275 000

Notes

1: The income is fixed and inflation prone for the next 8 years, therefore a high yield of 14 per cent has been adopted. Assuming investors in similar, fixed income freehold interests would require a return of 12 per cent, with an uplift of two per cent for the risks attaching to a life interest.

2: By adding together the Years' Purchases for the two lives, the period when both the man and the woman are expected to be alive is double counted. The Years' Purchase for this period – the joint continuation period of the two lives – must be deducted.

3: The Years' Purchase for the joint continuation period must be obtained from the tables showing the appropriate figures where the *man is the older* of the two tenants for life. In the eleventh edition of *Parry's Valuation and Investment Tables*, this is on page 296. If the *woman were the older of the two*, it would be necessary to refer to the Years' Purchase figures on page 300. The difference in the Years' Purchase figures arises from the differing life expectations of men and women.

4: This is the Years' Purchase for the life of the longest survivor of the two tenants for life.

5: The Years' Purchase for the longer of two lives is greater than the Years' Purchase for 8 years, indicating the expectation of at least one of the lives extending beyond 8 years. However, the lower Years' Purchase is adopted to reflect the uncertainty of survival.

6: Assuming freehold yields for this type of property, when let at full rental value on 5 year reviews, are 7 per cent, a risk premium of two per cent has been added because a life interest is involved.

7: This is the Years' Purchase for the longest survivor of the two tenants for life and is therefore the Years' Purchase for the total length of the life interest.

8: Receipt of full rental value is deferred for 8 years.

(ii) *The reversioner*

From the valuation of the tenants' for life interest, it is evidently unlikely that the reversioner will receive income from the property during the next 8 years. Any income will therefore arise after reversion to full rental value and will commence when the longest surviving tenant for life has died.

Full rental value   £45 000 pa
YP in perpetuity [see note 1]
    at 9 per cent [see note 2]   11.111

less YP for longer of two lives aged 45 (male) and 40 (female) deferred 8 years at 9 per cent [see note 3]	5.118	5.993
Capital value		£269 685
	say	£265 000

Notes

1: After both tenants for life have died, the interest of the reversioner will be the freehold in perpetuity.

2: See note 6, valuation of tenants' for life interest.

3: Receipt of full rental value is deferred for the remaining lifetime of the longest surviving tenant for life. See notes 7 and 8, valuation of tenants' for life interest.

(b)(i) *The tenants for life*

The life interest in this case is for the joint continuation period of the two lives. The interest will exist only for so long as both tenants for life remain alive – when *either* the man *or* the woman dies, the life interest will come to an end and the freehold interest will pass to the reversioner.

The approach to this valuation is similar to part (a)(i), except that only the Years' Purchase for the joint continuation period is utilised. Since the life interest can be expected to cease at an earlier date than in part (a)(i), this will result in a lower valuation.

Rent received		£10 000 pa	
compare YP for the joint continuation of two lives aged 45 (male) and 40 (female) at 14 per cent	6.501		
with YP 8 years at 14 per cent	4.639		
adopt the lower YP [see note 1]		4.639	£ 46 390 [see note 4]
reversion to full net rental value		£45 000 pa	
YP for the joint continuation of two lives aged 45 (male) and 40 (female) at 9 per cent [see note 2]	9.250		

less YP 8 years at 9 per cent [see note 3]	5.535	3.715	£167 175 [see note 4]
Capital value			£213 565
		say	£210 000

Notes

1: The Years' Purchase for the joint continuation of the two lives is greater than the Years' Purchase for 8 years, indicating that both tenants for life will probably survive beyond 8 years. The lower Years' Purchase is adopted, as explained in part (a)(i), note 5.

2: This is the Years' Purchase for the total length of the life interest – the period during which both lives survive together.

3: Receipt of full rental value is deferred for 8 years.

4: Not surprisingly, both tenants for life are still expected to survive for at least the next 8 years, therefore the value of the term income is unaffected. The reduced value is in the reversionary element, since *only one, not both* of the tenants for life has to die for the life interest to end.

(ii) *The reversioner*

As in part (a)(ii), there is unlikely to be any value arising from the term income.

Full rental value		£ 45 000 pa
YP in perpetuity at 9 per cent	11.111	
less YP for joint continuation of two lives aged 45 (male) and 40 (female) deferred 8 years at 9 per cent	3.715	7.396
Capital value		£332 820
	say	£330 000

The value of the reversioner's interest is greater than in part (a)(ii), since the freehold interest will pass to the reversioner at an earlier date – after only *one* of the tenants for life has died.

BIBLIOGRAPHY

Baum, A., 'The Valuation of Reversionary Freeholds: a review', *Journal of Valuation*, Vol. 3, No. 1 (1984).

Baum, A. and Crosby, N., *Property Investment Appraisal*, Routledge (1988).

Baum, A. and Mackmin, D., *The Income Approach to Valuation (3rd edition)*, Routledge (1989).

Baum, A. and Ming, Y.S., 'The Valuation of Leaseholds: a review: Part I', *Journal of Valuation*, Vol. 3, No. 2 (1985).

Baum, A. and Ming, Y.S., 'The Valuation of Leaseholds: a review: Part II', *Journal of Valuation*, Vol. 3, No. 3 (1985).

Baum, A. and Sams, G., *Statutory Valuations (2nd edition)*, Routledge (1990).

Bowcock, P., *Property Valuation Tables*, Macmillan (1978).

Britton, W., Davies, K. and Johnson, T., *Modern Methods of Valuation (8th edition)*, Estates Gazette (1989).

Butler, D. and Richmond, D., *Advanced Valuation*, Macmillan (1990).

Crosby, N., 'The Investment Method of Valuation: A Real Value Approach 1', *Journal of Valuation*, Vol. 1, No. 4 (1983).

Crosby, N., 'The Investment Method of Valuation: A Real Value Approach 2', *Journal of Valuation*, Vol. 2, No. 1 (1984).

Crosby, N., 'The Application of Equated Yield and Real Value Approaches to Market Valuation: 1', *Journal of Valuation*, Vol. 4, No. 2 (1986).

Crosby, N., 'The Application of Equated Yield and Real Value Approaches to Market Valuation: 2', *Journal of Valuation*, Vol. 4, No. 3 (1986).

Darlow, C. (Ed.), *Valuation and Development Appraisal (2nd edition)*, Estates Gazette (1983).

Darlow, C. (Ed.), *Valuation and Investment Appraisal*, Estates Gazette (1988).

Davidson, A.W., *Parry's Valuation and Investment Tables (11th Edition)*, Estates Gazette (1989).

Enever, N., *The Valuation of Property Investments (4th edition)*, Estates Gazette (1989).

Harker, J., Nanthakumaran, N. and Rogers, S., *Double Sinking Fund Correction Methods, an Analysis and Appraisal*, University of Aberdeen (1988).

Hawkins, D.J., *Boynton's Guide to Compulsory Purchase and Compensation (6th edition)*, Longman (1990).

MacLeary, A.R., *National Taxation for Property Management and Valuation*, E. and F.N. Spon (1991).

Marshall, P., *Donaldson's Investment Tables (3rd edition)*, Donaldsons (1988).

Millington, A.F., *An Introduction to Property Valuation (3rd edition)*, Estates Gazette (1988).

Rees, W.H. (Ed.) *Valuation: Principles into Practice (4th edition)*, Estates Gazette (1992).

Richmond, D., *Introduction to Valuation (3rd edition)*, Macmillan (1994).

Rose, J.J., *Rose's Property Valuation Tables*, Freeland Press (1976).

Ryde, W., *Ryde on Rating and the Community Charge*, Butterworth (1990).

Scarrett, D., *Property Valuation. The five methods*, E. & F. N. Spon (1991).

Trott, A. (Ed.), *Report into Property Valuation Methods (Interim Report)*, RICS (1980).

INDEX

Anderson Williamson
77 Eglantine Av